The Life of Lou Gehrig

Told by a Fan

The Life of Lou Gehrig

Told by a Fan

Sara Kaden Brunsvold

The Life of Lou Gehrig
Told by a Fan
by Sara Kaden Brunsvold

Edited by Andrew Yankech
Cover design by Tom Wright
Typesetting by Desktop Edit Shop, Inc.

Published by: ACTA Sports
            5559 W. Howard Street
            Skokie, IL 60077
            800-397-2282
            info@actasports.com
            www.actasports.com

Library of Congress Number: 2006921000
ISBN-10: 0-87946-298-1
ISBN-13: 978-0-87946-298-7
Printed in the United States of America
Year: 12 11 10 09 08 07 06
Printing: 10 9 8 7 6 5 4 3 2 1

Contents

To Gehrig fans,
who keep his legend alive and dynamic.

*Don't write a line about Gehrig
until you study his record.*
                          —Bucky Harris

Introduction

I won't even pretend to be the official Lou Gehrig biographer. That honor, in my opinion, belongs to Ray Robinson, a man with a much more impressive resume than mine. I've never written for major newspapers, my name has never been uttered by Bob Costas (to my knowledge), and I have absolutely no affiliation with the Yankees.

What I *do* have to my credit is an unwavering, deep-rooted admiration for Lou Gehrig, both as a man and as a ballplayer. I have made the pilgrimage to "Yankee Country" and have spent years doing research and connecting with fellow Gehrig fans from as far away as South America.

People ask me all the time why I chose Gehrig, the Iron Horse as he would be known, to be my hero. After all, I was born decades after he died and grew up half a continent away from where he did. That, and I'm a girl. Obvious comparisons, however, can be deceiving. No one in my family passed on Gehrig fandom to me, but what they did pass on was the same heritage that Gehrig had—German-Lutheran. Gehrig grew up in a poverty-stricken, hardworking city family; I grew up in a hardworking farm family that had survived the 1980s farm loan disaster by the skin of their teeth. Gehrig played stickball in a sandlot flanked by high rises. I played Wiffleball in a grassy yard flanked by fruit trees. Different locations, same passions, same morals.

The most important reason why I chose him as my hero, and why I've invested so much of myself into writing this biography, is quite straightforward: I would love it if my children chose to emulate him.

Over ten years ago I started researching Gehrig all because

of a happy accident. After getting through all of the Steinbeck and Hemingway in the local library, I decided to go for a "fun" book, something that avoided such depressing metaphorical paradoxes as the Dust Bowl and a large fish carcass. I browsed through the recommended reading list and my eye stopped on *Lou Gehrig: Courageous Star* by Robert Rubin. "Well, hey," I thought, "I'm a sucker for courageous stars." So I dived in. My only prior exposure to the name and life of Lou Gehrig was a reference to him in the movie "The Goonies." Within a few hours I had read the very short book. Rubin may not be Steinbeck, but I was captivated by the story he presented nonetheless. I hungered for more information on Gehrig, but living in a farm town in the Midwest is not exactly conducive to researching a Yankee great, especially without Internet access. Over the next decade I amassed an extensive Gehrig library of biographies, articles, videos, pictures, as well as rare tidbits about him.

> *Gehrig fans have e-mailed me priceless stories about how this man has affected their world.*

Through the website I created based on all this information, Gehrig fans have e-mailed me priceless stories about how this man has affected their world. For instance, a young gentleman named Ed Renauer, Jr., wrote about his grandmother's date with Lou Gehrig in the 1920s. Lonnie Woods wrote to tell about the gift he sent to Lou's widow and the handwritten letter he got in return. F. K. Eitler wrote about his uncle who did legal work for Gehrig in the last years of his life. And Lucille Lasky-Nuzzi wrote about what it's like to be a Gehrig fan visiting Yankee Stadium and the Baseball Hall of Fame.

On top of these stories piled countless others. What is most amazing is the array of ages and backgrounds of these fans and how Gehrig made such an emotional impact on people who weren't born until years after he died.

One evident thing about all of these fans and admirers is that they revel in stories that have not been discussed very often, or even at all, by Gehrig's previous biographers. This apparent void inspired *The Life of Lou Gehrig*. The aim of this book is to present biographical facts, such as pivotal life events and his career accomplishments, while never failing to highlight the stories that fill the space between these facts.

Lou Gehrig was a legendary baseball player and valiant victim of a horrible disease, but he was also a human being whose life should not be portrayed solely by a regurgitation of dates and record book statistics.

The Life of Lou Gehrig includes and goes beyond the basic facts to convey the very human side of one of the most intriguing people of popular American culture. It has his statistics, of course, but it also has his cures for hitting slumps, his favorite foods, even his attempt at comedy. It is part encyclopedia and part novel, but wholly honest, interesting, and in honor of him.

Chapter One
The Sandlot Years

The trail of the Iron Horse begins in a shabby, one-room apartment in Yorkville, New York. Along the walls lie piles of other people's laundry to be washed for money. The cupboards hold just enough rations to get the family through to the next payday. In the only bed of this abode, a woman loudly sputters incoherent German as she brings a life into the world. The woman is Christina Fack Gehrig. Her husband, Heinrich Gehrig, waits anxiously with their infant daughter, Anna. This is the night of June 19, 1903.

Before the night has completely settled in, a fourteen-pound boy with blond fuzz will be born. They will name him Heinrich Ludwig after his father and watch him until he falls asleep.

Little do his parents know that their baby's tuft of blond hair will eventually be thick, dark brown. Those sweet baby ears will one day hear 62,000 people in a single hallowed stadium chant his name. His tiny, perfect mouth will spill out German words initially, but then later will deliver one of the most famous lines in American sports history. His little hands, so tiny and precious, will one day shake the hands of Columbia University's finest, rest on the shoulder of his beautiful wife, sign autographs for awestruck children, and hold a bat as impressive as the 493 major league home runs it hit. And those chunky stems called legs will bloom into bold strands of muscle that will overcome everything except a paralyzing disease.

This little human will be, as Cal Ripken, Jr., would call him, "the great and courageous Lou Gehrig."

◆ ◆ ◆

The matriculation of this night was long in coming, and the baby's birth was seemingly timed by fate. 1903 was significant in the baseball world. The team known as the Highlanders (or Hilltoppers because their ballpark, Hilltop Park, was the highest elevation in Manhattan) had just arrived in New York, up from Baltimore. Later in 1913, just four years before Lou graduated grammar school, the team's name would change to the Yankees. The first World Series was also played in 1903, featuring the best of nine between the Boston Red Sox and Pittsburgh Pirates.

Heinrich Ludwig, nicknamed "Louie" by his mother, fought his way to childhood successfully, but the sister that came before him and the two siblings that came after him did not.

His parents already had their own adventures in the New World, but none of their experiences included a baseball diamond. Both his mother and father were born into Lutheran families in the Old Country—Germany; she in Wilster, Schleweig-Holstein (now dispersed) in 1881, he fourteen years earlier in Adelheim, Baden. He immigrated to America in 1888, driving deep into the land of liberty to Chicago. Unsatisfied with life in Chicago, he moved to New York City just before the turn of the century where he met newly arrived Christina. Heinrich was thirty-two, Christina eighteen. They married on November 27, 1900, and immediately started building a family in that shabby Yorkville apartment at 1994 Second Avenue.

Yorkville was a poor section of Manhattan dominated by German families. Sanitation was a challenge, and so was surviving past infancy. Heinrich Ludwig, nicknamed "Louie" by his mother, fought his way to childhood successfully, but the sister that came before him and the two siblings that came after him did not. Anna, born in 1902, died in 1905. Sophie, born in 1904, died in 1906 from diphtheria. And the youngest, a second boy, was not alive long enough for the medical records to include his name. Only Louie survived. His display of endurance must have been encouraging to his parents, for they knew that the rest of his life would not be any easier. "He's the only big egg I have in my basket," Christina said. "He's the only one of four who lived, so I want him to have the best."[1] But giving this little buffalo the best was no small task.

"Mom" was laborious, part out of habit and part out of necessity. "Pop," a skilled foundry worker, was constantly ailing from one condition or another and frequently unemployed. Subsequently, Mom worked practically nonstop to earn enough money to keep the family going: taking in laundry, cooking, and cleaning for those further up the economic ladder. Both parents knew only a life of strife and work, and that was the biggest lesson they passed on to their only surviving child. Louie was barely out of diapers when he joined the fray, mostly hauling loads of laundry for Mom. Whenever and wherever she needed him to fill in, he did his best, despite small hands and a young mind dreaming of sandlot games.

Louie's chunkiness stayed with him throughout his childhood. His head was a wavy mop of sandy blond and his mouth was the threshold of a bottomless pit. "He never left the table hungry," Mom said, "and I can say he had a terrible appetite from the first time he saw daylight."[2] Despite meager means, Mom always had a full meal waiting for her boys on the dinner table. After cooking authentic German meals for her wealthy employers, she would bring home leftovers and groceries to prepare meals. Her German cooking was highly regarded by her clientele, and cherished by her son: pickled pig feet, sauerbraten, roast pig, jaeger schnitzel, and pickled eels. The last, according to myth, was the source of the power hitting which would make Louie famous. Pickled eels were widely thought to be his favorite food (although he never publicly acknowledged this). With such rich and heavy foods, how could the boy look like anything but well-fed?

Clothing was a bigger problem. Mom and Pop got by on the same few articles of clothing, but their son, bulging wider and taller every month, was hard to keep covered. Mom had to constantly patch and mend his clothes, making them look like a patchwork quilt. Louie may have looked hideous in them, but she would tell people resolutely, "Maybe his clothes were torn, dirty, and rumpled after playing, but he was always clean and neatly dressed when I sent him off to school."[3] Rarely did he have more than a few shirts, and never did he have an overcoat, even on the coldest of New York winter days.

His peers never let him forget these symptoms of poverty. He was harassed by the other kids for just about everything: his clothes (or lack thereof), his unruly hair, his chunkiness. But what cut the deepest on this little boy with an innate desire to play was their blatant refusal to let him join in on the games that took place in the sandlot just steps from his building—namely the game of baseball. "You're too young. You're too fat. You're too slow. You're too poor," they told him. "You don't even know how to play!"

"Never mind them," Mom would tell him. "You have better things to do than join in on bummers' games." That's all sports were to her—games bummers enjoyed. Neither she nor Pop understood the American fascination with sports when there were so many other things to be concerned with, and they never bothered to learn about any of the sports Louie adored. Mom made sure that the pressure of education fell early and hard on Louie. It was essential that he go as far as possible with school.

Louie began his scholastic voyage at Public School 132 on 183rd Street and Wadsworth Avenue at age five. Every day he set out for school in a shabby shirt, short pants, seven cents in his pocket for lunch, and a wish that he could be everything he wasn't that day—athletic, educated, and rich. Mom constantly emphasized that he was never to miss a day of school, for education was his ticket from the torn-collar life to the blue-collar—a big jump for them. Often she would lay the "Your Uncle Otto in Germany is an engineer!" speech on him. She kept a close eye on his progress as he learned to read, spell, add and subtract, never letting him slack for even a single moment. As with many children of immigrants, school was a big transition for him because for the first time he was hearing English more than his parents' native language. He was also feeling the first ounces of the weight of responsibility to his future and his family. The family's future, not just his future, would be determined in part by how far he went in school. The further he went, the better the odds of survival.

Around the same time he started school, the Gehrig family moved to another poor neighborhood called Washington Heights, a mere six miles from the Polo Grounds, the new, temporary home of the Highlanders. Unlike Yorkville, Washington Heights was not German-dominated. It was more Irish and Hungarian, with Germans a small minority. The new apartment was slightly better, having two rooms. Louie slept on a cot next to the kitchen stove.

A new neighborhood did not immediately help Louie get a welcome into the sandlot games. He was still poor, fat, shy, and he had little experience in playing games. Christmas would change things. Pop gave him a catcher's mitt, a fairly lavish gift for a family of their situation. He was the only boy in the neighborhood who had one. That mitt meant the world to Louie. It didn't even matter that it was made for a right-hander and he was left-handed, a mistake resulting from Pop not understanding the mechanics of baseball. The new glove was Louie's salvation—it got him into virtually every neighborhood game of baseball. But an "in" was only the first step. For all his love of baseball, he had minimal skill. His most noticeable flaw was what the kids called his "bucket foot." Instead of keeping his feet next to the makeshift home plate, Louie developed a bad habit of pulling his back foot away, out of the batter's box. He swung with "one foot in the bucket." This messed up his swing's accuracy tremendously, resulting in very few hits. His bucket foot was a perfect symbol for young Louie's naturally low self-esteem. Forever unsure of his ability, he backed away from the ball. Forever unsure of himself, he found it hard to make friends.

Fielding was even tougher for young Louie, in no small part due to the challenge of using a right-hander's mitt. His coordi-

That mitt meant the world to Louie. It didn't even matter that it was made for a right-hander and he was left-handed.

nation was so lacking, even the youngest of the children on the lot wondered how he was able to walk. Louie was no quitter. He kept at it until he could successfully catch and hit, and the kids were impressed at how fast he could run despite his blubbery thighs jiggling with every stride. The more he improved, the more they let him play, and the more he grew, at a more rapid pace than any of his comrades, the less they joshed him. Though his personality was one of a pacifist, his physical presence to other six- and seven-year-olds was intimidating. On one occasion another kid dared to harass him and ended up pinned to the ground, bawling his surrender. After that, Louie didn't have to worry much about the other kids jumping him, but they still teased him...cautiously.

School was the highest priority to him, thanks to the constant prodding of his mother. The pride she displayed in having a son so concerned with his studies rubbed off on the boy. He became quite proud of his unbroken attendance record. Every day, every week, he was there at his desk. Childhood is full of illness landmines, however, and Louie stepped on one during second grade—a horrid flu that may have very well been pneumonia (no doctor ever saw the boy for history to have an accurate record). Mom tucked him in and reluctantly left for work with Pop. Alone in the small apartment, Louie's mind would not let him rest easily. He was missing a day of school. He was not meeting his obligations. There was only one choice of action so far as he was concerned. He got out of bed and put on his clothes hurriedly to make it to school before roll was taken.

Every day, every week, he was there at his desk.

When he walked into the classroom pale and sweating, his teacher recognized the illness torturing his body and turned him right around and took him to Principal Halligan's office. Louie insisted on staying. "For heaven's sake," Halligan said, "you're dripping wet and you can't even sit up straight. Go home."

"But my attendance record," Louie moaned.

Halligan laughed to himself at the boy's naive but persistent need to remain a faithful workhorse. "I'll mark you present for the day if you promise to go home directly and rest until you're better."

Louie nodded his head, then headed home with an eased conscience.[4]

Once again, Louie had proven himself a fighter in the worst of conditions. The situation at home brought its own difficulties. By this point in Louie's life, he began to realize the true dynamics of his parents. Pop meant well for the most part, but he sometimes let his status as head of household blind him from doing the right thing. For instance, he often chose to spend his days at the local turnverein, a place that was half social club and half health club for German men. There he sipped beer in the comfort of his fellow countrymen, spoke politics in his native language, and escaped the toil at home that his wife was forced to face alone. This unbalance in the home workload distribution caused friction between Heinrich and Christina, and Louie picked up on it. It was kind of hard for him not to, as the Gehrig parents had their fair share of shouting matches. Mom's income paid for the majority of the cost to put the "young ox," as he would later call himself, through school. Louie recognized that Mom was the one who kept the family together, and he sided with her in almost all instances. He helped her out where he could. Every day he awoke early to catch an at-dawn sandlot game, went to school, ran errands for Mom or a neighbor for small change, then went home for supper and homework. He worked harder than any child his age because he had to, and because he wanted to take as much of the burden off Mom as possible. Pop he respected, but Mom he adored.

Undeniably, Louie was much closer to his mother than his father. They were fighting their own little war together—day in, day out—sweating in sync and sharing the task of carrying on. They even shared their own kind of joy together without Pop...or rather, because of Pop. One night Pop stayed out late with his pals playing pinochle and came home more than a little bit tipsy. As soon as he had passed out for the night, Mom got up and searched his pockets. In a household that rarely saw

a spare penny for a candy for Louie, the $17 in pinochle win-
nings Mom found in Pop's pocket was a fortune. She stashed
the money, and when dawn began to break, she woke up Louie
and told him to quietly and quickly get dressed. Without telling
him where they were going, she led him to the trolley to ride out
to Coney Island. Louie's eyes grew wide as could be when he
saw the dipping coaster and the line of rides stretching across
the horizon. Mom smiled at him and showed him the cash. All
day long the two rode rides and stuffed themselves on conces-
sions.

When Pop found out what happened to his money, he felt
guilty enough to promise to lay off the card playing and beer
drinking—a promise that lasted for two weeks.

This is not to say that Pop was an alcoholic or abusive to his
family. He truly strived for the best for his family, but he faced a
dilemma. On the one hand, he had to juggle his status as head
of household, which included a responsibility to provide for his
family. On the other, he had to maintain a certain image to his
German neighbors and roots. If he did not do and spend as he
pleased at the turnverein like the other men, he might be seen
as weak or emasculated. Louie understood this quirk about his
father's life and did not love him any less for it.

Despite his relatively mature way of life, young Louie was ram-
bunctious at heart. He didn't enjoy causing trouble, but he did
revel in play, especially when it came to baseball. Many of the
boys in his neighborhood also had jobs or commitments after
school, so in order to fit in time for baseball the boys woke up
at dawn and met in the sandlot for a game. Neighbors would
complain about the noise, but the local patrol policeman, whom
the boys nicknamed "Fishcakes," would usually just give them
a warning to keep it down. When Fishcakes fell ill, however, his
replacement, a tall, skinny fellow the kids labeled "Beanpole,"
was not as compassionate to the boys and he repeatedly dis-
banded their games. The boys dreamed aloud about extraordinary plots of revenge, but it was Louie who actually came up
with a plan.

Few times in his life did Lou Gehrig openly display his playful cleverness, mostly because he clung to his dignity with white knuckles. Desperate to get in some game time, he didn't hesitate to whip out his imaginative thinking. The plan he developed was so astute that the other boys couldn't wait to put it into action.

The plan involved hanging a homemade dummy from a chimney pipe on the roof of a building. From the street, the dummy looked like a man who had hung himself. Boys hid on either side of the door that opened to the roof with a wire held taut between them. Louie, with his good-boy reputation, had the job of baiting the cop. "Sir! Sir!" he called to Beanpole. "Come quick! There's a dead man on the roof!" Having no reason not to trust the boy from a good family, Beanpole hurried after Louie to the point on the street where the "man" could be seen. Like a flash, Beanpole ran up to the roof and flung open the door. Just as they had hoped, his legs caught on the wire and he fell flat on his face. The boys laughed hysterically until they saw his angry expression. Then they fled. Thankfully he was not hurt, though he did inform Louie's parents of the trick. While Mom was infuriated at Louie's disrespect toward an authority figure, Pop could barely keep a straight face. He loved slapstick comedy and the vision of Beanpole hitting the rooftop with a thud and a thin cloud of dirt puffing up around him was classic. Pop did give Louie a punishment, then winked at him when Mom wasn't looking.

While Mom was infuriated at Louie's disrespect toward an authority figure, Pop could barely keep a straight face.

◆ ◆ ◆

When Louie decided to join the Public School 132 baseball team in fourth grade, Mom was a little relieved that he was spending his energy on games rather than fooling officers of the law. Games, she decided, were fine so long as they didn't disrupt his school work or his chores. The grammar school coach needed a catcher and put Louie behind the plate for the first practice. Louie had some difficulties but seemed good enough to use during the first game. The coach, however, was not accounting for the shy boy's nervousness. This was Louie's first organized baseball game, played in front of parents, umpires and, most troubling of all, girls. As a batter he was so nervous at the plate that he kept a foot in the bucket. As a catcher...well, he was benched after one game. The next practice he was moved to right field, where he would have comparatively ample time to shake off the nervousness when a ball came his way. Louie didn't let his escapade as catcher keep him off the field, though. A persistent boy if ever there was one, he practiced harder and longer and made it on the Oval Team of the Park Department's one-hundred-pound-and-under league, a shining milestone in his young life.

One day at the swimming hole, Louie got it in his head that he wanted to swim the mile-wide river to the Fort Lee Ferry on the New Jersey side.

Playing organized baseball didn't keep Louie out of trouble. In fact, his brushes with the law increased. Louie spent hot summer days swimming with his friends in the Hudson River at 181st Street. They used a protruding rock as a diving platform. On a particularly hot day, they decided to go skinny dipping. They were caught and arrested. Pop didn't laugh at that stunt. Nor did he laugh when Louie and friends were arrested for stealing a ride on a trolley. Louie's friends suspected that Pop gave Louie a beating for it. The pinnacle of his stunts came the summer he turned eleven. One day at the swimming hole, Louie got it in his head that he wanted to swim the mile-wide river to the Fort Lee Ferry on the New Jersey side. And he did, with a strong stroke and powerful kick that kept him from being swept by the tide. His friends were amazed and cheered him on. But when Pop found out about the dangerous stunt he boxed Louie's ears. Mom screamed at Louie, but he could barely hear her over the ringing of his eardrums.

In his parents' opinion, the stunts were warning signs that

their son was headed for a life of crime. So Pop turned to his turnverein for instilling the discipline in Louie that he could not. When Louie—or Lou, as he preferred by this age—was twelve, he began to attend the traditional German gymnastics classes taught there. In addition to getting him away from the negative influences of the streets, the gymnastics burned off the lingering baby fat that coated his body.

Lou's best friend, Mike Sesit, who was among the crowd reprimanded for stealing a ride on the trolley, joined him in attending a turnverein at 85th and Lexington. "Lou was about 158 pounds then," Sesit said, "mostly belly and ass." The boys took their turns on the parrallel bars, rings and mats. Steadily, Lou's body took shape, giving him the appearance of being carved out of a block of iron. The muscle bulk came faster than coordination, and Lou struggled with balance and timing. "His body behaved as if it were drunk," Sesit recalled.[5]

In addition, Sesit remembered, Lou occasionally complained of sharp pains in his back and legs during workouts, but Lou never quit. When the boys were not working out, they frequented *konditorei*, German coffee houses, that dotted the neighborhood.

The turnverein soon served another purpose for both Lou and his father: that of a safe haven. On May 7, 1915, a German U-boat sunk the luxury liner *Lusitania*, killing over 1,100 passengers, including 120 Americans. Hatred for Germany escalated rapidly in the United States over the next few years. Anything with German influence was fair game for public scorn. German-Americans caught the brunt. Though not every German expatriate and their families were subjected to humiliation, those who were had terrible stories to tell. They were fired without just cause from their jobs. Beatings were common. Many were forced at gunpoint to recite the Pledge of Allegiance. Universities cancelled German language classes. Books written by Germans, in German, or about Germany and its people were banned from libraries. Kraut was renamed "Freedom Cabbage." The German-Americans were losing their culture, through no fault of their own, because of some misdirection an entire ocean away.

The Gehrigs, living in the world's busiest city, could not escape the hate. Like many other German families, they ceased speaking German in public and guardedly spoke it at home. Typical of their nature, though, none of the Gehrigs complained openly about the new restrictions inflicted on them. They carried on with their daily routine.

Lou was not lucky enough to avoid all torment for his heritage, however. On the lighter side, he was called "krauthead," "little Heinie," "dumb Dutchman," "kaiser." At other times, though, he was accosted by older boys at school, who were also "hyphenated Americans," such as Irish, British, Polish, but who did not have the misfortune of being born with German lineage. Once, a group of boys physically taunted him to the point that he attacked with his stone-hard fists. A teacher broke up the fight before Lou was finished, but the bullies got his point. Lou's troubles were small relative to what other German-Americans experienced. In an effort to prove themselves more American than German, German-Americans Anglicized their names. The Gehrigs were no exception. Lou's official name became Henry Louis. Some families went so far as to change the spelling and pronunciation of their surnames. Mom's business as a cook of German foods may have suffered a bit, but she made up for it by performing other domestic duties. For the Gehrig men, the turnverein was the only place that boasted an all-German, all-the-time atmosphere in chaotic World War I America.

He led the pack in shot put, was the fastest relay runner, and played running back and tackle for the football team.

Discounting the troubles related to heritage, Lou had it as well as could be for a boy in his circumstances. By the time he was in the seventh grade, Lou was the best athlete of his grammar school's teams. He led the pack in shot put, was the fastest relay runner, and played running back and tackle for the football team. In his limited free time he played baseball on the Oval Team. Pop may have considered muscular development the highlight of Lou's achievements, and Mom may have considered academic progress the highlight. To Lou, however, the biggest achievement was establishing sports as his forte, especially since it had not been all that long since he was last shunned off of the sandlot.

In 1917 Lou graduated from grammar school. Pop, fifty at that time, was ailing and could not work. Mom had just taken a job as a cook in New Jersey, a trek that wore her out. Lou felt the strain of responsibility to family more than ever. Boys his age and of his social class rarely sought a high school education instead of a full-time job. A local delicatessen owner had offered him an apprenticeship and Lou suggested to his parents that he could "get working papers" instead of a high school diploma. Mom would not hear of it: "Your Uncle Otto in Germany is an engineer!"

Chapter Two
High School Hero

For Lou, the path to an Uncle Otto-esque life would begin with Manhattan's reputable High School of Commerce at 155 West 65th Street, where he began his studies in the fall of 1917. This all-boys school was a sort of technical school, teaching young men the workings of bookkeeping and similar careers. Most of its graduates went on directly to such jobs. Usually they did not proceed to university. But Mom was determined to get her boy to the highest possible level of education, regardless of the fact that both she and Pop were suffering physically and financially. So Lou continued to pack off to school every weekday wearing a khaki shirt and pants and thick brown work shoes with an apple for lunch.

Starting high school is a big step for any young man, and all the more important to a young man in Lou's position. His big step was at first a steeper one than he was prepared for. He was still wearing boyhood khaki short pants, for example, something for which his schoolmates teased him from day one. Being in a "big boy" school was undercut by his little-boy clothes. Unfortunately Pop's health continued to decline, which pulled the family's budget tighter than ever, and Mom told Lou he would have to continue to wear his short pants until the seat wore out. Then and only then would they spend the precious money on something as superficial as pants.

Lou refused to remain the dud. He already worked a number of odd jobs before and after school, and he began stashing a little money for himself before handing over the earnings to his mother. He eventually bought himself a pair of fashionable long pants. Mom would have been furious if she had caught him wearing his new pants, so Lou hid them in the apartment building's foyer. On school days he would dash out of the family apartment wearing his short pants. When he got to the foyer he made sure no one was around, took the long pants out of hiding, slipped them on over his short pants, and walked to school. In the afternoon, he reversed the process. This scheme worked, as Mom's attention was generally focused on whatever work was in her callused hands.

With one embarrassment under control, Lou tried to concentrate on finding his fit at Commerce, but even in long pants that feat was not easy. Though he pursued his coursework in earnest, he was not much more than an average student. His struggle in typing class epitomized his struggle with academics in general. Typing teacher Mollie Silverman Parnis said of him, "He could hit a baseball without missing a stroke but his thick fingers just couldn't seem to find the right keys on the typewriter."[1]

"When I got there and saw so many people going into the field and heard all the cheering and noise, I was so scared I couldn't see straight."

She encouraged him as much as possible, a favor he would repay in his first year with the Yankees by sending her roses from every American League city. He could have made up for academics, as many a young man can today, by proving his worth on playing fields, but Lou did not consider himself talented enough to compete on a high school level. Grammar school games and sandlot entertainments were nothing like what he thought high school ball was. The other kids didn't see it that way, and they hounded Lou to join Commerce's athletic teams. Only a teacher, an authority figure, could finally convince him. Lou said on the issue, "Some of the kids had told my bookkeeping teacher that I could hit the ball a mile in the park. The teacher ordered me to show up for a school game. I went up to the stadium on a streetcar. When I got there and saw so many people going into the field and heard all the cheering and noise, I was so scared I couldn't see straight. I turned right around and got back on the streetcar and went home. The next day the teacher threatened to flunk me if I didn't show up for the next game. So I went."[2]

The world was never the same again.

At some point during his tenure at Commerce, Lou played on every school team: soccer, basketball, football, baseball, hockey and wrestling. Mom was none too happy that Lou's time was packed with sporting events, which left less time for studying. She was convinced that he was headed for a life as a bummer and not one as an educated man with a well-paying job. Lou's numerous games were cut down dramatically when a doctor told him that he had a small heart. At the time, a small heart was considered to be a condition that restricted an athlete (today it is widely believed that a small heart's ability to pump blood more efficiently is advantageous to an athlete). Always one to obey authority, Lou dropped all sports except football, soccer and, his favorite, baseball.

His success in sports improved Lou's self-image and how others thought of him. In football, which showcased his power on the line and remarkable punting, he felt confident. In fact, he was so confident that when the coach kept playing him as a lineman, Lou went to the coach and threatened to turn in his jersey if he couldn't play in a position where he could carry the ball. Initially the coach was angry for the impudent threat, but soon he gave in and put Lou in the fullback position. This allowed Lou to punt, pass and carry. Enormity of build and strength no doubt provided Lou his noticeable confidence on the gridiron. Even his own team feared his size. In one practice, teammate Leonard Lyons absorbed the brunt force of Lou's tackle, a force Lyons likened to a speeding locomotive. Lyons consequently decided to be a kicker. Lou's football talent would earn him Metropolitan All-Scholastic Honors.

Lou's first year of baseball was not quite as successful. In his freshman year on the Commerce baseball team, the spring of 1918, he started at first base, the youngest starter on the team. His batting statistics were surprisingly sour: an unbelievable

.150 batting average. This was what Lou had been afraid of and why he was so hesitant to compete on a high school level in baseball. The ability to hit a ball a mile in the park does not necessarily translate into the same ability on a real ball field. Baseball Coach Duschatko had given the kid the benefit of the doubt, being convinced by a friend of Lou's that he was a shy boy who had immense talent in his rippling muscles. Though Duschatko never spoke negatively of him, Lou didn't need someone else to say anything to know he was a disappointment—the worst possible thing that he could be in his opinion. His friends wouldn't allow him to wallow in his baseball mishaps, however, so he forgot the self-pity and kicked around a soccer ball.

The fall of 1918 brought Gehrig into his sophomore year at Commerce and an opportunity to play soccer, a sport he rarely had the chance to play. Joining the team was a stroke of luck. One day after school, classmate Oliver Gintel and other boys were practicing on the soccer field and the ball got away from them. Lou happened to be walking on the sidelines and stopped the ball. "Kick it!" Oliver yelled at the husky boy. With a natural swing of his leg, Lou kicked the ball from one end of the soccer field to the other. The boys stared in stunned silence. For the next few weeks, Oliver was relentless in his goal to get Lou into a Commerce soccer jersey, advances Lou tried to shrug off. Finally, to shut Oliver up if nothing else, Lou showed up at soccer practice and performed the same stunt. The coach was hooked too. With Lou on the team, Commerce won the Winter Championship three straight years. On one astounding Saturday in the fall of 1920, Gehrig played against Commercial High School of Brooklyn in both soccer and football. In the morning he kicked the winning goal in soccer, and that afternoon he threw a forty-yard touchdown pass to gain the win for Commerce, 9-6.

Off the field, meanwhile, Lou managed to form close relationships with fellow Commerce boys. Mike Sesit was still around, playing sports with Lou. Another buddy of Lou's was Ed Rosenthal, a young man from a moderately wealthy family who was destined to found Warner Communications. Ed's father was a mortician and was able to afford plenty of food and clothes for his family and then some, but Ed never let that go to his head. Ed and Lou often could be seen sharing their lunches together.

Lou's sophomore year also ushered in a new head baseball coach, the man whom Lou would ultimately credit with molding him into a slugger. Coach Harry Kane, a veteran of World War I, was immediately taken with Lou because of his size, his underdeveloped talent, and, most of all, his dedication to improving himself for the sake of the team. Despite the school paper's assertion that Lou was "woefully weak at the bat,"[3] Kane saw that Lou was a powder keg, if he could only learn how to harness his power. Kane jumped into building Lou Gehrig into a hitter. He started by trying to break Lou's habitual bucket foot (the habit of pulling his back foot away and out of the batter's box would not be completely broken until Lou's college coach got a hold of him). Next, he worked with Lou on his biggest weakness—the inability to hit southpaw curve balls. A lefty himself, Kane threw curves at him for hours until Gehrig was able to spot the pitch and adjust appropriately to rip into it.

Kane recalled hearing opposing coaches tell their lefty pitchers, "Feed Gehrig nothing but curveballs. He can't hit 'em." He could only grin with anticipation as the next season started. Because of Coach Kane's help, Gehrig's second-year statistics soared over his previous season's. His batting average doubled to an even .300.

"He was the greatest athlete I ever coached," Kane said of his star pupil later. "He was almost as big then as he was when he was at the height of his career with the Yankees, and he had the same team spirit and eagerness to win. It was a pleasure to coach him, for he constantly wanted to learn and improve his play, and when a weakness cropped up in his play, he worked at it until he had eradicated it."[4]

Despite all of Lou's achievements and praise in athletics, and the fact that Mom began collecting newspaper articles that mentioned her Louie, sports were still frowned upon by his mother. Pop was more understanding, saying that the fresh air and exercise was invaluable to a growing boy. Throughout it all,

Lou knew his first priority was school, then work, then sports. He kept a string of various jobs to help bring in cash for his family. He had a weekend job with a local grocery, and during the week he would run errands for neighbors and help Mom with whatever jobs she had on her schedule.

Towards the end of his high school years, Mom landed a housekeeper/cook position with the Columbia University fraternity house of the Sigma Nu brothers. Pop was also hired on as janitor and handyman. By helping Mom serve the boys, Lou entitled himself to free meals, which put some much-needed ease on the family's food budget. The brothers were barely tolerant of the bulging, shy high school boy they labeled "Little Heinie" or "Little Dutch Boy" to try to get a rise out of him. Lou usually responded with a smile and silence, a move that left some brothers with the opinion that Lou was too dumb to speak. They teased him, played mean tricks on him, did everything but tie him to a tree during a lightning storm. This began Lou's distaste for Columbia University.

They teased him, played mean tricks on him, did everything but tie him to a tree during a lightning storm.

He was glad to go back to his high school world. Once he showed up to baseball practice covered from head to toe in black dust. While his teammates snickered over coal-miner jokes, he explained to Coach Kane that he had to take over Pop's job as janitor for the day because Pop was ill.

Lou rarely complained about his demanding schedule. One of the few times he did openly complain was during an extra-innings baseball game that was eating into his chore time at the Sigma Nu house. There was considerable distance between the house and Commerce's home field at the Catholic Protectory in the Bronx. Coach Kane remembered Lou sulking around the dugout and being rather irritable. Finally, Kane told Lou that if he wanted the game to end, he'd better go out there and do it himself.

That's exactly what Lou did, hitting to break the tie score in the next half-inning.

Baseball very quickly became Lou's strongest sport. He even found other teams on which he could play. The first time he began to earn money for playing baseball was with the Minqua Baseball Club sponsored by the Assembly District Democratic Club of West 181st Street. Minqua played against semi-pro teams from neighboring democratic districts for a guarantee of $35, the battery receiving $5 each. Gehrig batted in the bottom of the Minqua lineup on various fields, such as Floyd Bennett Field and the Bronx Reservoir Oval. He preferred to pitch—not for the glory, but for the higher cut of the money. The money was more than welcomed by Mom, but she held on tightly to her belief that baseball was foolishness.

All the extra experience on the field in front of crowds against semi-pro players helped mold Lou into the most versatile player on the Commerce team. He played outfield, pitcher and first base by his senior year. Though the shortstop Bunny Bonura was considered the best player, Lou ranked high in value to the team. With two outstanding players, Commerce easily earned the title of city champions in the Police Athletic League. New York's *Daily News* approached Coach Kane about putting together a championship game between the top teams in New York and Chicago. The proposed game date was June 28, 1920, Commerce versus Lane Technical High School, played in Chicago at Wrigley Field, home of the Cubs. Kane was not about to pass up the opportunity to spread Commerce's name and image halfway across the country and accepted the offer.

At the next Commerce practice, Kane gathered the boys and made the announcement. But before they could go, he said, the boys would have to get permission from their parents to travel to Chicago. Lou instantly realized how difficult this could be. It was a struggle just convincing his mother to let him play baseball in New York. How on earth could he ever get her to agree to let him go to Chicago?

As expected, Mom said no. Lou enlisted Coach Kane to change her mind. Knowing that Commerce would be crippled without Lou's talent, Kane went to the Gehrig apartment to talk to Mom in private. Lou waited anxiously in the hallway outside the apartment listening to the muffled voices of his mother and coach. Eventually Kane and Mom came to an agreement— Mom would grant permission only if Kane would promise to personally watch out for Lou and make sure he was tucked in safely at night. Kane knew she was overprotective and worried about her son, so he promised her that Lou's sheets would be pulled tightly around him every night. Lou was relieved, and a bit embarrassed for a being mama's boy.

The Commerce team was scheduled to leave on a Wednesday and return on the following Sunday, a total of five days. A group of about 100 students and a band were there for their farewell at Grand Central Station. In all, nine Commerce players went to Chicago: Eli Jacobs, pitcher; Al McLaughlin, catcher; Lou Gehrig, first base; Al Rosamundo, second base; Bunny Bonura, shortstop; Sewell Johnson, third base; Schacht, Starke, and Strum in the outfield. The train ride, a first for all the boys, was an unforgettable venture. They got endless kicks out of the Pullman beds. On the way to Chicago the boys' story quickly spread from car to car and other travelers visited them to give their best wishes. Among the visitors was former president and then-current Supreme Court Justice William Howard Taft, perhaps the most avid baseball fan ever voted into the White House (he began the tradition of throwing out the first pitch in 1910). He shook the hand of each boy and offered his tips on playing. Another prized visitor was comedian Joey Frisco, who performed an impromptu show to keep the boys rolling with laughter. Lou and his teammates felt like royalty, like media darlings—like big league players.

They arrived in Chicago on Thursday, and while many were anxious to see Wrigley Field, the first stop was the hotel for room assignments, two boys per room. Then they were off to the field on Friday for practice. It took a while to adjust to the big league park. The vastness made them feel like dots more than princes, and when they saw gigantic Lake Michigan after practice, they had trouble believing it was only a lake and not an ocean itself.

Saturday was game day. The turnout was an incredible 10,000 baseball fans. The last World Series game played at

Wrigley in 1918 attracted only 27,000. Photographers and motion picture cameras packed the sidelines just as they would at a big league game. Gehrig walked out onto the field and nearly froze with stage fright, but he kept himself busy with warmups. The nervous jitters nagged the team for the first half of the game. Eli Jacobs wasn't pitching well, and his catcher Al McLaughlin turned his left ankle so bad that Coach Kane had to carry him on and off the field. McLaughlin refused to give up, which justified his appointment that year as team captain. Then again, with no replacement players, Kane and McLaughlin didn't have much of a choice anyway.

His reputation as a power hitter had preceded him to Chicago, and Lane Tech kept its outfield playing deep waiting for him.

Gehrig managed to play without error at first base, but on offense he struggled. His reputation as a power hitter had preceded him to Chicago, and Lane Tech kept its outfield playing deep waiting for him. Lou's first five times at the plate were unproductive, but his team still managed to rack up a winning 8-6 score by the final inning. Lou's sixth time at bat, however, validated his reputation. Ninth inning, bases loaded. The first pitch zoomed by, and Lou didn't touch it. The second pitch was perfect, and Lou teed off on it as if it were stopped midair in front of him. The ball soared over the fence, hopped over Sheffield Avenue, and landed on a porch facing the park. With his homer, he sealed the Commerce victory over Lane Tech 12-6.

The press was infatuated with Lou's power and pressed Kane for the inside scoop on the muscle-bound young man. Kane bragged, "He was always a great kid in a pinch, and I would have bet my life he was going to slough one this time."[5] Before Commerce was able to make it back to New York, the press had already embraced Lou, both in New York and Chicago. The Sunday edition of the New York *Daily News* ran a picture of a smiling Lou as he crossed home plate after his grand slam with a caption that read "Louis Gherig [sic], Commerce Slugger." In the article he was deemed "the New York lad known as the

Babe Ruth of the high schools."[6] The *Chicago Tribune* said, "Gehrig's blow would have made any big leaguer proud, yet it was walloped by a boy who hasn't yet started to shave." The *New York Times*, which also erroneously spelled Lou's surname, as "Gherrig," wrote, "the real Babe Ruth never poled one more thrilling."[7] (Misspellings weren't a big deal to Lou; even his own high school couldn't spell his name correctly in the 1921 Caravel yearbook, where it appeared as "Gherig.")

At 11:15 am on Sunday, Commerce's heroes arrived at Grand Central Station and were welcomed by a swelling crowd of 5,000, including the Orphan Asylum Band. The crowd cheered each boy as he stepped off the railcar, and it cheered the loudest for Lou. He smiled his shy, deep-dimples smile as they carried him and his teammates to the cabs waiting to whisk them back to Commerce's gymnasium. A second large crowd was assembled at the school and the boys were honored with a congratulatory speech by the superintendent, who slipped in a special mention of a grand slam by one hitting prodigy.

The Lane Tech game gave Lou such publicity that universities took interest in him. By the time he graduated, Lou had sports scholarship offers from twenty-four universities—more than enough choices for a boy that social convention assumed would not even go to college. But both fate and his mother would determine his choice of university.

During the fall of 1920, the Commerce football team played De Witt Clinton High School in an exhibition game on Columbia University's South Field. In the stands was Columbia's manager of athletics and recent alum Bobby Watt. While working at the Sigma Nu house, Mom had met Watt and he had kept a vague memory of her quiet, unimpressive son. Little did he know that the stalwart young fullback who flabbergasted him with backfield talent was the same boy. All he knew watching the Commerce fullback run, pass and kick with skill was that the kid was the addition that would make his Lions team gleam. When Watt found out whose son his prospect was, he was thrilled. Signing Lou on with the Lions was nearly a sure thing.

He played up how close Lou would be to home when he paid a visit to Lou's mom. It didn't take much convincing for Mom to agree to Columbia. Watt would later tell reporters that he had no idea that Lou Gehrig played baseball, as Columbia only looked at him for football.

Fulfilling the pattern that had been set when he was big enough to carry a basket of laundry, Lou did what his mother wanted and agreed to enroll at Columbia University.

Chapter Three
Big Man on Campus

In a scene from *Pride of the Yankees*, the feature film based on Lou Gehrig's life, a young Gehrig is being reprimanded by Mom for hitting a ball through a butcher's window. To get across to her son that silly neighborhood games will never lead him to a great future, she draws his attention to a framed picture of a respectable looking man on the living room wall. "Don't you want to be an engineer like your Uncle Otto?" she demands. Lou mumbles, "Sure, Mom, sure. Whatever you want me to be," as he stares longingly at the baseball the butcher had given back to him. Mom's point was that respectable men did not play bummers' games.

In real life there may not have been a picture of Otto on the living room wall, but his precedent certainly loomed over Gehrig's head. Now that he was about to be a "collision," as Mom pronounced "collegian" with her thick German accent, Mom expected him to follow in Otto's footsteps. At the time German-Americans were making a name for themselves in the world of engineering, a fact Mom was all too happy to use for her cause. Gehrig submitted, in typical fashion. He was bound for Columbia University and its pre-engineering program.

Though there was no formal Ivy League in 1921, Columbia University already had the strenuous academic prerequisites the league is known for today. The academic demands were much more than Gehrig's relatively meager credentials could deliver. After he graduated from Commerce in February 1921, he immediately enrolled in Columbia's Department of Extension, a crash-course program that was designed to prepare him for Columbia's arduous entrance exam. Gehrig was an average student, but the thing that set him apart was his tenacious dedication to improving himself. He did not view the extension program as a put down, but rather as a surmountable challenge. He studied harder than ever and rapidly advanced. In June he completed the program, passed the final exam, and passed the entrance exam. He was officially a Columbia University incoming freshman and therefore officially received a football scholarship for the fall of 1921.

Meanwhile, he got a taste of college ball. Because he was not a full-time student, he was not allowed to play with Columbia's baseball team during official games over their summer season. However, his new coach, Andy Coakley (himself a former major league star), gave him permission to practice with the team, which Lou did with zeal. He even got to play in an exhibition game on April 5. He was there to get experience with college-level baseball, but the game nearly led to the end of his college career. The Columbia Lions played an exhibition game against the minor league Hartford Senators of the Class A Eastern League. Alton Durgin, the opposing pitcher, thought he could handle college batters well enough, but he wasn't expecting a seventeen-year-old boy to whack two home runs off of him, gaining the only points the Lions had on the board. If Durgin was surprised, his manager Arthur Irwin was shocked. After the game Irwin approached Gehrig and asked him if he knew who John McGraw was. Of course Gehrig knew. He was the manager of the New York Giants. Irwin offered to introduce Gehrig to Art Devlin, the man who could set up a tryout for Gehrig with McGraw and the Giants.

Gehrig met with Devlin, and the next afternoon they were at the Polo Grounds, the home field of the Giants, with McGraw and his team. For four days Gehrig tried out with men who were older with more experience and newer fielding gloves. Gehrig was a kid in patched clothes with a tattered first baseman's mitt. Regardless, he tried to prove himself for baseball's "Little Napoleon," as McGraw was called for his short stature and even shorter temper. The young Gehrig didn't do too poorly, which is to say that he managed to sock about six pitches into the stands, although McGraw was stubbornly unimpressed. The more McGraw basically ignored him, the more uptight and nervous Gehrig got. He felt out of place and lost what little self-confidence he had. On the fourth day his nerves got the best of him and he ruined a routine play by letting a grounder pass through his legs.

"Get this fellow out of here!" McGraw barked. "I've got enough lousy players without another one showing up!"[1] Against the objections of Devlin, McGraw demanded that Gehrig leave the field. Devlin did offer Gehrig an alternative, however, after they left the stadium. The Giants had a working arrangement with the Hartford Senators, he explained, and they could go back to Irwin and arrange to sign up Gehrig to play ball with the Senators for the summer. It was still professional ball, and Gehrig knew that the manager already liked what he had to offer, no tryout needed.

Both Devlin and Irwin assured him that many college players played for professional teams under assumed names and never got in trouble.

If this sounded too good to be true, it was. The one rule Devlin and Irwin both violated with such a proposal was this: If a college athlete plays for a professional team, he forfeits his amateur status and therefore cannot play at the college level. According to Gehrig, both Devlin and Irwin assured him that many college players played for professional teams under assumed names and never got in trouble. Both encouraged him to sign with the Senators under the name Lou Lewis.

Devlin and Irwin weren't completely upfront, however, giving Gehrig a half-truth. It was true that many college players played under assumed names for pro teams without getting in trouble...but only because they never got caught. Those who did faced harsh punishments. The first baseball star from Columbia University, Eddie Collins, was caught in 1906 playing for the Athletics his last college summer and was banned from college ball his senior year under this same rule. Chances were good that Gehrig did not know of Collins' fate and trusted the counsel of two authority figures, signing with Hartford on June 2, 1921. The Hartford newspapers nearly blew his cover when they announced that "Lefty Gehrig" was the newest addition to the Senators. Behind the scenes someone put the gag order on stating his real name, and for his semi-pro debut on June 3, he was referred to as Lou Lewis.

Lewis had a disappointing first game, getting no hits and one sacrifice in three at-bats. June 4 was a better day, with a triple in his first at-bat, helping the Senators win 5-3. The next day brought two hits, a 10-2 victory, and the first of the comparisons to Ruth that were routinely sprinkled in articles on Gehrig for the majority of his baseball career. After a couple of days off, Lewis was back at it on June 8, hitting a double. After being in the Senators' lineup for two weeks and helping them earn first place in their division, Lewis had played in twelve games and earned a .261 average, which included twelve hits, one double, and two triples. What the papers didn't mention was how much the young slugger longed to be back in New York with his parents. Unbeknownst to him, June 15 was to be the date he returned home. Andy Coakley had been tipped off that his incoming baseball star was playing for Hartford. Coakley had not believed it until he showed up to the Senators' ballpark on June 15 and saw his prodigy sitting in the home dugout. Coakley informed Gehrig that choosing to play with Hartford may have eliminated his eligibility to play with Columbia, despite what Irwin and Devlin had said. Coakley told him to get his butt back to New York, an order Gehrig gratefully followed.

Once they had arrived in New York, Coakley went to the board at Columbia to defend a naíve boy's mistake. He suggested that he could write to all the other schools that Columbia played baseball and football with to explain the situation and to ask if it would be acceptable for Columbia to retain the right to play Gehrig on the condition that he sit out all sports his freshman year. The board agreed and Coakley went to work. The letter went to schools such as Colgate, New York University, Rutgers, and Cornell. All of the schools replied that the punishment suggested was sufficient, and in fact many stated that it could even be lessened if Columbia saw fit. Gehrig was unconditionally benched until the fall of 1922.

Gehrig felt betrayed that he had been lied to and was consequently being forced to abandon the one thing he truly loved.
At the same time, he was grateful not to be kicked out for good.
He was left with ample time for studies. Gehrig became a freshman at Columbia in the fall of 1921. Though he still worked out
with the football and baseball teams, being told to ride pine during games was difficult. Sports was really the only comfort he
had in college. On a campus populated by well-dressed, well-
financed young gentlemen, Gehrig was a round peg shoved
awkwardly into a square hole. Many fraternities pursued him,
but only because they liked the idea of having a star athlete
among their members. He chose to rush Phi Delta Theta. Phi
Delta was not interested in assisting Gehrig in his college matriculation; they took him in because of his reputation as an athlete. The brothers ignored him altogether when they weren't
chiding him or playing tricks on him, not caring for how hard
and busy his life was. Early in the morning, he had to be at the
Sigma Nu house where Mom still worked to help her serve the
brothers breakfast. After the school day and practice, he would
go back the house to help her serve supper, clean up, then
study to try to keep up with the grueling coursework. Many
times he fell asleep in a chair studying, still in his clothes, because he was too exhausted to make the trek back home. To
this day Columbia and Phi Delta Theta like to drop Gehrig's
name as one of their own, but Gehrig was quite clear during his
life that he wanted nothing to do with either once he was out of
college. The day he died he still owed his fraternity a small
amount of money, his own little quiet rebellion.

In the classroom things were somewhat easier because the
other kids' attention was on the professor instead of him. He
had wonderful professors who showed him the respect that
some of his classmates did not. Because of his bulk, he was
easy for professors to spot in the crowd and call on to answer a
question. Such was the case in his American History class with
Professor Robert L. Schuyler. The much smaller kid who sat

next to him, Vernon B. Hampton, remembers that Gehrig always had the answer because he was a disciplined studier, just as he was a disciplined athlete. "I was always glad that Gehrig had done the studying, for all too often I didn't know the lesson myself," Hampton admitted[2].

During his first summer break in college, Gehrig found different teams on which to play. The unbelievable thing was that he chose to play in a semipro league again. He played every Sunday with the Westinghouse team from Morristown, New Jersey, as "Lou Long," an alias inspired by the surname of a teammate's fiancée. He also played with a team from Yonkers under the name "Gerry" on West New York Field, where he reportedly holds the record for the longest home run. It was well-known in his time that he played semipro ball in the summer of 1922, but for whatever reason the athletic department at Columbia looked the other way. One possible explanation is that playing games on the weekend for a little extra cash was considered more acceptable than signing with a Class A team.

With his playing eligibility fully reinstated, Gehrig returned to Columbia in the fall of 1922 for football season. A valuable player to his team, he split up his time on the field between the backfield and the line. Punting was his specialty. Later on in his life when he lived in New Rochelle, Gehrig would go to the football field and spend hours punting just for the pure fun of it. Bill McKenna, his high school football coach, would say of Gehrig, "He had perfect form, and compared favorably with the best professional I have seen."[3]

Columbia's football coach, Buck O'Neil, used Gehrig's punting as much as he could, but Gehrig excelled on the field in other ways as well. In the first game of the season against Ursinus College, Gehrig and All-American running back teammate Wally Koppisch together scored all five touchdowns for the Lions, Koppisch with three and Gehrig with two. Paul Gallico (who would later write the first biography of Lou Gehrig) praised Gehrig's performance in the university's *Alumni News*: "Gehrig is the beef expert who has mastered the science of going where he is sent, for at least five yards. His plunges seemed to carry force."[4]

During the season Gehrig helped whip Amherst, Wesleyan, New York University, and Middlebury. The biggest game was against Colgate on Thanksgiving day; it was also the last game of the season. Despite the pain of a separated right shoulder, Gehrig scored the Lions' only touchdown on a forty-yard pass reception. He actually scored two touchdowns but the first one didn't count because of a foul committed by Koppisch. His determination to play in spite of an injury would continue throughout his Yankee career, and it was not lost on his Lions teammates and the opposing team. Even after the dismal loss to Colgate, 59-6, the opposing coach lauded Gehrig's performance to sportswriter Grantland Rice, "His right arm and shoulder were useless. But he stuck to his job."[5]

His own coach was no less impressed with the steamroller named Gehrig, and his teammates would rave about him for years after what would be his only season with the Lions. Robert Pulleyn was on the squad with Gehrig and said of him, "He was a battler. On the football field Lou worked with everything he had."[6] Another teammate said, "They stomped all over Lou, but they could never crush his grin or spirit."[7] One player who was particularly glad to have Gehrig on his team was tackle John Donaldson. During practice one afternoon Donaldson dislocated a finger. Gehrig calmed him down and after looking at the injured finger expertly took John's hand and popped the finger back into place.

As much as he enjoyed football, Gehrig looked forward to the upcoming baseball season even more. On defense he was a coach's dream utility player, covering first base, outfield, and the mound. Coakley gave this evaluation of Gehrig: "Lou was a fair outfielder, a first baseman without any glaring weakness, and a good pitcher. In the outfield he covered a lot of ground, got most of the drives hit his way, and got the ball away fast with his strong arm. As a college pitcher he didn't have much stuff, but he did have a better fastball than most college pitchers. Some days no college team could beat him."[8] As pitcher, he earned a 6-4 record with eleven starts. In five games he struck out ten or more hitters. The highlight game was against Williams on April 18, 1923. On the same day that Babe Ruth christened the brand new Yankee Stadium with a home run, Gehrig was setting a Columbia-record seventeen strikeouts, a mark that would not be matched until 1968.

For important games Coakley said he used Gehrig as the first baseman because that was his best position. Coakley admitted that Gehrig was a good college baseman but at that time not that great on the professional level. "There were things he never could have learned in college baseball and things that nobody could teach him because the only place to learn them is in the major leagues."9 In one season with the Lions he spent ten games at first, eleven as pitcher, and three as a combination of pitcher and first baseman. The only time he filled in as a right fielder was during a game against Rutgers.

On the same day that Babe Ruth christened the brand new Yankee Stadium with a home run, Gehrig was setting a Columbia-record seventeen strikeouts.

On the offense Gehrig shined. He hit a school record of seven home runs, most over four hundred feet long. His final tallies for the season were fairly outstanding. He finished with a .444 batting average, .889 slugging percentage, six homers, two triples, six doubles, twenty-eight hits, five stolen bases, and twenty-four runs in sixty-three at-bats. This performance record earned the *New York Times* label "the best college player since George Sisler,"10 a label he had worked relentlessly to obtain.

Similar to the problem he had in high school, Gehrig's only batting weakness was hitting curve balls, but this time from right-handed pitchers. Coakley saw it and terminated it by having right-handed pitchers feed him nothing but curve balls during practice until he could swat them all. Coakley was not the only witness to Gehrig's dedication to the game and to improving himself. Bored during class, Columbia student Bill Corum would gaze out the window and watch Gehrig on South Field practicing endlessly. (Corum would go on to be a well-respected sportswriter and one who played an important role in Gehrig's final days with the Yankees.) Gehrig could often be found playing baseball or catch with students on campus well after practice had ended just so he could be playing. John Donaldson, the football teammate with a dislocated finger, witnessed one of the spectacular payoffs of Gehrig's tenacious dedication to practice: a Gehrig home run that clunked off the sundial that stood more than 400 feet from home plate on Columbia's South Field. The home run is Columbia lore now. "And there was Lou standing there in his baggy knickers, grinning from ear to ear," Donaldson recalled. "You don't forget things like that."[11]

Lou would never forget April 26, 1923. This was the day a New York Yankees scout came to watch Columbia play. The scout was Paul Krichell, the most respected scout of his time because of his innate knack for spotting worthwhile talent (thanks to his handiwork the Yankees had the core of their legendary 1927 infield). When Yankees spring training camp broke, Krichell set off back north to nose around the college fields looking for new talent. In those days, scouting was not as organized as it is today and scouts chose games to attend at random. Krichell had consulted the paper to find out which teams were playing in New York, and upon seeing that New York University was playing too far away that day, he decided to pop over to New Brunswick, New Jersey, to watch the Columbia-Rutgers game. The train he chose to ride to the game was coincidently the same train that Columbia's team was on. He located Coach Coakley and asked if there were any players he should watch in particular. Coakley mentioned he had a lefty pitcher, but he wasn't slated to start for another week. At the insistence of Krichell, Coakley said he would consider starting this lefty pitcher that day.

Krichell sat in the stands waiting for a lefty pitcher who never materialized. He didn't think his time was wasted, though. There was a granite statue of a kid in right field that caught his eye—

not so much for his fielding abilities as for his hitting abilities. Twice the kid sent pitches screaming out of the park. Krichell was ecstatic with his new find and rushed to talk to Coakley after the game. Forgetting all about the lefty pitcher, Krichell demanded to know more about the kid in right field. He was dumbfounded when Coakley informed Krichell that the kid in right field was also the lefty pitcher. Coakley invited Krichell to watch the kid pitch against New York University a week later.

Krichell agreed and hurried back to the Yankees front office to speak with general manager Ed Barrow. He was unable to stop smiling as he proclaimed that he had found another Babe Ruth and insisted that Barrow sign him right away. Barrow, a practical man, urged Krichell to take another look to be sure, and if the kid came through again then they could consider signing him.

Krichell was on hand April 28 for the game against New York University. Gehrig, however, was oblivious that anyone other than his teammates and a handful of fans were there. Pitching as promised, Gehrig put in a good show with eight strikeouts and two walks versus six hits allowed. Krichell, of course, was not there to see Gehrig on the mound; he was there to see Gehrig in the batter's box. The boy did not disappoint. In the ninth inning Lou went to bat with the score tied 2-2. With the ease that power hitters exude, he cranked a pitch over the outfield, across 116th Street, nearly to the library on the other side of the street. The crowd watched from a distance as the ball descended, narrowly missed the college dean, and bounced off the library steps. At the time, it was the second-longest home run ever hit on South Field, but that record would not stand long. Only a few weeks later, on May 19, Gehrig hit a ball that bounced off the steps of the journalism school over 450 feet away. Krichell had seen enough, and he cornered Gehrig after the game.

After determining that Gehrig had not yet signed with any other major league team, indeed he had not even been approached by any, Krichell invited Gehrig to Ed Barrow's office the following day. Intimidated by the daunting turn of events, Gehrig asked Coach Coakley to accompany him.

Upon their arrival, Barrow immediately jumped into offering

Gehrig a contract for the remainder of the 1923 season at a $2,000 salary, plus a $1,000 signing bonus. (It is important to note that many Gehrig biographies claim he received $1,500 as a signing bonus. According to his wife, however, the Yankees cut a check for $1,500, but Gehrig only actually received $1,000. Supposedly he was not aware of the other $500 as it was taken by "a friend" as a sort of finder's fee. When Gehrig did find out about the $500, he severed ties with his "friend.") The sum was more money than Gehrig had ever seen in one place, let alone in his own hands. Barrow told him the offer was on the table if he wanted it. Wisely, Gehrig said he had to take a few days to think about it.

He wanted to please his mother, but he also wanted to make sure she had what she deserved. At the time, she was missing work because of double pneumonia. Pop was also ill and unable to work. Gehrig's small wages earned waiting tables at the fraternity house could not cover rent, food, and the mounting doctor bills. His gut was telling him to go with baseball, but he needed an unbiased, authoritative figure to justify his notion. So he sought out a trusted professor, Archibald Stockder, who taught Gehrig's business class. After listening to Gehrig's dilemma, Stockder's answer was definitive: Play ball. For the wise assistance, Gehrig used part of his Yankees earnings to send Stockder a box of Corona cigars with a handwritten thank-you.

The sum was more money than Gehrig had ever seen in one place, let alone in his own hands.

Telling Mom that he was dropping school to play with the Yankees was infinitely more difficult than it was to get her to agree to let him go to Chicago for the high school game. There was yelling, there was an extended guilt trip, and there was sobbing on Mom's part. It broke his heart to break hers, but he knew it was for the best. He would tell the reporters later of his decision, "Mom's been slaving to put a young ox like me through college. It's about time I carry the load and take care of them."[12] Though he loved baseball tremendously, the love of the game was not the deciding factor—it was the promise of a better life. "The money they put before me was enough to turn any kid's head," he explained later in life. "I was still not sure I wanted to go into baseball as a steady profession, but I decided to grab what I could of it. That's the wrong way to look at baseball and I soon changed my mind."[13]

A few days after the offer Gehrig signed with the Yankees, using the signing bonus to pay off the family medical bills and spending the remainder on a vacation for his parents—their first vacation ever. The only stipulation Gehrig put on the signing was that there be no public announcement until after Columbia's season was over, the last game being June 9 against Penn.

During the hush-hush period, an odd situation presented itself, according to legend. Supposedly, a National League team in the Midwest had empowered the Yankees' then first baseman Wally Pipp to find the home run phenom they had heard about and offer him the first baseman's job with their club. Pipp did so, catching Gehrig walking across campus one day. Gehrig uncomfortably lowered his eyes as he replied to Pipp's offer, "Thank you, Mr. Pipp, but I've already signed with the Yankees." With that Gehrig continued on his way, leaving Pipp faint with the idea of the young slugger nipping at his heels for the spot at first.

Chapter Four
The Ox Is Farmed Out, 1923-1924

Mom had wanted her son to envelope himself in the world Uncle Otto knew, but Lou was quickly wrapped up in a world of Uncle Charlies hurled by pitchers above any caliber he had faced. That world was Yankees baseball. In 1923, Colonel Jacob Ruppert took sole ownership of the Yankees after his fifty-fifty partnership with Captain Tillinghast Huston dissolved. Ruppert wanted nothing short of the best baseball team in the world. The Yankees had won the league pennant in 1921 and 1922, but lost the title to their archrival the Giants each time, leaving Ruppert anxious to finally take the championship. This was the environment Gehrig entered in 1923. Within a couple of months he would turn twenty and Ruppert liked the look of the six-foot-one kid with nearly 200 pounds of muscle and pudge. "We knew we were getting a grand prospect when we signed Lou Gehrig to a Yankee contract," Paul Krichell told reporters. "He had everything you looked for in a youngster…speed, power, a good arm, an excellent batting eye, and a burning desire to become a great ballplayer."[1]

The Yankees manager was Miller Huggins. Upon Gehrig's arrival at the clubhouse Huggins got down to business by taking Gehrig out to the field for his first major league batting practice. Even though Huggins trusted Paul Krichell's scouting report, he wanted to see for himself the marvel that Gehrig supposedly was.

Huggins was short, scrawny and feisty, some comparison to

the brawny, shy Gehrig as they walked out to the field of Yankee Stadium. Gehrig tried to keep himself calm, a definite feat as he and Huggins walked past the living legends already on the field: Babe Ruth, Waite Hoyt, Wally Pipp, Everett Scott. As they reached the batting cage, Huggins asked Joe Dugan to step aside, then told Gehrig to grab a bat.

All eyes in the stadium turned to Gehrig. Blindly he grabbed the first bat he touched, a hefty one made to the preference of the reigning home run king. Unbeknownst to him, it was Babe's favored bat. As he walked to the plate, he noticed the name inscribed on the barrel. "Oh, no," he thought. Using a power hitter's favored bat was nearly as bad as washing his lucky cap, but Gehrig didn't want to look like he didn't know what he was doing, so he held on to it and stepped in the batter's box with quivering knees. Ruth gave no objection. Perhaps he, much like Huggins, was curious to see if this kid had what it took to rumble with the big boys. They were in for quite a delightful treat.

After testing everyone's patience by letting the first handful of pitches go by without a swing for fear the bat would fly out of his sweaty palms, Gehrig dug in and whacked the next pitch into right center. Next pitch...crack...into the stands. Next pitch...crack...into the stands. Gehrig was not only using the home run king's bat, he was slugging the ball into a section of the right field bleachers that had been dubbed Ruthville.

"Atta boy, Lou! Show the Babe how to hit one!" came cheers from the sparse crowd gathered to watch batting practice. These joyful yells were from a group of Columbia boys there to watch their classmate vie for a spot in the lineup. Gehrig acknowledged the cheers by continuing to bounce balls off the stands, feeling more at ease now that he had shown himself that Yankee Stadium wasn't really all that massive. He tingled with joy and relief.

When Huggins finally pulled Gehrig out of the batting cage, he felt confident and proud. He had, after all, just proved he could slug with the best of them. "We didn't know what else he could do or in what position he would end up," Hoyt commented on Gehrig's first batting practice. "But it was a cinch that a young fellow who could hit like that couldn't be kept out of the major leagues."[2] As for the home run king's opinion: "That kid sure can bust 'em."[3] Ruth's comment foreshadowed Gehrig's nickname among the Yankees during his first years with them—Buster.

During that first year with the Yankees, Huggins tried him as first baseman, pitcher and outfielder. In every position, though, Gehrig was as awkward as a toddler. His underdeveloped talent and lack of seniority placed him "in the lumber business," sitting on the bench picking splinters out of his pants, which caused some confusion for his parents the first time they came to the stadium to watch him play. They couldn't find him. While Gehrig explained later that he had been sitting on the bench the whole time, his father wondered what kind of a job paid a man to sit on a bench.

While Gehrig focused on improving his fielding, the reporters focused on his rawness. Niven Busch of the New Yorker magazine wrote that Gehrig "was one of the most bewildered recruits anyone had ever seen."[4] He was awkward on the field, and he was awkward off the field when trying to converse with the media or other players. While in Cleveland during his first tour around the American League network, Gehrig saw Babe Ruth chatting with the legendary Tris Speaker before the game. The Babe noticed Gehrig staring admiringly at them and called him over. To Gehrig's amazement, Speaker addressed him. "Hear you're the kid that's going to make Swiss cheese out of Babe's record," Speaker joked. "I hope you do. He's getting too fresh." Gehrig was terribly flattered that a player like Tris Speaker would even know who he was, but he was overwhelmed to be compared to the Sultan of Swat. "Tris Speaker had been a boyhood idol," Gehrig told people when he recounted the story. "And the first time we passed each other on the diamond, he smiled and nodded to me. I lived in a glow for days after that."[5]

Gehrig's professional debut with the Yankees was on June 15, 1923, four days before his twentieth birthday. He replaced Pipp at first base in the ninth against St. Louis, but he never got a chance to bat. Three days later his first major league at-bat was bitter-sweet. He swung hard at the pitches offered up by Detroit's Ken Halloway, even got a chunk of the second pitch and sent it roaring down the right field foul line, but he never got a ball to go fair. His next plate appearance, against Bonnie Hollingsworth of the Senators, also resulted in a "K," and he returned to the dugout downtrodden. Ruth called out to him, "You took your cuts anyway. You didn't just stand there and watch the balls go by."[6]

Gehrig's others chances to prove himself were few and far between since he didn't play on a regular basis. When he did have an opportunity the pressure nearly always got the better of him. Finally, on July 7, he knocked out his first major league hit, a single against St. Louis. The next time he went to bat against the Cardinals, he knocked out a double and gained an RBI.

He had begun to prove himself offensively, but on defense he was still waiting for the moment of truth. Late in July, Huggins threw him a chance and started him at first base. The Yankee pitcher for the day was a calloused veteran named "Bullet" Joe Bush who was looking for his twentieth consecutive win of the season and had little patience with the greenhorn. Early in the game it was obvious that Gehrig's inexperience was showing through. With runners on first and third, the Senators bunted up the first base line. Gehrig pounced on the ball, checked the runner at third, looked at second, then acted as if he was going to throw to first for the easiest out. For reasons even Gehrig himself didn't understand, he couldn't get himself to throw the ball. He stood there with a perfectly fielded ball in his left hand, unable to throw it. His hesitation allowed the third base runner to score. The Senators had the lead.

Bullet Joe was boiling. He screamed and angrily snatched the ball out of Gehrig's hand and marched back to the mound muttering to himself. For the next few innings Gehrig suffered quietly at first and in the dugout, wishing he could either be invisible or find a way to make up for his dumb mistake. In the seventh inning Washington was still leading 5-2 with two Yankees on base, bringing up Ruth. With a sly grin, the Senator manager intentionally walked Ruth to get to the blundering rookie Gehrig.

Then he yanked his pitcher to bring in a lefty reliever. Statistically speaking, lefty versus lefty usually favors the pitcher. Bush railed against letting Gehrig get up to bat with Huggins, but to no avail. Huggins ordered Gehrig to the batter's box.

Gehrig bounced the very first pitch off the right field fence for a standing double that pushed all three preceding runners across the plate. The next batter brought in Gehrig. The score remained Yankees 6, Senators 5 for the rest of the game. Bush had gotten his win. Not one for sentiment, Bush approached Gehrig in the locker room after the game, much calmer than their previous encounters that day. "Thanks for the game, kid. You may be stupid with that glove, but you can sure pound the ball."[7] Bush couldn't have been any more congratulatory as far as Gehrig was concerned.

In the time Gehrig spent with the Yankees in the summer of 1923 he earned eleven hits, appeared as a pinch hitter thirteen times, and maintained a .423 batting average. But both Gehrig and Huggins knew that his defense would have to drastically improve in order for him to break into the lineup permanently. Huggins knew that with the roster already full of star starters, the only option was to send Gehrig to the minors where he could get the valuable playing time he needed. The Yankees had a working relationship with, of all teams, the Hartford Senators. Gehrig was going to play for the same team for which he had played back in 1921 that caused his temporary suspension from collegiate sports. Arthur Irwin, the manager in 1921, had been replaced by Paddy O'Connor, a friend of Miller Huggins who once coached under him. The Yankees General Manager Ed Barrow signed off on Gehrig going to Hartford in August on option (meaning he remained property of the Yankees and could be called back at any time) with one simple instruction for O'Connor: "Play this kid at first base every day."[8]

Hartford's Bulkeley Stadium was a speck of dust compared Yankee Stadium. The crowds Gehrig played in front of wouldn't have filled a New York subway train. When traveling, the players fanned themselves with old scorecards on a hot coach bus and dreamed of hotels with showers that actually worked. The minor leagues were a sort of boot camp for ball players. The season was 154 games long, filled with games against teams from cities such as Bridgeport, Waterbury and Pittsfield. It was a hard summer for any young man, but especially for a kid of Gehrig's socio-economic circumstances and personality.

Harry Hesse was his roommate during the 1923 season at Hartford. He recalled, "I had been rooming with him for several days before I realized that the guy didn't have a dime. Not a dime. He didn't have money for clothes. He looked like a tramp."9 Lack of money, homesickness, and low self-esteem caused Gehrig to begin his season with Hartford in a horrid batting slump. The reputation the press had given him prior to his arrival had built him up to be a baseball god among mortals. Such praise rattled him. When he couldn't deliver on his reputation, the press got antsy, and Paddy O'Connor got impatient. Disappointing his manager was the worst thing that could happen in Gehrig's mind. He struggled hard to reverse the slump, but kept falling deeper. The more Gehrig went "for the collar," the more O'Connor fumed at the Yankees for sending a lackluster kid. He was a longtime friend of the very scout who started the hubbub over Lou Gehrig, Paul Krichell. O'Connor blasted Krichell too. Krichell advised giving Gehrig more time. Gritting his teeth, O'Connor followed the advice of Krichell and attempted to wait out the slump.

Gehrig felt the pressure more than ever. According to legend, he found a surprising solution to his problem. The story goes that one night he was invited out by the hooligans of the team to a speakeasy. Rarely in his life would Gehrig touch alcohol; particularly hard liquor, but that night he downed glass after glass of gin. The next day he went to the ballpark in hangover anguish. The sound of his cleats on gravel made his head throb. In the batter's box he could barely keep his eyes focused—but he hit the ball...repeatedly...with distance. The apparent cause-and-effect of the alcohol gave Gehrig misguided hope. That night he tested the idea by sneaking a quart of gin into his hotel room and chugging for all he was worth. Again the following day he was sluggish, aching, miserable…and slamming the ball all over the park. He had found the cure to his slump, or so he thought.

For roughly two weeks Gehrig allegedly kept himself perpetually in some stage of drunkenness. In the height of his bender, he kept a little medicine bottle filled with gin tucked in his uniform. Between turns at bat he would stealthily nurse on the miracle liquid. His teammates may have gotten a laugh out of seeing this, but when O'Connor found out what was happening he took it upon himself to help his naïve first baseman.

For roughly two weeks Gehrig allegedly kept himself perpetually in some stage of drunkenness.

While Gehrig did lay off the booze after his talk with O'Connor, his batting slump returned with a vengeance. His batting average fell to an astounding low of .062. O'Connor was a hair's breath away from exploding with frustration. He wired an urgent telegram to Ed Barrow that read, "Gehrig of no use to this ball club. Please recall him."[10]

Barrow immediately wired Krichell at his scouting stop in Spartanburg, South Carolina: "Proceed at once to Hartford. Gehrig in a bad slump. Talk to him."[11] "At once" and "immediately" were among Barrow's favored expressions, and he meant them sincerely. "At once," Krichell went to Hartford's next game to watch the young star. Neither Gehrig nor O'Connor were aware of his presence in the bleachers that day, which is how Krichell preferred it. In four times at bat, Gehrig failed to put the ball in play, and each time he returned to the dugout completely sullen. After the game Krichell approached Gehrig, whose eyes brightened to see a familiar face so far from his beloved New York, and Krichell invited him out to a nice dinner.

During the meal the two discussed Gehrig's slump. Gehrig let all his stresses and frustrations pour out: He was homesick, he was penniless, his parents were struggling with their health, and the press kept hounding him for more results. Krichell immediately recognized the problem. Gehrig was suffering from too much pressure, both internal and external. His expectations were too high. Krichell explained to his young prospect that even the best hitters with an average of .400 still failed more often than they succeeded—six times out of ten, to be exact.

At that moment, Gehrig had a small revelation of why the bender had worked so well: At least when he was drinking he was relaxed. He decided to give Krichell's advice a whirl. After all, he had nothing to lose by trying it.

Meanwhile, O'Connor was at the nearest telegraph office dictating a long telegram to Barrow asking for permission to bench Gehrig. As luck would have it, the telegram reached Barrow's office on Labor Day Saturday, when Barrow had taken a rare day off. O'Connor regretted sending it because that same day, Hartford played a game in which Gehrig burst out of his slump with a game-winning home run. The next day he hit in practically every plate appearance during the course of a doubleheader to win both games. On Monday O'Connor called Barrow's office to recommend that Barrow ignore the telegram. In Gehrig's last month with Hartford in 1923, he hit homers at a record pace—twenty-four home runs in fifty-nine games. His average soared to .304 and he drove in fifty-four runs. A newspaper reporter covering the turn of events declared, "Lefty Lou at present ratio would hit fifty-seven homers in full season,"[12] a feat only Babe Ruth had accomplished back in 1921 with fifty-nine home runs in a full season.

Girls in particular were a Mount Everest challenge to Gehrig.

Gehrig's confidence grew with every point his average raised. He was so comfortable on the field that he even took a turn on the hill against New Haven, a game that ended in a favorable 6-4 score. Hartford ended their season with fanfare by winning the Eastern League Pennant.

The confidence Gehrig found on the field did not carry over into his private life, though. As roommate Harry Hesse put it, "He was a guy who needed friends but didn't know how to go about getting them."[13] Girls in particular were a Mount Everest challenge to Gehrig. Hesse suspected that his roomie had never been on a date and took it upon himself to fix that problem. If

Gehrig was shy around legendary players like Tris Speaker, he was even more so around the fairer sex. He hardly spoke at all to his lovely date, and when she tried to talk to him he would blush and mumble something unintelligible, if he responded at all. Making friends among his own gender wasn't much easier. Gehrig was so used to being shunned—for his size, for his heritage, for his slow wit—that when he had a chance to make friends with new people he sometimes got overeager. One night his teammate Zip Sloan wandered through the hotel halls drunk and looking for a playful tussle. He was carrying around a rag doll monkey he had bought for his daughter and fumbling his way from room to room. Just as Gehrig and Hesse were settling down to sleep, Sloan came in their room. Hesse didn't want any part of a tussle and pulled the covers over his head and pretended to be asleep, so Sloan decided to jump on Gehrig instead. Gehrig fought back. When it suddenly became awfully quiet, Hesse switched on the light and saw Gehrig with his head thrown back squeezing Sloan between his thick thighs in a scissor lock. When Hesse yelled, Gehrig opened his eyes and saw Sloan's blue face and limp body. Immediately Gehrig released him, and Sloan rolled unconscious off the bed. The rag doll monkey lay in a pile of its own sawdust on the floor next to him, an unfortunate casualty of war.

In the good ten minutes it took to revive Sloan, Gehrig was frantic. He hadn't meant to hurt his teammate. His only goal was to keep Sloan from getting too out of hand and obnoxious. "That incident taught me a lesson," Gehrig said. "I didn't know my own strength. I never cut loose after that."[14] He held fast to that decision, and as a result many people, namely his teammates and the reporters, considered him a square. Little did they know, but little did Gehrig explain.

Back in New York, Wally Pipp turned his ankle during the last days of August and Huggins needed a replacement. So Gehrig was called back up to finish out the season with the Yankees. He played in thirteen games in September 1923, four of which he started at first. In that short window of time, he earned a .423 average, slapping out four hits in a single game. On September 27 the world got a sneak peek of the future Yankees' Murderers

Row when Ruth hit a triple and Gehrig followed him up by slugging out his first major league home run, against "Wild Bill" Perry. The Yankees claimed the pennant that year, and their Word Series rivals were the Giants, the same match-up as 1921 and 1922. Huggins was thoroughly impressed with Gehrig and was hoping to use the hot-hitting youngster in the World Series campaign. The Yankees owner, Colonel Ruppert, asked Commissioner Kennesaw Landis for permission to use Gehrig as a replacement for the injured Pipp. The rules spelled out that a player must join the team prior to September 1 for eligibility in postseason play, a requirement which Gehrig did not meet, but only just barely. In years prior, there had been exceptions made in cases of injuries. Taking this into account, Landis in turn appealed to the opposing team's manager, the very same John McGraw who had cut Gehrig from Giants tryouts, for his blessing. By this point, McGraw may have realized that he had failed to detect the goldmine in the young Gehrig. With bitterness in his heart, he refused permission. He had let Gehrig slip through his fingers before, and was not about to let the young slugger play against him.

Huggins had no choice but to tape up Pipp's ankle, play him, and do without the bat of Gehrig. Gehrig's first World Series was spent on the bench, but it was one sweet view of the action. The Yankees went on to take the victory away from the Giants. McGraw's biased refusal to welcome Gehrig had done him no good.

After such a rocky first season in professional baseball, Gehrig wondered if he was going to be signed again next year, and he would wonder that every year for the entirety of his career. He pondered going back to school or finding a steady job instead of hanging his hopes on a bummer's game. "By the time I had enough money to go back to college, it was too late," he said later in life. "I was part of baseball and baseball was a very big part of me. However, I went out that first winter and got a job with the electric company just in case."[15]

Gehrig was signed again, of course. Baseball was clearly the right career for him, though some aspects of being a professional ballplayer were hard for him to adjust to. When Gehrig first joined the Yankees he was an interviewer's nightmare. He was so nervous that he stammered through even the simplest of statements. Then again, this trait was evident to everyone who tried to get to know him, not just to interviewers. He rarely spoke at all, even to his own teammates. Some of the players would joke that all he would say was "hello" at the beginning of spring training and "goodbye" at the end of the season. Needless to say, he wasn't always a worthwhile source of quotes to a reporter trying to get a juicy story. Because of his habitual shyness, Gehrig was often pegged as standoffish and cold. The reality was he feared speaking to reporters. He admitted he was exceedingly self-conscious and worried that he would say something dumb. To get a story on him, sometimes reporters had to derive it from other sources. For instance, Niven Busch of the *New Yorker* wrote about Gehrig's odd habit wrought during a poverty-stricken childhood of not wearing an overcoat, a tidbit he learned from a Yankee executive.

The story went that the Yankee executive spotted Gehrig walking outside on a frigidly cold day in only a sweater. "For heaven's sake, Lou," the exec said, "here's $100. Go buy a coat."

"Oh, no, that's alright," Gehrig responded. "I'm so used to not wearing a coat that if I did wear one I'd feel too dressed up."

"Are you sure? God forbid you get frostbite on your throwing hand."

"I'm quite sure. I have enough money saved if I change my mind."[16]

The habits Lou acquired in his hard-knock life didn't always make sense to those who never had to go without. His conservation of money was the most publicized habit he had. Teammates would also joke about it, saying he probably still had the first dollar he ever earned, which may well have been true. In his estate his survivors found a check made out to him for exactly $1.00 dated October 1, 1914, the year Gehrig turned eleven. For the 1924 season Gehrig was to receive $3,000. Players were not paid salary until the season started, however. For the veterans of the team who had been paid handsome salaries the previous season and still had full bank accounts, this wasn't a problem; but Gehrig was not so fortunate. When he had signed with the Yankees, he told his mother that she was not to work another day in her life, that he was going to foot the bill for everything. Everything, he learned, cost a lot of money. Doctor bills, rent, food, clothes; all of these add up very quickly. By the time Gehrig left for spring training in New Orleans in February 1924 he had in his possession a seriously un-classy cardboard suitcase and $14.00 that his mother had given him. The expenses of essentials such as hotel stay and a set amount for food were paid by the Yankees' front office, but the incidental expenses such as cab fare, tips, and entertainment were solely up to the player. Veterans such as Ruth could drop $14 as tip for a cheeseburger meal and not think twice. In Gehrig's case, dime tips were excruciatingly hard for him to leave.

In the evenings he would watch his older teammates dress up in fancy clothes to go out on the town, then the next day he'd silently listen to their animated conversations about their escapades.

Gehrig, however, was creative in his methods of hanging on to every penny he could. Instead of heading to the movies or one of the many restaurants, he entertained himself by walking the city's streets since he enjoyed learning about new places. At the same time, this furthered his sense of isolation from the rest of the team. In the evenings he would watch his older teammates dress up in fancy clothes to go out on the town, then the next day he'd silently listen to their animated conversations about their escapades. He walked the city and counted the days until they went back home.

It was during one of those many walks that he ran into Dan Daniel, a reporter who traveled with the team for the *World-Telegram*. Daniel asked Gehrig what was wrong and was astounded to hear of Gehrig's money shortage. How could a player for the New York Yankees not have a lot of money?

When Gehrig mentioned he was considering a second job,

Daniel urged him to seek out Huggins and ask for an advance. Gehrig resisted this idea so Daniel sought out Huggins to tell him that his up-and-coming first sacker was pounding the pavement and was too shy to admit it. Huggins could see Gehrig was having problems trying to fit in with the team, so the next day Huggins took Gehrig into his office, handed him a check for $100, and asked him to stop looking for another job. Huggins also arranged for Gehrig to room with two other young players, Hinkey Haines and Benny Bengough. Gehrig was thankful for the extra money and a chance to befriend someone his own age, but he realized that even with the extra money his budget remained as narrow as a needle. To make matters worse, both of his new roommates joined the older players in their expensive nightly adventures. Benny and Hinkey implored Lou to join in, but Lou just shook his head and gave some mild excuse. He was baffled by how they found the funds to go out, but he was too timid to ask them about it. Then one night, a glum-looking Bengough stayed in with Gehrig. When Gehrig found out it was because Bengough was also out of money, he was ecstatic—much to Bengough's chagrin.

Gehrig proceeded to lay out his scheme for making money, which included getting wait jobs at one of the fancy restaurants he had spotted during a walk. Bengough was reluctant, but Gehrig assured him there was nothing to waiting tables. He had been doing it for years at Columbia. Bengough consented, but their hopes were dashed when they visited the restaurant they wanted to work at. Through the restaurant's main window they could see a table full of Yankee players. There was no way they could risk being seen by fellow players.

With the wait job plan a bust, Gehrig was back to trying to figure out ways to skim off the cream of daily expenses. Instead of taking cab rides he walked to and from the practice fields. When it came to food, he devised a scheme: "I was glad the team worked out every day from eleven to one," he told people later, "so I could just skip lunch."[17] In this way, the board money given to him by the front office could go toward other expenses. With his finances now somewhat bearable, though by no means great, he could focus on what he was supposed to be doing in the first place: learning baseball.

Wally Pipp played a pivotal role in Gehrig's practice time. A college man from Georgetown University, Pipp was a level-headed gentleman and was not intimidated or insulted by Gehrig's presence. He went out of his way to help Gehrig improve his sacking skills during spring training in Florida, showing him how to stretch for throws and how to properly field a bouncing grounder so as to prevent taking one in the kisser. Patience was the key with a kid like Gehrig, who was skilled enough, but severely underdeveloped for a big leaguer. It took many hours of instruction for him to blossom. Manager Huggins watched Gehrig closely and saw the improvement Gehrig was making, but he also saw how illogical it would have been to play a rookie who was still raw. Before the Yankees broke camp, Huggins told Lou that he would be sending him back to Hartford after the home opener. First, though, he wanted to keep Gehrig on for the experience he would gain during the trip north. Gehrig was thoroughly disappointed, but took the news well.

After the Yankees broke camp, they played their way north and opened the regular season in Boston. The next stop was Washington, then it was back to New York for the home opener. During those games Gehrig was utilized as a pinch hitter and a relief first baseman for a couple of innings. He garnered six hits in twelve at-bats, making his average a clean .500. After that he packed off to Hartford for another season of sweaty bus rides. The 1924 season went much smoother than the previous one. In the clean-up spot of the lineup, Gehrig came out swinging, literally. There were no slumps or hidden bottles of gin. In 134 games, he knocked out 186 hits, ninety-three for extra bases, thirty-seven were home runs, which earned him a .369 average. June 17, 1924, was a landmark day, as it was the day he would hit his only minor league grand slam. With his hot bat to Hartford's advantage, the team sailed into the top of the standings. Manager O'Connor was jigging for joy until Gehrig asked him for permission to take a couple of days off to return to New York. June 19 was his birthday and his mother had hoped he could spend it with her and his father. O'Connor balked at the nineteenth, but mentioned they had a free day on the twentieth and allowed Gehrig to go home then.

Subsequently, Gehrig spent his twenty-first birthday at the ballpark playing against Worcester. The birthday luck was certainly with him as he hit one double, one triple, and one home run to help gain Hartford the 9-8 victory. The next day he caught a train home. This season in Hartford, his hitting was impressive, but the twenty-three errors he committed at first base reiterated his rawness.

In late August, Huggins called him back up to lend a hand in the Yankees pennant race. On September 4 Gehrig replaced Ruth and his sore left arm in the outfield and got two hits. He would go on to see ten more at-bats and gain another four hits before the pennant dreams were killed with a three-game losing streak to Detroit.

Despite his contributions to the team on the field, some of the older players whom he described as "clannish and sullen toward rookies"[18] had little problem remaining distant from him. Waite Hoyt and Bob Meusel got kicks out of playing practical jokes on him. With his quiet, slow-witted manner, Gehrig was an ideal victim of such hazing. At times he would come to batting practice hoping that the vets wouldn't crowd him out of taking some cuts, which happened frequently, only to find that his favorite bat had been sawed into four pieces. "[That] kind of meanness was hard to understand," he said.[18] Gehrig complained to Huggins that the players' taunting was robbing him of valuable practice, so Huggins arranged for coach Charley O'Leary to show up to the stadium an hour early to throw pitches for Gehrig. The teasing and practical jokes, of course, were not completely curtailed. Carl Mays was guilty of the worst of it. Mays' incessant hounding finally pushed Gehrig over the edge one day in the locker room. Gehrig got up in Mays' face, clenching his bulging muscle and seething with anger, daring him to fight. Mays wisely declined.

Not all of the veterans were showboat hazers, though. Wally Pipp, for one, was extremely congenial to Gehrig. And gentle, patient Huggins became more of a father figure than a coach to

Gehrig. Huggins loved Gehrig as an essential addition to his lineup and as the son he never had. Gehrig was forever grateful to both men and showed them nothing but respect. Babe Ruth loved to tease, but he also admired the young kid Gehrig for his drive and hustle. In a quote to the reporters, Ruth joked that when Buster came to the team he was "loaded to the decks with hog fat and [the Yanks] took it off him. He still has some of it above the neck. But he's working on that."[19]

That hog fat above the neck would land Gehrig in trouble a number of times. On September 21, 1924, the Yanks were playing Detroit, and the infamous Ty Cobb was Detroit's coach at the time. In the game Gehrig singled off of the Tigers' Earl Whitehall to score two men. Cobb did not take too kindly to that or to Gehrig's reputation as the never-lets-loose type of man made well-known by the newspapers. When the half-inning ended, Gehrig was in the dugout grabbing his mitt. Cobb took his position in the third base coach's box alongside the visitor's dugout and started throwing belligerent remarks at Gehrig, poking him with insults about everything from fielding ability to heritage. As he often did at that age, Gehrig took it to heart to the point that anger overtook him. He charged out of the dugout toward Cobb, accompanied by Everett Scott. Cobb stood unstirred with hands poised arrogantly on his hips and grinned slyly as the umpire Tommy Connolly thumbed both players out of the game. Cobb's psychology had worked perfectly. In his naiveté, Gehrig honestly thought Cobb hated him. Cobb was just using strategy to rid the Yankees of their star rookie for the remainder of the game, whereas Cobb's true opinion of Gehrig was much different: "Lou Gehrig was the hustlinest ballplayer I ever saw, and I admired him for it."[21]

One of Gehrig's glaring weaknesses was the fact that he was unable to accurately gauge his own worth. He feared being shooed from his hometown team. After the end of the 1924 season, he began hearing rumors that minor league teams in Atlanta, Louisville and St. Paul wanted his services on their teams. The rumors were a result from the fact that Huggins was in a tough spot. Gehrig still needed experience at first base which he probably would not get if he stayed up with the Yankees. But five of the seven American League clubs refused to let Huggins send Gehrig down to Hartford again without first offering him up for trade or sale. The December issue of *Evening World* presented Bozeman Bulger's theory that Huggins was contemplating trading Gehrig and "Bullet" Joe Bush to the St. Louis Browns in exchange for pitcher Urban Shocker. The theory was based on the fact that the Browns' current first baseman, the college player to whom Gehrig was compared while at Columbia, George Sisler, was having eye problems. The Browns supposedly wanted to replace Sisler with Gehrig, and Huggins supposedly wanted to replace Bush with Shocker. Huggins was irritated by Bulger's presumptions. "That's the silliest thing that was ever written," Huggins said on the matter. "If I'd have traded Gehrig at that stage of his career, I should have been shot at sunrise."[22] Part of Bulger's theory proved astute, though. Huggins did indeed trade for Shocker, and "Bullet" Joe Bush, who had believed that Gehrig would gum up his milestone twentieth win in 1923, was gone from the Yankees. Gehrig, on the other hand, stayed.

Chapter Five
Growing Pains, 1925-1926

Huggins had the highest of hopes for his 1925 team and their ability to regain the top spot. The Yankees set off for spring training in February to a new location: St. Petersburg, Florida. Training rolled on in a breezy, tropical manner, and soon enough April came as did the first of many troubles. On April 7, as the Yankees were traveling north by train, Babe Ruth suddenly began complaining of stomach pains. Before long he was suffering from fever, incessant vomiting, and delirium. Some teammates tried to laugh it off as a digestive tract rebellion from the hordes of hot dogs and beer the Babe was often spied consuming. The pains worsened. While the rest of the team stopped in Asheville, North Carolina, for a preseason game, Ruth continued on to New York and his personal doctor, accompanied by nearly every sportswriter who toured with the Yankees and wanted to stay on top of the big story. His stomachache overtook the front pages of newspapers across the nation for weeks. W. O. McGeehan dubbed his ailment the "belly ache heard around the world."[1] Ruth would be within thirty yards of his bed and toilet until the end of May.

Meanwhile, back on the Yankees tour train, Miller Huggins fretted. The Babe's illness, whether Huggins wanted to admit it or not, was an omen. Replacing Babe Ruth was a job no manager wanted, but Huggins had it. If only he could get that slugger Gehrig into the lineup. He and the writers who considered themselves experts on Yankees strategy twirled their writing pens and chewed their nails, searching their brains for a way to get Gehrig's bat into the order. Some had idle talk of using

Gehrig for a pitcher, since he did have the Columbia record for most strikeouts in a game. But Huggins was too good of a baseball mind to use a budding first sacker as a moundsman. With a stellar infield including Wally Pipp at first, Aaron Ward at second, Everett Scott at short, and Joe Dugan at third, there was no switching option so far as Huggins was concerned. There was no option other than to wait for the opportune time, keeping Gehrig on the bench, the very option Gehrig feared the most. After watching Pop for numerous years not work due to one ailment or another, Gehrig thought that not working was synonymous with being lame. Impatient with bumming on the bench, Gehrig made a rash decision. He went to Huggins' office, packed suitcase in hand, and demanded to be put on the list of players being sent to the minors in St. Paul, Minnesota. At least there he could get some playing time.

Anyone who truly appreciates baseball knows that success is only ten percent physical, but ninety percent mental.

Incredulous at Gehrig's audacity, Huggins informed the young player that he still had a great deal to learn about the game of baseball, things that playing in the minors could not teach. Playing time in the minors was good for experience, but it failed to teach the intricate ins and outs of professional ball. No, he told Gehrig. His place was right there on the bench.

When the words had time to percolate in his mind, Gehrig realized exactly what Huggins was trying to get across. He had been looking at the bench all wrong, as a sort of Purgatory. He realized Huggins was trying to make him think of the dugout as a classroom. Gehrig saw that he was working after all; he was being paid to learn. Epiphany complete, Gehrig didn't focus on how much playing time he was granted. Instead he focused on Huggins' dugout seminars. Anyone who truly appreciates baseball knows that success is only ten percent physical, but ninety percent mental. With his manager's guidance he was able to pick up on pitchers' telltale signs of what pitch they would throw, which batters had a tendency to pull the ball, which runners were likely to steal in a given situation, and many of the countless other situations a baseball game could present. When he looked back on how much he had to learn that first full season with the Yankees, Gehrig commented, "Sometimes I wonder how in the world I was ever able to make it."[2] He made it by playing baseball as a career, a hobby, and a religion. Baseball was his life.

"Only Lou's willingness and lack of conceit will make him into a complete ballplayer," Huggins told reporters. "That and those muscles are all he has."[3]

Gehrig did manage to see a few innings here and there as a pinch hitter or a replacement for Pipp in the last innings of a game, dreaming of the day when he could break into the line-up for good. As he was learning to appreciate his limited playing time, veteran shortstop Everett Scott saw his playing time dwindle. At the time, Scott was known as the "Iron Man of Base-ball" for his ongoing consecutive games streak. No one else in baseball history had attempted the feat, preferring instead to seek glory in home runs a lá Ruth or sending strikeout victims back to the dugout as Cy Young did. On May 5, 1925, Huggins finally decided to bench Scott due to his waning offensive production. Scott's streak had begun in June of 1916, coming full circle at 1,307 consecutive games. To a ballplayer, including Gehrig, the appropriate time to finally call it quits was when his legs began to fail him, and Scott had not yet neared that point. "The lively ball ended my string," Scott bemoaned, "not bad legs." He had to settle for sitting on the bench with Gehrig and watch his replacement, Pee Wee Wanniger. When his baseball career ended, the Iron Man became the proud owner of the finest bowling alley his hometown Fort Wayne, Indiana, had ever known. Scott's fate seemed fitting for the 1925 Yankees, who were quickly dropping in the ranks and befouling the Yankee dynasty's reputation. Huggins' hopes of a winning season were knocked to the ground by hitless innings and kicked in the teeth by subpar defense. The former World Champion Yankees were virtually unrecognizable to their fans.

◆ ◆ ◆

Ruth rejoined his teammates on May 26, at first remaining on the bench until he felt up to playing again, which was on June 1. The day he reentered the game was important in more ways than one. Of course the legendary slugger was finally back in the line-up, but June 1 was also the start of a record that would grow in importance over the years: It was the start of Lou Gehrig's consecutive games streak. Gehrig pinch-hit for Pee Wee Wanniger in the ninth against Washington's legendary "Big Train" Walter Johnson. Gehrig failed to get a hit, but unbeknownst to him, and everybody else, it was the first game played that would be followed by thousands more. On June 1, though, all the fans knew and saw was a less-than-graceful showing by the team, including a bumbling Babe and a fumbling freshman Gehrig, and the Yankees losing their fifth straight game.

There are differing accounts of how the morning of June 2, 1925, unfolded in Yankee Stadium. Some say that Wally Pipp had an old eye injury that flared up, giving him a headache as painful as a migraine. Some say Huggins was fed up with Pipp's lack of hits and told him to take a rest, then to protect the veteran's pride he told the press that Pipp was in pursuit of aspirin for a headache. Still others claim Pipp had been beaned previously and was prone to headaches, one of which cropped up that morning. According to Pipp himself he was taking batting practice that morning from a young college boy named Charlie Caldwell, Jr., who was eager to make a good impression. The only thing Caldwell's inaccurate arm made an impression on was Pipp's forehead. In those days batters didn't wear helmets. "I just couldn't duck," Pipp explained. "The ball hit me on the temple. Down I went. I was too far gone to bother reaching for any aspirin tablets, as the popular story goes."[4] So far gone was he that he reportedly spent two weeks in the hospital. Regardless of how the morning of June 2, 1925, actually went, the important part is that Pipp was disabled. Huggins had his long-awaited opportune moment.

That morning Gehrig was in no hurry, having adjusted to day after day of feeling his butt go numb on the bench. Though he did take a turn at batting practice, he did not witness Pipp's fall. After he took his practice, he moseyed to the locker room to change into his game jersey. As the starters headed for the dugout, Gehrig decided he had been seeing too much of the dugout and took his time, stretching out on the trainer's rubbing table. He didn't think anything of the sound of cleats headed toward the table and kept staring blankly into space. Then he heard Huggins ask if he was tired.

As embarrassed as Gehrig was to be caught like this before a game, he was more shocked to hear the news from Huggins: He was going to start at first. Huggins walked back to the dugout without further commentary.

In a blur of excitement, Gehrig snatched up his glove and rushed after Huggins. He had to check the lineup card posted in the dugout to be sure he hadn't imagined the encounter. Sure enough, his name was sixth in the order, adjacent to "1B." He was starting at first base!

Even if Gehrig performed poorly he would fit right in with the rest of the success-challenged lugs on the team.

Huggins might not have been so willing to replace Pipp with Gehrig for good had the Yankees not been having one of the worst years of their club's history. Huggins knew all too well that his new first baseman was still wet behind the ears, but he had no other first baseman, and even if Gehrig performed poorly he would fit right in with the rest of the success-challenged lugs on the team.

Gehrig did perform well, though. In his first three times at the plate facing Washington's George Mogridge, he gained two singles and a double. Altogether he had five at-bats, three hits, and one run. In his new corner office at first base, he garnered eight putouts with one assist. With his help, the Yankees broke their losing streak by beating the Senators. Gehrig hummed happily all the way home.

Shortly after gaining Pipp's old spot, Gehrig himself was nearly knocked out of the game. During a game he was caught in a double play as he ran to second. The infielder pivoted and threw to first. Gehrig didn't see the ball coming right at him. It slammed into his forehead, knocking him unconscious. Watching his second-string first baseman crumple to the ground,

Huggins threw up his hands in helplessness, wondering how many first basemen one team could go through. To his great relief, though, Gehrig came to after a little coaxing and refused to leave the game. It had taken this long to get in, and he wasn't about to let a bump on the head knock him out.

The more Gehrig played the more aggressive he was at improving in every way. His daily pursuit to improve and stay in the game caught the eye of reporters and fans, and definitely caught the eye of Pipp. For generations after, "Wally Pipp" was a threat used by parents, teachers, drill sergeants, and other authority figures to would-be slackers. "You don't want to be a Wally Pipp, do you?" In the dictionary of cultural lingo, his name meant "a person who decides to be lazy and regrets it thereafter." In reality, Pipp was anything but a lazy player. At the ripe age of thirty-two, in his twelfth season with the Yankees, Pipp was all-around a better-than-average player and extremely dedicated to his team and his responsibilities on it. His nickname among the press was Pipp the Pickler for his knack of successfully placing hits in a pinch. In 1924 he set a personal high of 113 RBI. Not a single person who knew Wally Pipp thought he was on the decline in 1925.

Gehrig didn't care how others perceived his first start. All he cared about was that he was the Yankees' starting first baseman. In his musings on Gehrig, New York writer Frank Graham wrote, "He was happier than he ever had been before. He was a Yankee now in all truth. Out there at first base every day, playing every game."[5] Gehrig shared his joy with his parents, especially his mother. After becoming a regular, Gehrig started the tradition of giving her extra money every time he hit a home run.

◆ ◆ ◆

Since he was seeing so much playing time, he had ample opportunity to prove his worth. Sometimes he did it in unexpected ways. On June 24, he gained his first stolen base—home plate. He may well have been the first player to achieve such a feat on a first stolen-base attempt. In his career Gehrig would steal home fifteen times, seven of which would occur in June. In the base paths, he used his size to his advantage. His aggression in combination with his bulk made for quite an intimidating sight to infielders.

His fielding improved to the point that it more and more closely resembled that of a major league player. Those who appreciated his impeccable work ethic helped him as best they could. Without any bitterness whatsoever, Pipp continued working with him on improving his skill. Umpire Billy Evans often officiated Yankee games, and one day he noticed Gehrig was making a major error in his footwork at the base. He pointed it out to Gehrig and told him the proper way to arrange his feet. Gehrig corrected it on the next play, but it didn't feel quite natural. The next day Gehrig had Coach Charley O'Leary at the stadium at 10:00 a.m. to practice. Hour after hour, from morning until game time at 3:30, O'Leary fed Gehrig throws until the footwork became automatic. With every problem that popped up in his play Gehrig did the same thing. Poor O'Leary suffered from lack of sleep for quite a while, but he respected Gehrig for working so hard to improve. Paul Krichell said of Gehrig's doggedness, "No player in the history of baseball ever drove himself harder to make himself a ballplayer, to overcome his shortcomings and to perfect his play on field and his techniques at bat."[6]

One area Gehrig was particularly weak in was playing cut-off for the right and center fielders. A game against Detroit finally implanted the lesson in his brain. With a runner on second, Ty Cobb came to bat. He singled to Meusel in right, and the runner on second had sights on home. Meusel had a missile launcher for an arm, but the fact that he was not going to be able to hit the catcher on this play was obvious to everyone...except Gehrig. Assuming Meusel's throw had enough umph to get to the catcher, Gehrig let the ball go instead of cutting it off. Of course Meusel's throw was short, allowing the runner to score and Cobb to take second. Huggins was furious. Normally so calm around his prize pupil, Huggins ripped into Gehrig in the dugout at the change of the inning, threatening to fine him if he made that same mistake again. After the game, Gehrig was leaving the stadium with some fellow players when he asked with some reluctance just what Huggins was talking about. Only one of his shocked companions could find the words to explain how to properly cut off a throw. Lou was embarrassed for having not known how to handle the play. "I don't think Lou was ever caught that way again," Waite Hoyt said of him later.[7]

Gehrig didn't, however, learn one lesson from the previous year, and that was not to take to heart jabs from Ty Cobb. During a tight game, Gehrig endured insult after insult from Cobb. The batter's box offered no shield. At one point Gehrig singled but screwed up in running the bases and was tagged out between first and second, to which Cobb sneered, "You ain't got the brains or the guts to run the bases!" The insult seemed to bounce off of Gehrig, so Cobb pulled out the big gun and made a disrespectful comment about Gehrig's mom. That did the trick. Gehrig rushed the Detroit dugout, headed directly for Cobb. At the last second Cobb scooted to the side, and Gehrig soared headlong into the roof of the dugout. There was a dull thud when he hit the ground, knocked unconscious. Cobb laughed. Huggins rolled his eyes. When Gehrig came to, Cobb offered to call it a truce.

Gehrig accepted, and the relationship between the two men calmed down. Cobb would later pick Gehrig as his choice for all-time greatest first baseman. The truce, however, was not valid between Gehrig and the rest of Detroit's team. Earl Whitehall, considered one of the best pitchers of the time, was on the Yankee Stadium hill for the Tigers one afternoon. Gehrig was at the plate for the Yankees working his way through an at-bat, trying to use his newly acquired knowledge of pitchers and situations to guess what Whitehall would throw next. He did not expect a high and tight pitch at his chin. Gehrig, slightly overreacting, flew backwards onto his duff. Promptly he rose to his feet, indignantly screaming at Whitehall for what Gehrig considered an attempt to hit him. None of the other players thought Whitehall tried to hit Gehrig, least of all Whitehall. The more experienced players saw Whitehall's brush-back as a sign of respect, which it was. Pitchers tend to brush back the best hitters, a group in which Gehrig did not yet place himself. Once more his naiveté got the best of him and he took a few steps toward the mound, the universal sign of a challenge, and Whitehall never backed down. He took a few steps, only to be separated from Gehrig by the umpires. He did, however, challenge Gehrig to meet him under the stands.

Yankee Stadium's layout was such that the visiting team had to pass through the home dugout to get to their locker room. After the game, Whitehall met Gehrig in the narrow tunnel that connected dugout to lockers. There they threw jabs and hooks at each other as irritated teammates passed by on their way to the showers. Then Gehrig lost his footing and slammed his head onto a concrete stanchion. While he was down Cobb gave him a couple of kicks, which Ruth saw and responded to harshly in Lou's defense. A couple of the other players got into a brief match too, but it all amounted to little, and the players went on their way. Bob Meusel carried the unconscious Gehrig to the locker room. Within a few minutes Gehrig woke up and groggily asked the blurry figures in front of him who won. No one answered him, and all the blurry figures walked away from him, irked by his childish reaction.

> *They threw jabs and hooks at each other as irritated teammates passed by on their way to the showers.*

After that incident, Gehrig settled down and started to attack with only his bat and not his fists, or forehead. On July 23 he banged out his first major league grand slam, off of Washington's Firpo Marberry. Not that this was a sign that his hitting that summer was worthy of legend. In the first few weeks of being in the lineup he was replaced by a pinch hitter six times. As with many things, Gehrig took it personally, and thought Huggins saw him as a weak hitter after all. In fact, Huggins said of his developing power hitter and the successful future ahead of him, "What I wouldn't give to be that kid right now." Other observers judged Gehrig's ability in a similar fashion. For instance, Babe Ruth's second wife Claire described Gehrig's power in her autobiography as "a Mack truck running into a stone wall at 100 miles an hour."[8]

The self-deprecating rookie fit well into the 1925 lineup. That year was called the "black year" in Colonel Jacob Ruppert's reign. In a list of top ten signs a ball club is having a bad year, the top two for the Yankees were the facts that the Sultan of Swat was pinch-hit by a man who hit less home runs in his career than Ruth did in one season, and that the Tigers trounced the Yankees 19-1 in a single game. The Yankees never recovered and finished in seventh place.

Gehrig was sorely disappointed in his team's lack of success. His personal totals were only marginally better than the league average. He finished a bit higher than the league average of .292 with a .295, which encompassed twenty homers, nine triples, twenty-three doubles. Scoring seventy-three runs was helped out by his six stolen bases. His proudest achievement, no doubt, was playing in 126 games—nearly a full season's worth.

"He's going to be a great ballplayer, that kid Gehrig," Huggins said. "When he came here, he didn't know a thing; he was one of the dumbest players I've ever seen. But he's got one great virtue that will make him: He never makes the same mistake twice. He makes all the mistakes, all right, but not twice."[9]

Gehrig made it a goal to find the mistakes he made in his play and then prevent them in the future. With the selfless help from coach O'Leary and Wally Pipp, Gehrig was able to improve, even if he did it slowly. He didn't learn fast, but he did learn, which was a blessing when Pipp was traded to Cincinnati at the end of the 1925 season, leaving Gehrig with a decent boudoir of first-base skills. On the one hand Gehrig was disappointed to see Pipp leave the team because of all the kindness Pipp had shown him. At the same time, he was overjoyed to be *the* Yankees' first baseman, not the kid who replaced the Yankee first baseman. "That was the greatest thrill of my career, the knowledge that I was the regular first baseman of my hometown team," he said. "At last I could go to my parents and tell them that I had regular work at good pay, so long as I could hit the ball and hustle."[10]

In preparation for spring training in 1926, Gehrig put in his first order for a personalized Louisville Slugger—a thirty-five-inch, thirty-seven-ounce chunk of wood with a large barrel and knob connected by a medium handle that fit snuggly into his muscular hands. With only small modifications, these specifications would remain the same for the rest of his career.

Gehrig eased into his role as Yankees first baseman. He knew for sure he would always come to the dugout and see his name on the roster tacked to the wall. The smile never left his face. "He has come much faster than I dared to expect," Huggins said of him on the tour north after spring training. "Lou has become an influence to the entire team. You get a player with that kind of spirit, and it spreads like a contagion to the other players."[11]

After the disastrous 1925 season, few in the sports world dared hope that the Yankees would bounce back in 1926. Among those few who did believe were Gehrig and Huggins. The starting lineup was rather different than the lineup used to kick off the previous season. Ruth, Meusel and Earle Combs handled the outfield work; Gehrig, of course, dug in at first; and veteran Joe Dugan was afire in the hot corner. That handful alone made for a threatening offense. Herb Pennock, Waite Hoyt, Urban Shocker, Bob Shawkey, Dutch Ruether, and Myles Thomas did rotations on the mound with Pat Collins behind the plate. New to the lineup were Mark Koenig and Tony "Poosh 'em Up" Lazzeri at short and second, respectively. These two kids, and the strong but raw kid at first base, were the main reason why nearly everyone in New York scoffed at Huggins' insistence that 1926 was going to be a good year for the boys of the Stadium. "If these kids fail me," Huggins told the unbelievers, "we'll wind up in sixth place. If they come through, we'll win the pennant."[12] The only reporter who agreed with him was Fred Lieb, a reporter who often traveled with the team and had befriended the Gehrig family.

Opposing teams were not impressed with Huggins' fortune telling either until the Yankees' bats starting whacking some sense into them. Some pitchers who had faced Gehrig in 1925 were not completely convinced of his much-hyped power. They would sometimes intentionally walk Babe Ruth, who was shifted in the lineup that season to bat directly before Gehrig, to get to the young first baseman. It only took a short time of Gehrig ripping the seams out of the ball with his Mack-truck force to convince the cynics that he was just as much a threat as Ruth. Of course, after Gehrig came Bob Meusel in the lineup. If the pitcher got through Ruth, he'd have to face Gehrig. If he survived Gehrig, or even if he gave up a hit or worse, he'd still have to face Meusel. No other time was this triple threat clearer than in a game against the Cleveland Indians. The pitcher for the day was Joe Shaute, who got it into his head that pitching all three right-field-loving hitters outside would curb their productivity. All three batters slammed a pitch into the body of Shaute's third baseman Rube Lutzke—Ruth to the shoulder, Gehrig to the shin, and Meusel to the stomach. After the shot in the belly, Lutzke fell to the ground and didn't move. His teammates rushed over to check on him.

It only took a short time of Gehrig ripping the seams out of the ball with his Mack-truck force to convince the cynics that he was just as much a threat as Ruth.

"Are you hurt?"

Lutzke glared at the inquirer. "Am I hurt! A guy would have been safer in the World War!"[13]

The Yankees were back. With their rekindled confidence came a mood for fun. Sportswriter Paul Gallico described the Yankee club as such: "They like their likker."[14]

Huggins was strict when it came to the proper way for a baseball player to entertain himself. Booze and women were not on the list of acceptable pleasures. Threats of suspension and fines were made, but the players had their fun anyway. Gehrig, however, was a man after Huggins' own heart, and he kept his alcohol intake extremely limited. There were better things to spend his money on, and there were better ways to spend his time. All of the hard work and perseverance he had invested into baseball were coming back two-fold. He had a firm hold in the lineup, a flourishing reputation as a power hitter, and his own share of the media's attention, however small it was compared to his much more colorful teammate Babe Ruth. "Buster" soon gave way to other nicknames, such as "the

Crown Prince" to Ruth's "the King." Prince and King caused pitchers grief with their bats and the infielders grief with their feet. In 1926 they accomplished the feat of a double steal, with Gehrig stealing home for a 12-11 victory over Boston.

The Yankees rolled their way through the majority of the season, laughing all the way to the bank and then laughing harder with female companions at a choice night spot. Toward the end of the season, though, things started to slip. Their confidence was so high they seemed to put on the autopilot instead of remembering that they were playing other professionals who were serious about winning. Underestimating the teams they had rolled over in the first part of the season, the Yankees lost games at a more frequent rate, until their comfortable lead over the league was chipped away to a two-game lead over second place in the last few weeks. Their fans held their collective breath and prayed hard, and sure enough, as Huggins had predicted, the Yankees won the pennant from second-place Cleveland by beating St. Louis.

Despite the fantastic voyage, Gehrig still nitpicked his performance, taking a glass-half-empty approach. Huggins saw some of these flaws too and talked to Gehrig about them. Among the things Huggins pointed out were playing too close to the bag and knowing when to come in on a bunt. Gehrig described how he set about erasing these errors from his game, "In the beginning, I used to make one terrible play a game. Then I got so I'd make one a week, and finally I'd pull a bad one about once a month."[15]

Another thing Huggins addressed was the curious drop in his hitting productivity during 1926. Huggins had noticed that Gehrig had been forcing himself to hit to the left side instead of following his natural tendency to hit to the right. When Huggins questioned Gehrig about it, the young man's response was that he figured since pitchers were pitching him outside it would be more efficient to hit to the left. Astounded, Huggins tried to contain his agitation. He calmly informed Gehrig that he loved seeing balls thrown to his leftys disappear into the right field stands.

"This league has a lot of short right-field fences," Huggins point-ed out. "Start hitting to the right again like nature wants you to anyway, and we'll all be better off."[16] Gehrig did, and they were.

If ever there was one who took instruction, Gehrig was it. Though he would get thrown out for arguing a handful of times in his long career, his record of early showers was miniscule compared to those of the egomaniacs and hotheads on the Yankee team. So rarely did Gehrig challenge an umpire's deci-sion that American League President Ban Johnson used him as an example of sportsmanship in his address to boys on field etiquette.

The hardest thing for Gehrig to learn, and he never fully real-ized it, was accepting his own imperfection. Even though he had tremendous talent, too many times he dwelled on what he was doing wrong instead of what he had done and was doing right. The shortest of slumps would trigger depression. In 1926 his hits tapered off for a bit and he made himself so miserable over it that Huggins, contrary to his teetotaler attitude as a manager, slipped him a ten-dollar bill and begged the slugger to get a couple of drinks and relax.

The difficulty he faced in accurately evaluating himself was nothing compared to the difficulty he had in reading other play-ers. Being a college grad, Gehrig was a big believer in "giving it the old college try," and had the infield chatter to match. In one game as he returned the ball to Waite Hoyt he cheered, "That's the old fight, stick in there!" Hoyt snapped back, "Let me pro-vide my inspiration, would ya, kid!"[17] Gehrig's go-get-'em atti-tude grated on the nerves of more players than just Hoyt (al-though Hoyt would later praise Gehrig for his efforts).

Opposing players were no less difficult for Gehrig to read. Clearly he had trouble getting along with certain pitchers and at least two managers (McGraw and Cobb). In a game against Detroit, Tiger Frank O'Rourke was pivoting to throw from sec-ond to first to finish a double play when Gehrig barreled into him. "I thought a truck hit me," O'Rourke recalled. The om-nipresent umpire Billy Evans called interference on Gehrig, causing both Gehrig and the batter to be called out. As Gehrig walked off the field, O'Rourke snarled unrepeatable remarks.

Gehrig started back at him but was shouldered away by a Tiger. The next day the Tigers and Yankees played again. While O'Rourke was taking infield practice, he spotted Gehrig, arms crossed, hat brim low, staring at him from first base line. Knowing he had to pass Gehrig to get to the visitor dugout, O'Rourke kept taking throws as long as he could in hopes that Gehrig would get tired of standing there and leave. Alas, O'Rourke's throwing buddies grew tired much sooner than Gehrig did, and O'Rourke had no choice but to walk toward the dugout. When he was close enough, Gehrig held out his hand for him to stop.

"Frank," Gehrig said in a gentle tone, "I'm sorry I went into you so hard yesterday. I shouldn't have done it."

O'Rourke sighed with relief. "Forget those names I called you, young fellow."

They shook hands. "Lou smiled at me," Frank later told an interviewer. "We were firm friends after that."[18]

Gehrig's confidence in his ability to make friends and his ability to play baseball wavered as much as the wind. But he needn't have worried so, particularly about his baseball career. No matter if he slumped or not, by the end of the 1926 season no one among the opposition considered him a weakling. The Senators' Walter Johnson could attest to that. In Johnson's admirable career he gave up only ninety-seven home runs in nearly 6,000 innings pitched. Only twice was he taken deep more than once by the same batter in a single game, once by Jack Fournier, who hit two inside-the-park homers, and once by a kid named Lou Gehrig, who slugged two of Johnson's pitches out of Washington's Griffith Stadium on August 13, 1926. It was Gehrig's first major offensive accomplishment during his consecutive games streak. Even with this phenomenal achievement, Gehrig still did not recognize that he was quickly becoming one of the elite hitters in the game at the age of twenty-three. Failures overwhelmed him in his self-evaluation.

Gehrig finished the regular season with a .313 average, sixteen homers, and 107 runs, and he may have done better had he not experimented with hitting to the left. He also finished with his first opportunity to play in a World Series. On October 2, 1926, Yankee Stadium was packed with 61,658 fans, including Mom and Pop Gehrig, for the first game in the Series against St. Louis. Mom was aflutter, telling all the neighboring attendees that their Louie played first base for the Yankees and he was once a college man. For the Series, Huggins slipped Gehrig down to the fifth batting slot. Gehrig proved his worth in any spot in the order by hitting in the only two runs the Yankees earned to beat St. Louis 2-1. Other memorable feats occurred that Series. First of all, Ruth hit three home runs in one game (Game Four), a feat no one had accomplished before in post-season play. Most people, however, remember the 1926 World Series for Grover Cleveland Alexander versus Tony Lazzeri in the seventh and decisive game.

Lou Gehrig described Alexander as "a tricky old bird with perfect coordination and without nerves. You never knew what he was going to do and while you were still trying to guess he did it!"[19] The day of the game there was a cold drizzle over New York, driving away 25,000 ticket holders. Jesse Haines had been laboring on the mound for St. Louis, and had managed to keep his team ahead of the Yankees 3-2 by the seventh inning. He walked Earle Combs, who was bumped to second by Mark Koenig with a sacrifice. Then he intentionally walked Ruth to get to Meusel. Meusel got to first, but caused a force out with Ruth at second. He also intentionally walked Gehrig, who was hoping for a chance to be the Series hero, for the opportunity to get the third out against Lazzeri with the bases loaded. In a bold move, St. Louis manager Rogers Hornsby pulled Haines and brought in the aged and allegedly hung over Grover Cleveland Alexander to face Lazzeri. Alexander was a show master. He purposely walked slowly from the bullpen to the mound to let Lazzeri agonize a little longer, and then when he finally got to the mound, he threw his five practice pitches in rapid-fire succession. According to Gehrig, Alexander liked to pitch like that. "The effect he always gave on the mound was of a pitcher working in batting practice."[20]

Bam, bam, bam, bam, bam. Alexander was finished with his

practice pitches. Lazzeri stepped in. Gehrig led off from first as Alexander delivered his first pitch—a strike. The second pitch— a strike. Third pitch—crack! Not a soul breathed as the ball soared far up the line, toying with the Yankees' hopes before it bent foul. Gehrig's heart was racing with excitement as he regained his leadoff stance. This close to a Series win! One pitch would determine it. Alexander threw the ball, a hard pitch that zipped toward home. Lazzeri swung...and missed.

The side was retired, and the score did not budge the next two innings. The game ended when Ruth, not known for his quickness, made the odd and fateful decision to try to steal second with two outs. He wasn't even close to being safe, leaving many wondering what Ruth had been thinking. With that, the Series win escaped the Yankees' grasp in 1926. Gehrig was beyond disappointed. So what if he had a noteworthy Series average of .348 and a perfect 1.000 fielding percentage? His team had lost.

The 1926 season provided Gehrig with numerous firsts—his first World Series and his first full season. It was also the season that kicked off some of his long-term offensive streaks: the first of twelve consecutive years he earned a .300 batting average or better, the first of twelve consecutive years he ended with at least 100 runs and RBI. With his Series bonus, he bought his family a house in New Rochelle, New York. For the first time his family lived in an upscale part of town and owned the roof over their heads.

Just as her son was self-conscious on the field, Mom was apprehensive in her new neighborhood. She struggled with the notion that the local merchants inflated prices because they knew that her son had money. Convinced the local butcher was dishonest, she bought a kitchen scale to double-check his measurements. She was, however, comfortable around certain Yankee players, taking a shine to the personable Babe Ruth. Many times he would come home with Lou to partake in Mom's massive suppers and conversations carried on in German.

It was becoming clear that Gehrig and Ruth were more than just an on-field duo. Photographers often snapped pictures of them standing side by side during batting practice or convers-ing on the sidelines. Inevitably people compared Gehrig to Ruth. They liked to see how the two stacked up statistically. After the Series more than one writer pointed out that Gehrig out-hit Ruth with a .348 compared to Ruth's .300, and that was with one less run than Ruth. The comparisons would never cease, which was fine with Gehrig at the time. He had a deep admiration for Babe Ruth. Their relationship was founded on that admiration. To Gehrig having a hero like Ruth take a liking to him was a bigger compliment than being recruited by Paul Krichell on the behalf of baseball's best-known team. After the World Series was over, Ruth and Gehrig departed on their first barnstorming tour together, a charade that was the brainchild of their mutual agent Christy Walsh, who saw nothing but dollar signs in taking the two biggest Yankee stars to the small towns where fans who only got second-hand accounts of the stars could have the chance to see them play and possibly even meet them. The two visited eighteen states, delving deep into the Midwest, to play exhibition games with top local players. As Walsh promised, the trip was well worth the money the locals shelled out to see first-hand Babe Ruth and Lou Gehrig wallop home runs.

The extra money was definitely welcomed by Gehrig (espe-cially after buying a house), but he had a much simpler reason for agreeing to extend his baseball play another month: "I be-long on the field," he told reporters.[21]

Chapter Six

To Be Young and a Yankee, 1927

A flurry of media rumors and gossip about Lou Gehrig opened 1927. Allegedly he had not won over the Yankee organization and they were contemplating a trade. Gehrig heard the heresy and fought it off furiously. "It can't be that anyone who can field any better than I do is needed," he told reporters. "If there's some mysterious guy who is being considered because he's supposed to be more effective in hitting left-handed pitching, that's a laugh. I can hit leftys as well as right-handers, and just as far."[1] His statement didn't quell the reports though, and Huggins didn't silence the issue until spring training by saying that he was satisfied with Gehrig. The team had already accepted Gehrig as the first baseman. They even experimented with a new nickname for him based on his gargantuan legs that led up to his broad derriere: Biscuit Pants.

Whether the unbelievers accepted it or not, Biscuit Pants was firmly planted in the Yankee lineup for the next twelve years. That lineup was first referred to as Murderers' Row in 1921, but not until 1927 did the foreboding nickname follow through on its promise. Huggins, sick of watching gutless pitchers and managers intentionally walk Ruth to try their luck with Meusel, had permanently flip-flopped Gehrig and Meusel in the batting order, putting Gehrig in the cleanup spot. Gehrig was a more consistent hitter than Meusel, therefore intentionally passing Ruth to get to Gehrig was like a manager stringing a KC strip around his pitcher's neck and making him walk into a lion's den. Passing two batters in a row would defeat the strategic purpose of an intentional walk, but even if a manager ate two walks, he still had to face Meusel and Lazzeri and Dugan. Pitchers had no choice—they had to throw to Ruth. The Murderers Row of legend was formed: Combs, Koenig, Ruth, Gehrig, Meusel, Lazzeri, and Dugan.

Much like the Yankee hitters, the Yankee pitchers were aces, especially Waite Hoyt. The most important addition to the team that year was the thirty-year-old rookie pitcher Wilcy Moore, said to be one of the first, and perhaps the best-ever, relief pitchers. After years of toiling in the minor leagues, Moore was "fixin' to go home" to his ranch when he was picked up by the Yankees from the South Atlantic League.

Even with the Row, the Babe was still number one in the eyes of virtually every Yankees fan, and some of the Yankees themselves. "Lou admired Babe as a ballplayer," a confidante of Gehrig wrote. "You had to, he was superb. Lou liked him as a man, too, and got a kick out of his shenanigans—even though he didn't want to copy them and couldn't. I think Babe liked Lou as much as he liked anybody."[2] Indeed Lou did hero-worship Babe, even playing personal assistant to him from time to time. While Ruth was notoriously horrible at remembering names and faces (he got his first wife's name wrong in his autobiography), Gehrig's mind absorbed such data. Along the American League circuit Ruth had a string of honeys. When he wanted female companionship in any given city, it was Gehrig's delegated responsibility to call up one of the girls. As for Gehrig, he seemed to hold little hope for finding a Miss Right for himself. Mom, as he told the press several times, was his best girl.

Babe Ruth was as carefree with his wallet as he could be with people's names. On long train rides Ruth was a regular at the poker table. Occasionally he would win, but he always bet extravagantly. Since he was the highest paid player in all of baseball, he could afford to throw bills around like leaflets inviting receivers to worship at his shrine. While Gehrig may have wished he could be so liberal with his money, there was simply no way he could be—he was the twenty-four-year-old sole breadwinner for his family. The one rule in baseball he never let out of his thoughts was that there are no guarantees; he could be cut from the team at any time.

Though Ruth and Gehrig seemed to be polar opposites, they did bond over a couple of things. Deep sea fishing, Gehrig's favorite relaxation activity, was one of them. The other was Mom's cooking. To show his gratitude, Ruth gave Mom a Chihuahua that she named "Jidge," a German-accented version of "George," Ruth's real name. Mom hosted many of the Yankees, including Bengough, Meusel, Koenig, Dugan and Lazzeri, a group nicknamed "Mom's boys." After partaking in the glory of Mom Gehrig, her cooking, and her beer, the other Yankees understood better why Gehrig was so close to her.

While 1927 may have begun swamped in meaningless rumors and gossip, it quickly shifted focus to more important things—like baseball. This was the season the Yankees bowled over the competition with a record-setting number of wins. It was the year Ruth declared he would break the home run record he set in 1921 and did. It was the year "Five O'Clock Lightening" struck with stunning vigor (the Yankees' batting productivity tended to surge in the seventh or eighth innings, typically played around five o'clock). The "lightening" pushed the Yankees into first place quickly and zapped everyone else into submission.

On July 4, while on a ten-game winning streak, the Yankees invited the Washington Senators to play a doubleheader in the Bronx. The Yankees whipped the Senators 12-1 in the first game. For the second game the Senators might as well not have bothered. The final score was 21-1. As Washington first baseman Joe Judge was leaving the stadium that evening, he uttered perhaps the most quoted lament from that season: "These fellows not only beat you but they tear your heart out. I wish the season was over."[3]

The Yankees trampled all over their challengers, regardless of day, place, weather or player conditions. After a game in Boston, the Yankees were to be shuttled by train to Detroit, an unusual jump because the season was usually meticulously scheduled so that teams had to travel the least amount possible between games. The Yankees' train was delayed in Boston. Then the next morning the diner car was taken off after an early breakfast, leaving the late raisers without a morsel. The team was due in Detroit at noon for the 3:30 game, but with the delay the night before they arrived at 3:00. The stadium was filled with fans. The Tigers were already dressed, warmed up, and spitting out sunflower shells in their dugout. Cancellation was not an option. So the Yankees were whisked from train station to stadium with a police escort. As they clamored for the dressing room, the hungry Yanks stopped at vendors to get whatever food was available—hot dogs, peanuts, beer, soda. As shirts and socks flew off, dogs and soda were shoved down, and the team hustled to the dugout. Waiving pregame warm-up and practice, the Yankees signaled they were ready to play ball. In the prime example of why the 1927 Yankees were so great, even with indigestion and cold arms, they still shamed the Tigers into an ignominious defeat: 19-2.

"Break up the Yankees!" rose the plea during the course of the season. Colonel Ruppert got goose bumps at the words. The team he had envisioned was his in all reality. Laments, pleas, appeals from opponents thrilled him to no extent. St. Louis Browns manager Dan Howley put forth the suggestion that every Yankee batter should be penalized one strike each plate appearance. It likely wouldn't have helped the opposition.

To Gehrig, winning was certainly tasty, but what he loved most about being a Yankee was the way they were treated around the country. He loved the traveling, the lovely diner car meals like the ones he used to serve for dime wages, the upscale hotels with bellmen who handled his bags for him. He had enough money to replace the shabby cardboard suitcase he had taken to spring training three years prior with a classy, professional one. He was a long way from hot bus rides and cracker box stadiums. His enjoyment off the field transcended into his on-field persona. When he was warming up, elation tinted his cheeks. One writer, Adie Suehsdorf, favored this image of Gehrig: "I'll always remember him in the last round of infield practice. The third baseman had made the play at home and left the field, likewise the shortstop and second baseman. Now the ball is thrown to Lou, who gathers it in and fires home. The catcher comes up the line a few feet and slams it back to Lou. Lou comes in a few feet, one-hands it, wheels, and fires. So it goes, once or twice more, until the two are throwing bullets to each other from only twenty-five to forty feet apart. Lou then breaks off with a wide grin and lumbers to the dugout. He experienced sheer joy in the whole ritual." His defense had improved dramatically since his baptism by fire in 1925. In fact he had progressed to the point where many considered him a worthy rival to Giants great Bill Terry. Suehsdorf stated, "Lou could dig the ball out of the dirt as well as Terry, maybe better." The defensive and offensive skills Gehrig possessed were essential to the team's success.[4]

On Labor Day, the Yankees ground Boston's nose into defeat. Winning the AL pennant was all but gauranteed. That night at Boston's Back Bay Station the team celebrated by way of a ceremonial burning of straw hats. The rest of the season was a sail on peaceful seas. So much so that toward the end Huggins granted the regulars permission to take themselves out of the lineup whenever they had the urge to take the day off to fish or lounge or sleep off a hangover. Gehrig, of course, did not take advantage of the offer, and his consecutive games streak continued unnoticed by everyone, including himself.

The pennant race no longer an issue, fans and reporters turned their full attention to the home run duel waged between Ruth, determined to break his own season home run record, and Gehrig. The duel began on April 16 when Gehrig banged out two homers and went into full throttle in the hottest months of the summer. On June 30 they were tied at twenty-four apiece. While fans loved the tension, they were rooting for Ruth, not the kid batting behind him. "The fans applauded Ruth's home runs, that's his business. Not so Gehrig's. He's just a first baseman," the *Herald-Tribune* reported. By July 5, Gehrig was ahead by three over Ruth's twenty-five, cueing the *New York Telegram* to print the headline "The Odds Favor Gehrig to Beat out Babe in Home Run

Derby." A few weeks later Gehrig still had a small lead at thirty-five to thirty-four. Fans bit their nails in anticipation of the next Yankee game and the next homer. The sluggers stayed neck and neck through mid-August, with thirty-eight home runs. On September 6 in Fenway, Gehrig hit a homer in the beginning of the game to pull his total to forty-five. Ruth answered with a home run of his own in the sixth inning, then went on to sock two more homers during that game and two more the next day. In the home stretch of September, Ruth raced ahead, swatting at an amazing pace. Gehrig couldn't keep up. In the month of September the Sultan of Swat hit seventeen home runs, more than anyone had ever hit in September before.[5]

The home run derby encouraged deep scrutiny of each man's style of hitting, which were perfect visual metaphors for their respective personalities. Ruth's swing was filled with easy, unmistakable grace; Gehrig's with down-to-business bluntness. Ruth's corkscrew swing derived power from the twisting of his skinny ankles, and the home runs it produced were high rockets that tickled the feet of angels before descending into the right field bleachers. Gehrig dug in deep and swung with stiff wrists, sending home runs on line drives that slowly rose the further away from home plate they went. Detroit's second baseman during Gehrig's time was Charlie Gehringer, whose name follows Lou's in the Hall of Fame register. From his experience in watching the two men for a number of years, he observed, "[Ruth] had that uppercut swing, so he never hit a hard grounder. Gehrig would knock your legs off, but Ruth the only thing he hit hard would be the air. But Gehrig? He'd hammer 'em."[6] Whereas Ruth's style limited him to almost always pulling the ball into right field if he didn't strike out, Gehrig's style allowed him to hit in any direction, and he did. The Browns' manager Dan Howley pointed out, "You can usually figure what the Babe might do, but you can *never* tell about Gehrig. Lou is likely to hit any kind of ball to any field."[7]

So much attention was being paid to the home run race, particularly to the boisterous Ruth chasing down his own record, that any achievements the other Yankees enjoyed were barely noticed. For instance, Tony Lazzeri hit two home runs in one game. It just so happened that Ruth also hit a home run the same game. The next day the nation's papers only discussed Ruth. "Fellows like Ruth and Gehrig can ruin an ordinary ballplayer," Joe Dugan commented. "They win so many games by their individual efforts that you wonder why you are in the lineup."[8] But Lazzeri and Dugan and the rest of the team respected that home runs were what Ruth was paid to do and they didn't have hard feelings.

Five times that season the duo of Ruth and Gehrig hit back-to-back home runs, as they would do many more times together.

Five times that season the duo of Ruth and Gehrig hit back-to-back home runs, as they would do many more times together. Rube Walberg, pitcher for Philadelphia, was a victim of these back-to-back homers twice. Once on April 23 and then again on September 2. He was the only pitcher to be so victimized. Other pitchers did not see one homer directly after another, but did see both men sock one out in different innings of the same game, an occurrence repeated ten times in 1927.

It was a spectacular show, but the fans wanted a winner in the home run king campaign. The tension reportedly got to Ruth the closer the season's end drew. A 1933 article signed off by Gehrig in *Liberty* magazine claimed that Ruth approached him one day in Yankee Stadium. "Say, young fellow," Ruth said, according to the article, "there's a lot of fun in this thing but the money is the thing we're after. The more balls we hit over the wall, the more World Series we'll get. Suppose we forget each other and remember that."[9]

Ruth didn't have to be afraid (if he was) of losing the duel. In the remaining forty-two games of the season, Ruth took a leisurely jog around the infield twenty-four times. At that rate he would have hit ninety home runs in a full season. Meanwhile Gehrig's churn rate decreased noticeably. His mother had suddenly fallen very ill, requiring immediate surgery. His attention was understandably on things more important than a game of baseball. At the end of every home game Gehrig rushed to the hospital to sit by her bed, pet her hand, and pray for her full recovery.

The last one Ruth was to hit in 1927 was the record-setting number sixty in the next to last day of the season, September 30. Tom Zachary from Washington was the opposing pitcher that day in Yankee Stadium. History was made in front of a meager crowd of 10,000, many of whom rushed the field to congratulate Ruth. The first person Ruth greeted after stomping on the plate was his grinning teammate Lou Gehrig. For the rest of his life, Gehrig would consider shaking Ruth's hand that day as one of the biggest rewards of his career. While few remember, Gehrig hit his last homer the next day, ending the amazing season with forty-seven hash marks in the HR column.

The media darling and his young cohort had a combined total of 107 home runs and 339 RBI. Their performance was a vital part of the equation for the Yankees to finish nineteen games ahead of their closest competitor, the Philadelphia Phillies. The Yankees won an astounding 110 games, a record that would stand for twenty-seven years. In twenty-two tries against the Browns, the Yankees succeeded twenty-one times. As a team their average was .307, and they scored 975 runs and hit 158 homers compared to the seven other teams' combined 281 homers. The pitchers made opposing batters work for their success, keeping a 3.20 earned run average. "I'll lay five bucks against one thin dime," John Kieran wrote in the *New York Times*, "there was never a team came crashing through, like Ruth and the rest of the Yankee crew, like Combs, Lazzeri and Buster Lou."[10]

Gehrig was exponentially happier with his team's performance that season than the previous season, but his focus quickly shifted back to his ailing mother. He approached Huggins to discuss an ominous possibility: not playing in the World Series.

Huggins, of course, was not willing to entertain this idea and told Gehrig as much. Gehrig went to his mother to discuss her care, still uncertain as to what he would do. Her response, while perhaps not as blunt as Huggins', was the same. She had come a long way from her previous mindset that baseball meant the death of respectability. Reluctantly he agreed to play, telling

himself that with the extra earnings he could buy Mom something pretty.

◆ ◆ ◆

The "enemy" to be brought down that World Series was the
Pittsburgh Pirates. During those days there was no interleague
play, so Series rivals faced each other with very little if any
knowledge of the opposing team's playing style. With the phenomenal Waner brothers on their team, the Pirates were cocky
and ready to take on the boys in pinstripes. Paul Waner, dubbed
"Big Poison," was the same age as Gehrig and could guzzle
more booze than Ruth. Lloyd Waner, "Little Poison," was three
years younger and slightly bigger than his brother. Between
them they weighed less than 300 pounds, but power comes in
all sizes. Combined the boys got 460 hits. They had known, of
course, about the home run derby, but thought that those
homers were inflated hits off poor pitchers.

   The Series started on Pittsburgh's home turf, Forbes Field, on
October 5, 1927. The day before, the Yankees had a chance to
practice at the stadium while the Pirates sat in the stands in
street clothes watching. Huggins saw the Waner boys and their
teammates in the stands and, according to legend, decided to
employ his master's in baseball psychology. Before Waite Hoyt
took the mound to throw batting practice, Huggins caught him
by the arm and whispered, "Let 'em hit it." Following his instructions, Hoyt served up nothing but fat pitches for the boys.
As Huggins was predicting, the Yankees smashed the balls over
the fences, one right after another. Ruth and Meusel sent a number of balls over the right field fence, but it was Gehrig's
whistling shot over the center field fence, a feat never accomplished by a National League player, that made the Pirates gulp.
Supposedly the Pirates were so intimidated they couldn't keep
their hands steady. The Waner brothers insisted in 1927 and
thereafter that their team was not scared into submission. Lloyd
said he may have commented to his brother something like,
"They sure are big, aren't they?" The rest, he said, was embel-
lishment by New York writer Ken Smith, who had overheard
their conversation.[11] Smith claims that Lloyd did indeed say

that, but then followed up his first question with another one, "Do they always hit like that?"[12] Whatever the reaction of the Pirates that afternoon, their manager Donnie Bush ignored the showoffs and told his players to do the same. No one believed the Pirates were immune to the unforgettable sight of Gehrig's hits soaring over the center field fence, however. "If they ain't nervous, they ain't human," Ring Lardner wrote in his *Evening World* article.[13]

Hitters the Pirates may have had, but nothing they could pull out was strong enough to plow a dent into the iron side of the 1927 Yankees.

Hitters the Pirates may have had, but nothing they could pull out was strong enough to plow a dent into the iron side of the 1927 Yankees. The Yankees dominated Game One, then Game Two. For a few days before the games in New York there were reports that the Pirate batters would rip into Herb Pennock, a lefty, because they had shredded leftys all season long. Huggins laughed at the reports and dared the onslaught by putting Pennock on the hill to start Game Three. Twenty-one batters later, the Pirates finally got a hit. And so the Series went, the Pirates forgetting what had made them so great to be able to play on the same field as the Yankees in the first place.

In the course of the games played in Pittsburgh, Gehrig had proven his smarts as a first baseman were dramatically better than they were when he broke into the lineup. Forbes Field had box seats that encroached on his territory behind first base, creating a tricky place to catch foul balls. Before the Series began, he carefully measured the distance he could go back and to the left before he hit the wall. This knowledge allowed him to make three catches against the wall, one of which he made while flipping over the wall into startled spectators, that he otherwise may not have made. Twice in one game he robbed George Grantham of a hit—a double up the line and a hard grounder between first and second. Writers, fans and players alike took notice. As sportswriter Ray Robinson put it, "Lou had come a long way in erasing his image as an artless baby hippo."[14]

Overall he batted .308 in the Series with a pair each of doubles and triples and five RBI. In the third game with two men on Gehrig slugged a pitch to the deepest part of center field and tried to leg out an inside-the-park home run. Though he didn't make it to the plate before the ball, thanks to a precise relay by the Pirates, the *Evening World* declared, "That was the most thunderous hit of the Series."[15] The Yankees went on to win the game 8-1. In the fourth game, played in New York, he came to the plate in the ninth with the bases loaded, score tied and zero outs. It was the perfect situation for Gehrig to make a hero of himself. The home crowd cheered him on, hoping to see him slug one over the Waner brothers' heads. Though normally a reliable hitter, he struck out. The important thing this time was that he had learned how to deal with failing to be the hero every time, and he did not get all worked up over it. Two batters later, Pirates pitcher Johnny Milsus threw a wild pitch and the third-base runner took home to win the game and end the Series in a comparatively anticlimactic fashion.

The Yankees had beat the Pirates in four straight games, the shortest Series in history, lasting only seventy-four hours, fifteen minutes. It was the first time an American League team had swept the Series. The Pirates left the Big Apple with a slouch, the arrogance purged from their posture. "The one thing I remember best about the Series," Paul Waner said, "is that I didn't seem to actually realize I was really playing in a World Series until it was all over."[16] He must have been too distracted by trying to convince himself that he wasn't intimidated. There was one thing for which the Waner brothers could hold bragging rights—they out-hit Gehrig and Ruth in the Series.

The most important thing to happen during the 1927 World Series, however, was that Lou Gehrig's mother came off the critical list.

◆ ◆ ◆

Expectedly, the press quickly tallied up the season stats to compare Gehrig and Ruth. Gehrig had outdone Ruth with an average of .373 compared to Ruth's .337. He was first in the league in total bases (447), doubles (52), and set a new RBI record with 175. Considering he batted after Babe Ruth in a season when Ruth set a new home run standard, Gehrig's RBI achievement is all the more remarkable. He was second in the league in batting average, hits (218), runs (149), triples (18), walks, and home runs. His home run mark of forty-seven was higher than that of the Chicago, Boston, Cleveland and Washington teams combined. This phenomenal rap sheet, in partnership with the fact that his presence in the lineup gave Ruth a chance to hit, earned Gehrig fifty-six votes, the majority by far, from the sportswriters association to win the American League Most Valuable Player Award on October 12, 1927.

This award was fortunately based on playing ability, not on the writers' personal opinion of a player. Gehrig didn't have the discipline to shoot the breeze with strangers or engage in small talk. He was raised to work, not chitchat. Reporters made him very uncomfortable, and when he was uncomfortable, he recoiled and kept quiet, which gave him the reputation of being standoffish. If a writer did corner him for an interview or a quick quote, he tried so hard to think of something to say that wouldn't make him sound like a blubbering buffoon that he spoke flatly and without vibrant diction. "When these writers would ask me questions," he told a friend, "they'd often think I was rude if I didn't answer right away. They didn't know that I was so scared...."[17] He didn't like the fact that reporters thought he was a slow-witted dud. The truth was he only came across that way because he was being put on the spot. In private he was not only articulate, but funny and insightful. Reporters didn't see that side of him and he didn't understand how to translate his private speaking into public. This shyness dogged him until the end of his career.

Having to deal with writers aside, Gehrig loved his job. With it he was able to provide more than enough for himself and his family. In 1927 he took home a salary of $8,000 plus a World Series bonus. It was more money than he had ever earned, even though it was only a fraction of Ruth's $70,000 salary and a day's pay for the run-of-the-mill Wall Street trader during that roaring decade. Most of the starters earned salaries between $7,000 and $12,000.

To make more money, Gehrig agreed once again to barn-storm with the home run champ. Ruth liked to tell people that he offered Gehrig more money for going on the month-long tour than Gehrig had seen all season. On October 11 they boarded a train at New York's bustling Penn Station to begin a three-week tour of the country. In the course of the tour they traveled 8,000 miles, with stops along the East Coast, in the Midwest, and then in California. Each town gathered their best players together to form the Bustin' Babes and the Larrupin' Lous, each team headed by its namesake. More than 200,000 fans around the nation paid to watch the two mythical players they knew only from newspaper pictorials. Every city Lou and Babe stopped in saw record attendances. Well over half of the twenty-one games on the itinerary were called early because overly eager fans rushed the field. A game in Ashbury, New Jersey, ended early after the two sluggers had knocked all thirty-six balls provided by the promoter into the lagoon beyond the outfield fence.

Gehrig was both flattered and overwhelmed by the massive crowds everywhere they went.

Gehrig was both flattered and over-whelmed by the massive crowds every-where they went. Babe the attention junkie basked in the attention as he stood on the back platform of their train to give one last curtain call to the hundreds of smiling, waving, shouting people at the station to see them off. While Gehrig allowed himself to be dragged out there with Ruth, he never enjoyed it. Cheers and applause didn't coax him out of shyness. Rather, it encouraged him all the more to avoid the spotlight.

By the end of the tour, Gehrig had seen more of California than many of his Yankee teammates, with stickers from Fresno, Santa Barbara, San Diego and San Francisco decorating his travel trunk. He had hit thirteen homers to please the people while Ruth rightfully outdid him with twenty-four. The biggest reward was the extra $10,000, one-third of Ruth's take-home earnings for the tour. "The kid's giving it all to his mother," Ruth told reporters, which was very likely what happened. Reporters asked Gehrig what his plans for the rest of the offseason were. "I plan to play a lot of basketball," he responded.[18]

In the next couple of years, Gehrig and Ruth would take an annual barnstorming tour for the fun and the money of it. Then Colonel Ruppert finally put a stop to it. Their earnings from the barnstorming tours was leverage the Colonel didn't care to resist during salary talks.

Gehrig knew that playing was only part of his job and that he had to make efforts to reach and affect the fans. After the 1927 season he teamed up with Ruth to perform a comedy skit for a phonograph recording. Maybe "comedy" is a stretch, for the two had no comedic timing and Ruth slurred his way through it, sometimes repeating a word in an effort to say it correctly before moving on to the next one, and sometimes he just butchered the lines, such as this priceless segment:

LG: Say, Babe, tell me something. Is it true that you eat twenty hot dogs during a baseball game?

BR: That's one of those fool lies. Why, twenty hot dogs during a game would kill any man.

LG: I know it.

BR: A man who would eat twenty hot dogs is a pig during a ball game.

LG: Of course he would.

One rarely discussed characteristic of Gehrig was quite apparent in the audio—his high-pitched voice. Looking at his body seemingly carved from a single six-foot-tall block of marble, most people assumed his voice was a deep baritone, but he actually sounded almost boyish, which should have helped the comedy. In the end, the skit was much funnier in writing. For instance, this *reads* funny:

LG: Do you remember when I first reported to the Yanks, Babe?

BR: [laughs] Do I? You were so green the groundskeepers tried to go over you with a rake.

LG: I was just a raw student.

BR: I don't know anything about the student part of it, but I'll tell the world you were raw. As a matter of fact, the first day you reported, I didn't see your face at all. I couldn't keep my eyes off your feet.

LG: What was the matter with my feet?

BR: They were so big I thought you were standing in a couple of troughs. Is there any truth in the story that you sell old shoes for bungalows?

The actual delivery dampens the humor this exchange holds on paper. They end the skit with the dialogue that perfectly describes their years together with the Yankees:

LG: Good-bye. See you all next season.

BR: How will they know you when they see you?

LG: They'll know you, won't they?

BR: Of course they'll know me.

LG: Well, wherever they see you they'll know I'm the guy that's right on your heels.[19]

Around this same time Gehrig also gave writing a go. His article "The Job of Playing First" was published in 1927 by D. Appleton and Co. as part of a project headed by Rogers Hornsby that presented accounts from major league players on how to play baseball like a pro. If Gehrig's reader is not a first baseman or doesn't have plans to play first base, the article is rather dull. It does include some standard, helpful bits of advice: "Always play the ball—don't let it play you"; "The ballplayer who loses his head, who can't keep his cool, is worse than no ballplayer at all." This last bit of advice no doubt came in part from Gehrig's own experience in his run-ins with a certain fiery Detroit manager.

These outlets allowed Gehrig's voice to be heard by fans while not pinning him in the hot seat. He enjoyed being known, but he didn't enjoy being famous. He was born a man of simple pleasures and high virtue, and that's not something that can be stripped from a man's psyche. Reporter Frank Graham wrote of him, "The modesty and the firmness of character that had been bred into him and nurtured by his parents kept him on a level keel."[20]

In the thousands of comparisons made of him to Ruth, this is one area in which Gehrig outshone his flamboyant teammate. Pete Sheehy, longtime clubhouse manager at Yankee Stadium, epitomized the vast difference between Gehrig and Ruth when he praised Gehrig for his dignity and honesty and said of the other guy, "Ruth never flushed the toilet."[21]

Chapter Seven
The Good with the Bad, 1928-1929

When it came time to negotiate contracts with Colonel Ruppert in 1928, Babe Ruth pulled Lou Gehrig aside to discuss business strategy. Ruth knew that if both he and Gehrig held out for more money, Ruppert would have no choice but to pay them what they wanted. He made Gehrig promise to hold out for $30,000 a year.

In reality, Gehrig knew that he would accept whatever Ruppert offered because, unlike Ruth, Gehrig didn't know what he was worth. Combined with his submission to authority figures, Ruth's advice was lost on Gehrig. At the end of the negotiations with the boss, Gehrig signed a two-year contract for $50,000, a total well below what he had promised Ruth he'd seek, but more than triple what he had been paid the previous year. Too shy to tell Ruth directly, he kept mum even after the papers broke the story. Ruth confronted Gehrig as soon as he read the headlines and found his excuse lacking.

To the reporters Ruth confided that he was upset only because he thought Gehrig was actually listening to his go-get-'em speech. From his point of view, his advice was thrown to the wayside, and the sultan didn't respond well to such treatment. The two men were never friends in the traditional sense; they were friendly so long as Gehrig was submissive. The one true friendship Gehrig would form was with teammate Bill Dickey, who first reported to the Yankees for spring training in 1928 as the new catcher. They initially bonded over one of Gehrig's favorite topics—hitting. In the minor leagues Dickey had been a good hitter, and he was frustrated that he couldn't get the hang of hitting major league pitchers. "Sometimes when I was at bat," he said, "I noticed Lou studying me. I didn't know him so well then, although I was a great admirer of his long before I even came to the Yankees."

One day in batting practice, Gehrig took Dickey aside. "I've been watching you. I think I can tell you what you're doing wrong."

Dickey recalled, "I was so pleased and surprised I could hardly answer."[1]

Gehrig explained to Dickey that he was hitting up on the ball, a technique that could work in the minors where pitchers were less experienced, but it would not work in the majors. With the same patience Wally Pipp had shown Lou, he spent an hour each day for a few days working with Dickey until the kid got it worked out enough to swing correctly nearly every time. For the next decade Dickey never had a bad slump, a phenomenon he credited to Gehrig's selfless instruction.

The schooling formed a companionship between the two men which deepened when they roomed together on road trips. Dickey was four years younger than Gehrig, but the age difference was of no significance. They were best friends who both limited their expenses and didn't enjoy booze like the other Yanks did. Together they would fish, an activity Gehrig used to enjoy with Ruth, off Long Island. The only big difference between the two men was the fact that Gehrig was very methodical in everything from pregame ritual to how he folded down his sheets at night, while Dickey, with his more freewheeling ways, sometimes left his bed unmade.

Theirs was not a hero-worship relationship but a genuine friendship. It was Gehrig's tenderness and humanity that appealed to Dickey. On more than one occasion Dickey witnessed Gehrig share this tenderness with young fans. After a hard loss, many players would stiffly walk past the youngsters outside the stadium asking for an autograph. From time to time Gehrig was guilty of this. The difference, Dickey pointed out, was that Gehrig would regret it and turn right around mumbling, "It wasn't that kid's fault we lost."[2] He would catch up with the kid and not only give an autograph but also stay and chat for a minute or two to make up for his rudeness.

Of course the everlasting tender spot in Lou's heart was for his mother. By the time the 1928 season got underway, Mom had fully recovered from her illness and was back in her role as den mother. She was a constant presence in St. Petersburg during spring training, in Yankee Stadium on game days, and on the team train for away games. To her son she was counselor when he slumped, medic when he endured various incidental injuries while playing every single game, and purveyor of home-cooked goodies. One of the roles she took on with earnest was defender of her offspring. The press liked to play upon the story of Gehrig's rise from poverty to posh, but Mom would tolerate no one saying her boy was a product of the slums. He was a collegian, she harped. No one on the Yankee squad resented Mom tagging along, especially when they got to join in on the consumption of her cooking. During a card game on the train, Gehrig got up from his chair and went to his room. A few minutes later he returned to the card table with a basket of Mom's fried chicken. The always-hungry young men on the team and in the press corps devoured the food and sung praises to Mom Gehrig.

No one on the Yankee squad resented Mom tagging along, especially when they got to join in on the consumption of her cooking.

Gehrig called Mom his sweetheart, his best girl, but those close to him saw his loneliness and longing for a young woman to love. Unbeknownst to Gehrig, his true love was alive and had brushed by him once in 1928. At a large party in Chicago, Lou was introduced to a fresh-faced young woman with hair as dark as his. Her name was Eleanor Twitchell.

"I thought he was a very nice young man," Eleanor said in her autobiography of their first meeting, "and a very nice-looking one. He was the first major league player I ever met, and, naturally, I was interested in his career because he was such a famous one. I followed it closely so that by the time we met again in 1932 I felt that I really knew him because I knew so much about him. He always swore, later on, that he remembered me from 1928, but I'm sure he didn't, and I used to tease him about it."[3] Gehrig was oblivious to Eleanor's interest and kept playing baseball and living with his parents.

It seemed to Lou Gehrig at one point in the 1928 season that he wasn't getting any love off the field and he wasn't getting any on the field either. Washington's spirited little Bucky Harris bunted down the first base line to try to score the runner on third, but when Gehrig fielded it cleanly and prepared to throw home, Harris stomped on his foot. Gehrig's throw was a mile off target, as was Harris' intention, allowing the run to score. Harris was proud of his achievement, until he saw Gehrig's face. "I've never seen a man look so surprised and hurt," Harris said. For the rest of the twenty-two games against the Yankees that season, Harris played in fear of retaliation from Gehrig with his gigantic biceps. "But Lou never did a thing," Harris said. "Every time after that when I got to first, he just gazed at me as though to ask me how I could do such a thing. I got feeling so ashamed of myself for what I'd done that I finally apologized to him. You should have seen the poor guy lighten up!"[4]

Once again Gehrig's tender nature showed through his iron exterior. Reputation means everything in baseball, and Gehrig's reputation was not as a tender heart but as a batter who put the fear of the Almighty into American League pitchers. In one game alone, Gehrig socked three home runs off a trembling White Sox pitcher. The feat prompted Gehrig's choice bat manufacturer, Hillerich and Bradsby, to create a magazine ad featuring him wielding his Louisville Slugger model and the story of his three-homer game. Some pitchers confessed they were more nervous with Gehrig in the box than with Ruth. Pitchers began to refer to Gehrig as "the hard number," the hardest number of the batting order to get through successfully.

For the most part the 1928 season started out with the same

Yankee domination as the 1927 season had. At the midseason mark they had distanced themselves from the second-place A's by seventeen games. Then, almost simultaneously, nearly every starter managed to get injured in some way. Lazzeri suffered from an aggravated shoulder, Ruth from charley horses, Pennock from a limp pitching arm. Bengough, Combs and Meusel also did time in the row of disabled benchwarmers. Gehrig walked off all of his injuries, never once sitting out a game. The onslaught of injuries created the perfect time for one writer to say, "The Yankees were held together by sticking plaster. But even so they are too much the best."[5] They were still in first place, though their lead had dwindled considerably. In early September the A's slipped briefly into the top spot in the midst of the incorrigible Ty Cobb's announcement of his retirement. On September 9 the Yankees and Athletics faced off in a deciding doubleheader. The Yankees won to regain the top spot, but their joy was cut short by the news that their 1927 teammate Urban Shocker had died in Denver from heart disease. Gehrig was not particularly close to Shocker, but the loss of someone whom he had known and worked with fairly closely was still emotional.

Playing a good portion of the season with taped appendages and sore muscles, the Yankees managed to break the century mark in wins, 102, finishing two-and-a-half games ahead of the Athletics to capture their third consecutive pennant. Going into the World Series against St. Louis, Ruth was still complaining of cramps and Gehrig sported a fat lip from taking a grounder to the face. The Cardinals were comparatively intact. They had star players like Jim Bottomley at first, shortstop Frankie Frisch, and twenty-game-winners Jesse Haines and Bill Sherdel. While these pitchers had faced Ruth and Gehrig in the 1926 World Series, they had yet to experience the matured Gehrig and the rest of Murderers' Row.

In the first game of the Series, Hoyt pitched the Yankees to a 4-1 win, two of the runs knocked in by Gehrig with a double and a single. Gehrig was no less productive in the second game. The first pitch he saw he belted into the right-field bleachers as the once-dominating pitcher Grover Cleveland Alexander hung his head. Yankee George Pipgras described the resulting home run, "It just kept rising and rising and finally hit the scoreboard. If you know where that scoreboard was in Yankee Stadium, you know what a clout that was."[6] The Yankees scored three of their runs on that homer. They went on to win 9-3. The home run was Gehrig's first postseason round tripper ever, and not the last he would hit in the 1928 postseason.

In the third game, played in St. Louis' Sportsman's Park, he slammed two more home runs. The first one was another first-pitch wallop off Jesse Haines that landed atop the right-field pavilion. The second could have been an out if not a triple but it got away from the center fielder. Gehrig with his deceptive speed was able to leg out an inside-the-park home run. After this score, Gehrig was determined to tie Ruth's record of three home runs in one postseason game to tickle the fancy of Mom who was sitting proudly in the stands. Unfortunately his last two plate appearances ended in walks.

His prowess at the plate was complemented by his ability in the base paths. Despite his apparent disgust with Bucky Harris' intentional spiking to score a run, Gehrig was not completely above dirty baseball. In the Series, as a matter of fact, he victimized the opposition in a similar way.

"The play was at second base," Gehrig recounted. "I gave Frank Frisch all I had and knocked him kicking. The ball rolled to short center field. Ruth had turned third and was headed for the plate. He hadn't seen me take Frish, but he knew I had—that's how we played in those days. Ruth kept heading for the plate, and when he got there he bowled Jimmy Wilson over. The ball had been retrieved by then. Frisch was still sitting back of second rubbing his leg when Ruth reached the dugout. It was dirty baseball, but that was the rule of the day."[7]

In the fourth game Ruth, so far silent in slugging for the Series, hit a blast early in the game. Then he did it again. And the next time he came to bat...bam, another one. Fans of Yankees and Cardinals alike gleefully tossed straw hats, seat cushions, and whatever else they could onto the field, thankful to have witnessed Ruth tie his own record of three homers in one Series game. Too many people were still yakking up Ruth's third blast to remember Gehrig's homer in the seventh that sealed the Yankees' victory 7-3. Gehrig had hit four home runs in the same Series, a feat achieved by no one else other than Ruth. The *New York Times* lamented on Gehrig's behalf, "Gehrig tied Ruth's record of four home runs in a Series, yet few knew he played."[8] Though Ruth did deserve praise, especially considering he set a still-unbroken Series slugging percentage record at .625, Gehrig's overall offensive performance is one of the best in Series history. His four home runs helped bump his Series batting average to a prestigious .545, and he also got six hits to drive in a record nine runners and scored five times himself. The perfect sign that Gehrig was the true hitting hero in the Series was the fact that he was intentionally walked (a sign of respect from pitchers) six more times than Ruth. Reporters asked him, "How do you feel about your performance in the Series?" With a noticeable gleam in his eye, he answered, "It was one of my greatest."[9]

"Gehrig tied Ruth's record of four home runs in a Series, yet few knew he played."

The 1928 World Series was definitely one of his best, and so was the 1928 season. He was second in the league in the home run category with twenty-seven; tied for most RBI with 142; tied for most doubles at forty-seven; second in slugging percentage (.648), runs (139), and hits (210). His season batting average was a very respectable .374.

On the train back to New York after the final Series game, the victorious Yankees celebrated with a round of drinks and rough-housing that entailed ripping each other's shirts off. No one was immune to the jubilation. Colonel Ruppert and his companion had just settled into their beds in their stateroom when two Yankees burst in and tore at their pajama tops. Ruppert struggled from under his assailant and turned on the light. He found Ruth grinning widely holding up his tattered pajama shirt. Across the room stood, of all people, Lou Gehrig. Gehrig was laughing as loudly as Ruth, and Ruppert could not hate the fun. All the players were tickled by Gehrig's uncharacteristic participation in such folly.

The train rolled into Grand Central Station an hour late on October 10. Thousands of fans had waited in the terminal to catch a glimpse of the heroes as they came off the train. The one player they were most anxiously awaiting was, naturally, Ruth. Gehrig received polite cheers, but the women screamed and the children yelped when the Bambino stuck his pumpkin-shaped face out of the railcar door. Gehrig certainly didn't mind, however. He was still much more comfortable on the rim of the limelight, perfectly content with Ruth hogging the rest.

Back in the pressrooms that winter, the baseball writers looked for a way to keep their writing hands agile. They relieved their idleness by formulating the theory that the American League would no longer stand the best hitters being indentured to one team. Break up the Yankees, they said. Obviously the Yankees would not let Ruth go, so who should be traded to make power more distributed? Who else than Lou Gehrig? Ever since Gehrig replaced Pipp in June 1925, he had never missed a game, and ever since Gehrig replaced Pipp writers went to great lengths to propose why he should not be on the Yankee roster anymore. They speculated on how much Gehrig would bring Ruppert if he decided to sell—perhaps $50,000, maybe even $100,000. The rumor continued to be tossed around up through spring training in 1929. Huggins shook his head in annoyance, and he insisted that there was no need for the renewed plea to break up the Yankees. "It won't happen and it isn't necessary. Time and the law of averages will take care of that.... One of these days they will fail. Empires, great private enterprises, and personal fortune have been broken up by time. Who do these people who have raised this cry think the Yankees are that they can go on forever?"[10]

Huggins, as was his habit, was right, and a bit prophetic. The coming season would be a doozie, not only for the Yankees but for the entire country. Ruppert sent out the warning in early 1929 to his players urging them to get out of the stock market.

The Roaring Twenties were sobering up, and genius business-man Ruppert saw the end on its way. Gehrig was not much of a ticker tape reader, and he had sunk most of his money safely into savings, putting only some in investments. Other Yankees, however, ignored Ruppert's warning and kept buying, selling and trading away.

Meanwhile Ruppert had put in an order for uniform modifications. The Yankees were to be the first team to wear numbers on the backs of their jerseys. The single-numeral numbers were assigned according to batting order; therefore Ruth received number three, Gehrig number four, and so on down Murderers' Row. Looking sharp and still feeling high from the 1928 Series win, the Yankees welcomed the new season with open arms.

The point Huggins was trying to make in his retort to "Break up the Yankees" was clearly shown by his team's sluggish performance. "The time will come," he had said, "when this team will crash."[11]

He didn't foresee that the crash would come so soon, but there it was, and the Connie Mack-led Athletics kicked the Yanks out of first place almost immediately. The A's had been top league contenders for years, finishing second for the previous three seasons. The 1929 season was their time to shine. Lefty Grove, George Earnshaw, Mickey Cochrane, Jimmy Dykes, Al Simmons, under the management of the incomparable Connie Mack, were determined to keep the Yanks out of first for the rest of the year.

Except for a few shining moments, the Yankee team did not play on par with 1928. Among the exceptional moments were a May day when Gehrig hit three home runs in three consecutive at-bats and an August game in which Ruth knocked career homer 500 out of the park. Besides that, the team cracked as easily as egg shells. Late in August they were beat by the fourth-place St. Louis Browns three games in a row. The slide in their performance was linked to the horrible imbalance of pitching versus offensive production. The two best pitchers, Waite Hoyt and Herb Pennock, won only nineteen games combined. The pitching staff's earned-run average rose to 4.17. The drop in Ruth's performance was at least slightly explained by the fact that his estranged first wife had been killed in a house fire in January. Meusel saw his batting average sink to an uncharacteristic .261. A second dose of tragedy befell the team at Yankee Stadium on May 2 during a sudden storm when panicked fans rushed for the exits and two people were trampled to death.

Gehrig slumped periodically throughout the season for various reasons. He also suffered a barrage of injuries. There were times he played with a torn muscle in his back and a broken thumb. At one point he strained his left ankle and favored that leg. Doing so caused him to get charley horses in his right leg, so he tenderly walked on his right leg instead, which caused a pulled muscle in his left leg. He was hit on the head while sliding home, and then he broke the middle finger of his right hand. "Every time he batted it hurt him," teammate Bill Werber said. "And he almost got sick to his stomach when he caught the ball. You could see him wince. But he always stayed in the game."[12]

To make matters worse, Huggins watched his team deteriorate as the team watched Huggins' health deteriorate. The more Huggins harped on his players, the bigger the bags under his eyes swelled and the smaller his appetite was. It was well known that Huggins was an insomniac, but his visible lack of rest worried Gehrig and some of the other players. Huggins himself did not see his health decline; he was too busy trying everything he could think of, including rearranging the batting order, to improve the team. For all his yelling and persistence, Huggins was ineffective in livening up his players.

Huggins' health declined in pace with his heavy hitters' averages. On September 20 he showed up to the stadium for the day's game so weak he could barely lift his jersey over his shoulders. Coach O'Leary and Coach Arthur Fletcher, a longtime friend of Huggins, noticed a large carbuncle on the side of his face. Against the advice of the other managers and players, including Gehrig, Huggins refused to leave the stadium. But by the third inning, Huggins changed his mind. The carbuncle was flaming and his body ragged with fever. The team doctor examined him in the clubhouse and ordered him off to St. Vincent's Hospital. Soon after he arrived, he was admitted as a patient and diagnosed with erysipelas, an infectious skin disease. Fletcher checked in on him one day and said their brief conversation was something along the lines of: "How are you feeling, champ?"

"See if you can do any better with this team than I have."[13]

It was the last instruction Huggins would ever utter. On September 25, just ten days shy of the season finale, Miller Huggins died at the age of fifty.

"He was my friend, a great little guy," Ruth said of the man with whom he was often at odds. "I got a big kick out of doing things that would help him."[14]

Out of all the Yankees, Gehrig took the news the hardest. He sobbed as if for his own parent. His statement to the press was, in typical fashion, to the point and as professional as possible: "When I first came up, he told me I was the rawest, most awkward rookie he'd ever seen or came across in baseball. He taught me everything I know. He gave me my job and advised me on salary matters. He taught me how to invest my money. Because of him I had everything a man could ask for in a material way. There was never a more patient or pleasant man to work for. I can't believe he'll never join us again."[15] Because of his bond with Huggins, Gehrig was chosen as a pall bearer, serving as escort to Huggins' body when it was sent by train from New York to Huggins' hometown of Cincinnati. The famed coach was laid to rest in Woodlawn Cemetery.

Gehrig was not just blowing smoke when he said that Huggins was an incredible manager.

Gehrig was not just blowing smoke when he said that Huggins was an incredible manager. Huggins was considered one of the best managers in baseball with his impeccable eye for talent and star potential. He still stands as a great coach alongside his peers Connie Mack and John McGraw.

After Huggins' death, Ed Barrow and Colonel Ruppert had the immediate task of finding a new manager. They attacked the list of possiblities. First up was Donnie Bush from the Pirates, but he had already signed with the White Sox. The next choice was Eddie Collins, who was playing for the Yankees' current enemy number one, the A's. Collins refused to leave Mack's team. Third in line was apparently Huggins' first choice as his replacement, Arthur Fletcher. Before joining the Yankees in 1927, Fletcher had apprenticed under McGraw. His experience and down-to-earth attitude made him quite popular among the players. He was a perfect fit, it seemed. But Barrow and Ruppert were disappointed by his "No, thanks." Fletcher had managed Philadelphia's team for five years and swore off managing ever again. No amount of money they stacked on the table could change his mind. Fortunately, there was a fourth choice, also among the Yankee ranks. Pitcher Bob Shawkey had joined the team from the Red Sox and possessed a brilliant baseball mind and a good rapport among the players. Much to Ruppert and Barrow's relief, Shawkey accepted the position.

In the mayhem, the Yankees continued to drop in the standings. Gehrig and his teammates suffered through the tough ten games left in the season. He saw his batting average drop seventy-four points since the end of the 1928 season, due in part to mourning and mostly to those periodic slumps throughout the season. His average actually fell under .300 the last few days of the season. During the last scheduled game, Philadelphia's third baseman Jimmy Dykes congenially held on to both bunts Gehrig laid down in his direction to help boost Gehrig's average to an even .300. Gehrig's bunts were insignificant to the outcome of the game and of the season. The Yankees finished second, which might sound impressive if they had not been eighteen games behind the first-place Athletics. The proverbial tide had turned. The Yankees would spend the next three seasons nipping at the heels of the Athletics as Mack took his crew of stars to the Series repeatedly.

The world of New York seemed to crash all at once. Huggins was dead, the Yankee empire seemed to be crumbling, and down on Wall Street the brokers were watching helplessly as the market imploded and sent seismic waves of economic crisis through the rest of the country. The Great Depression was at the doorstep. Ruppert's warning in early 1929 to his players to get out of the stock market proved valid. Many of his players had chosen to ignore the warning, and saw their savings all but disappear. Gehrig, however, lost only a fraction of his wealth.

Chapter Eight
A Leader in the Shadows, 1930-1931

With the collapse of the stock market came a 25% nationwide unemployment rate and cuts in the salaries of those fortunate enough to keep jobs. The Yankees were not immune to the effects of the Great Depression. Many on the team saw their salaries cut to under $6,000 per year. The top-billing players, such as Babe Ruth, retained the majority of their salaries. Ruth, who at that point had a new wife and two daughters to support, was the highest paid player in baseball with an $80,000 salary. Meanwhile Gehrig's salary was reduced to just over $23,000, down from his $25,000 salary in 1929, but the reduction didn't harm his ego or his lifestyle in any way. He remembered how to tighten the purse strings when needed.

Tough times continued for the Yankees. Bob Shawkey had won more than twenty games four times for the Yanks in his pitching days, but no one held expectations that he could drive the team to a pennant. The team had crumbled well before he took over, and as a result he was forced to reorganize the team and start from the beginning. He traded older players and called up kids from the minors. Meusel and Dugan left, Ben Chapman, Lyn Lary, Red Ruffing and Harry Rice arrived. The face of the team changed from familiar to unrecognizable. The players didn't know each other on or off the field, weren't used to each other's playing styles, and suffered loss after loss. Waite Hoyt put the dilemma into perfect, eloquent words. "Do you know what the trouble is with this team?" he asked reporters one night after a terrible game in St. Louis. "There are too many fellows on it who aren't Yankees."[1] To win, a team must be solid. To be solid, a team has to have the kind of kinship the 1927 Yankees had. Shawkey did what he could, but he didn't push the players to bond. If they were going to be more than teammates and become friends, they would do it on their own.

Regardless of whomever happened to be on the team with him, Gehrig bled Yankee blue. He understood the importance of selfless contribution to foster team unity and reached out to the rookies. Remembering all too well the days when he was a broke, lonely greenhorn, Gehrig did his best to help where he could. When he saw the new third baseman Ben Chapman struggling with the long throw to first, he volunteered to help. Much like he did with Bill Dickey the prior year, Gehrig spent hours working with the rookie. Time after time in their practices Gehrig had to chase a wild throw from Chapman in the air, to his left, or in the dirt. Chapman recounted the events after one grueling practice on an unapologetically hot July day. They trotted to the dugout for much-needed water. Chapman angrily threw his glove at the bench and grumbled, "Hell, I'll never be a third baseman. I'm a lousy fielder with a lousy arm." Then he noticed Gehrig cradling his swollen, discolored left thumb.

Gehrig caught his eye. "I think it's broken," he said quietly. It turned out that Gehrig had jammed it into the ground chasing a wild throw.

Ben was speechless with gratitude. Never would he forget the image of Gehrig dripping sweat and calmly holding his disfigured thumb. "You didn't hear a peep out of Lou," he said when he told the story. "Never a word of complaint about my rotten throw and what it did to his finger."[2]

For all the budding talent on the team, the Yankees could not keep up with the league-dominating Philadelphia Athletics. The A's were blessed with a tremendous offense that included Al Simmons and Jimmie Foxx and the stellar battery of Mickey Cochrane and twenty-eight-game-winning Lefty Grove. A rivalry emerged between the two teams. Games between the A's and the Yanks during that time could virtually shut down the city. For one game alone, over 85,000 fans packed into Yankee

Stadium just to brag to their friends the next day of what feats of legend they had seen. Seats filled quickly, as did the catwalks and steps, and people perched themselves uncomfortably on metal railings wedged between other fans for hours.

Gehrig grew particularly fond of Philadelphia's Shibe Park. Two of his record-setting accomplishments would happen in this cozy little stadium. The first was on May 22, 1930, when he tortured the Philly team with his dependable hitting, driving in a record eight RBI and propelling the Yanks to a 20-13 victory. The second would occur in 1932 when he matched the record for the most home runs hit in a single game.

People started noticing that Gehrig had the perseverance and reliability of a diesel engine.

As the 1930 season progressed, people started noticing that Gehrig had the perseverance and reliability of a diesel engine. No one, including Gehrig, yet realized he had played in a streak of consecutive games. 1930 was the fifth consecutive full season that he played without a game off. There were too many distractions between 1925 and 1930 (Ruth's sixty homers, 110 wins, the rise of the A's) for people to pay attention to something as mundane as a consecutive games streak. During Gehrig's day, players did not typically work out or keep fit the way players do today. Chain smoking and booze binges were commonplace among yesteryear's professional baseball players. Reporters asked Gehrig what was his secret to health. "Nothing to it," he replied. "Ten hours of sleep a night, a lot of water, a sensible choice of food, and you'll never have a day's worry in your life."[3]

In his case, a sensible choice of food included lots of fruit and fruit juice, vegetables instead of sweets and bread, and only the occasional alcoholic beverage. He didn't avoid sweets altogether, saying that he did eat a slice of pie when the notion hit him, but for the most part he stuck to nature's sweets. He admitted he was, quite frankly, addicted to fruit.

On game days he would eat a small breakfast, then skip lunch to prevent a full belly that would weigh him down. After the game, if it was played in New York, Mom treated him to quite the spread for supper. In the offseason he enjoyed ice skating. He was convinced that skating would keep the strength in his legs and the cold air would refresh his lungs. Teammate Waite Hoyt battled weight fluctuations around that time, and Gehrig suggested Hoyt join him at the ice rink. Much to Hoyt's delight, the ice skating was an offbeat way for him to drop weight successfully while increasing muscle. "Fitness was almost a religion with him," Hoyt said. "Those guys who thought Lou had the mind of a teenager didn't know what they were talking about."[4]

As the supreme compliment one man can give another, Hoyt stated to the press that if he were to have a son, he would find endless joy if the boy turned out like Lou Gehrig.

The 1930 season can be summed up in a single syllable: A's. No team could catch them, especially not the Yankees as they fumbled over their unsynchronized feet. The Yanks finished third, a distant sixteen games behind the league winners, although they led the league in runs, triples, home runs, batting average and slugging. It was one of Gehrig's best seasons, as he banged out forty-one homers, scored 174 runners, and earned a career-high .379 average. His individual performance was better than all of the top Athletics sluggers'. His RBI total and his total-bases tally (419) led the league. Regardless, he lost the league batting championship by a mere two points to Al Simmons of the A's.

Gehrig's results pleased the Yankee front office, but the team's performance did not, nor did Shawkey's easygoing approach. Shawkey was relieved of his duties. Ruppert and Barrow were again faced with the challenge of finding a new manager. At the urging of Barrow, Colonel Ruppert agreed to make an offer to Joseph McCarthy (no relation to the infamous Senator from Wisconsin), the Chicago Cubs manager who had just been released, even though he had questions about a manager crossing between the leagues.

Joe McCarthy had never played a single inning of professional ball in his life, a rare characteristic among managers. Growing up he had played cricket, and his professional experience consisted of managing minor league teams for a few years. He had earned the reputation as a natural leader with an incredible ability to develop players who went on to successful major league careers. He was called up by the Cubs in 1925 to heal the disjointed team, taking them to no less than fourth place every year. Then he led them to a pennant in 1929. They lost the World Series to the unstoppable A's. In 1930 the Cubs failed to finish first, so the Cubs cut him loose. At the age of forty-four, McCarthy was still a bachelor and unsure of who would sign his next paycheck. Then he received a call from Ed Barrow.

During the World Series of 1930, McCarthy met Barrow and Ruppert in a Philadelphia motel to discuss the opening on the Yankees staff. Ruppert made it very clear to McCarthy that he liked to win, but had been forced to eat loss after loss for the last two seasons. McCarthy announced his taste for winning as well, but was realistic: He pledged to do his best for the upcoming season, but promised to win by the following season at the worst.

McCarthy had only one misgiving about accepting the position. He had a tumultuous history with Coach Fletcher from his days in the minors. The previous season Fletcher had firmly declined the offer to become the manager, but many believed he had changed his mind by the end of the 1930 season. This concerned McCarthy greatly. After he accepted the job, he promptly phoned Fletcher to ask for a private meeting in Chicago. If Fletcher was uneasy around McCarthy, he didn't let on. Instead he told McCarthy that he did not feel slighted in the least by Ruppert and Barrow not offering him the position again, and he declared his loyalty to the new manager, despite any qualms they may have had in the past. With that wrinkle smoothed, they jumped into a lengthy conversation about the team and the American League in general, for McCarthy knew little about either. All he knew of the players was what he read in the papers, a fact McCarthy feared would eliminate his credibility in the players' eyes.

While Huggins and Shawkey had viewed spring training as an

informal way to warm up players for the season, McCarthy viewed it as an extension of the regular season. He demanded that the guys push themselves hard, keep fit and trim, and play their best every day, every game. The team's first exhibition game that spring was against a minor league team from Milwaukee. The Yanks trounced the opposition 19-1.

On the team bus after the game, one gleeful Yankee reportedly yelled, "How did you like that, Joe?! Not bad, eh?"

"Against a team like that," McCarthy growled, "we should have made thirty runs!"

In his seat Gehrig giggled to himself. That night he commented to Bill Dickey, "You know, Bill, I like this McCarthy. I like the way he thinks."

Dickey smiled. "Me too. He's our kind of guy."[5]

It should be no surprise that serious ballplayers like Gehrig and Dickey took to McCarthy's ways like fish to water. He believed that a disciplined team was a successful team. While Gehrig applauded most of McCarthy's new rules, such as the strict new dress code of jackets and ties in the dining room, he had trouble with some of the others. McCarthy despised smoking, forcing Gehrig to try to hide the smoking habit he could never break. For those ballplayers in it for fame and fortune, McCarthy was a thorn shoved into their side. Ruth, for one, resented McCarthy with passion. Many believed that if Fletcher had not accepted the manager position then it should have been offered to the Yankee player with the most seniority—in this case, Babe Ruth. Though Ruth did not openly say he wanted the job and no one nominated him for it, he felt cheated by being passed over for a National Leaguer. Ruth's resentment was picked up and furthered by those on the team who followed his lead. McCarthy still had to prove himself in the eyes of his players, and that would take time.

> *McCarthy despised smoking, forcing Gehrig to try to hide the smoking habit he could never break.*

McCarthy could, however, count on the support of Lou Gehrig, and that counted for a lot. One writer described the manager-player relationship as this: "McCarthy grew to look upon him as he might upon a son or a younger brother."[6] Another writer who traveled with the team, Stanley Frank, witnessed first hand a superb example of how much McCarthy influenced Gehrig. The team was traveling the American League circuit via train one night in 1931. Gehrig, Ruth, Frank and others in the Yankee family were playing a game of bridge. According to Frank, Ruth, having made a bad move, joked, "Hey, I butchered that one just like McCarthy handles the goddamn pitchers!" The others may have initially cracked a grin but they didn't dare laugh when they saw Gehrig intensely glaring at Babe. Torturously awkward silence ensued. No one moved.

"What?" Ruth asked as he looked Gehrig in the eye.

Gehrig threw down his cards and snapped, "You need to learn to control that big loose mouth of yours!" He got up and left the table. It was one of the first times Gehrig ever openly stood up to Ruth.

The next day Gehrig was still afire. He confided to Frank that he believed Ruth, as the game's biggest celebrity, should exemplify respect and integrity especially when reporters were around him.

"He should realize he has a responsibility to this team," Lou insisted.

"Oh, Lou," Frank said breezily, "he was drunk when he spouted off that stuff about McCarthy. Don't put too much emphasis on it."

"He shouldn't have been drunk either," Lou responded. "He's a professional, he should act like it." Gehrig had a point, but it was a moot one. It was the Babe, after all. He could do virtually anything and get away with it, because that's what the fans expected. At least Ruth remembered McCarthy's name.[7]

For the most part, Ruth and Gehrig still got along, despite their disagreement on McCarthy's worth. They still performed in exhibitions cooked up by money-hungry marketers. Just before the regular season began in 1931, the two Yankee big guns agreed to compete in an exhibition duel against the most unlikely of opponents—a seventeen-year-old girl. Jackie Mitchell was the first woman to sign a professional baseball contract, landing a hurler spot on the Double-A team the Chattanooga Lookouts. She dazzled her patron town with her staggering speed. On a sunny April day facing both hitters back to back in front of a crowd of fans and newsmen, she was no less dazzling. She dizzied both men with six straight strikes. Lou admitted he was thoroughly impressed, and agreed to pose with her for photographers. Immediately a heated debate began in the press over whether the contest was staged. Could a girl really possess the talent to whiff the two best hitters? Doubters used the detail that the contest had been postponed due to weather from its original scheduled date of April 1, April Fool's Day. The countless newsreels and headlines dedicated to the Mitchell debate finally got the better of baseball commissioner Judge Kennesaw Landis. After weeks of nonstop press coverage, Landis ended the nonsensical debate by voiding her contract. For the rest of her life Mitchell denied the event was staged. Gehrig and Ruth never mentioned it again.

The strikeout would not be Gehrig's only that season. He would, in fact, suffer a slump. It turned out to be only a short-lived departure from his usual production, but for all of his career Gehrig would carry the burden of unrelenting self-doubt and the unshakable paranoia that his skill would suddenly vanish, that he would walk up to the plate one day and not remember which end of the bat to hold. When a problem arose in his play, he reacted as any desperate man would. His teammates didn't suffer the same paranoid delusions, but they suffered vicariously through him. The 1931 slump had him asking everyone from the pitching coach to the peanut vendors for advice. One day he cornered Hoyt in the dugout.

"What am I doing wrong?" he asked.

"I don't know," Hoyt answered.

"Have you been watching me?"

"Yes."

"And you still don't know what I'm doing wrong?"

"No."

Gehrig sighed heavily and sulked as he returned to the clubhouse. When he was out of ear range, Hoyt told some nearby teammates, "I know what he's doing wrong, but I'm not about to tell him. He has asked everyone on the ball club what's wrong and everyone has a different answer. If I told him it would only add to his confusion. He won't come out of it until he gets so desperate he quits worrying." The others nodded.[8]

Gehrig was able to convince teammate Jimmy Reese to come home with him to discuss the slump. The two talked for hours about Gehrig's unfruitful plate appearances. His stance, his follow-through, the roll of his wrists, which way the wind blew, how bright the sun was. Early the next morning, Gehrig drove Reese to the park to have a private batting practice. Reese, an infielder, threw pitch after pitch, high, low, inside, outside, until Gehrig hit and hit and hit. Reese developed painful blisters on his fingers, but his arm was numb from the shoulder down so he didn't notice. Nearly every pitch he served up Gehrig reversed into fair territory. That afternoon's game, Gehrig broke his batting slump. With a smile as wide as the Mississippi, Gehrig said to Reese after the game, "I guess it worked."[9]

If the truth be told, Gehrig didn't need to worry about his hitting ability abandoning him. For athletes like Gehrig, hitting is like riding a bike—once a man learns, his body never forgets. Slumping was an inevitable occurrence that Gehrig never learned to accept. He loved riding roller coasters, but he couldn't stand the wavering of offensive production. When he was up in production, he was up high. When he broke out of the slump in 1931, he hit three grand slam home runs in a four-day span. For exactly this kind of thing, other teams always felt a special sort of fear with Gehrig at the plate if he was in a slump. They knew it was only a matter of time before he started punching out hit after hit. The A's premier southpaw Lefty Grove was notorious for throwing at batters who he felt challenged him, and he threw at them with the fury of a trapped grizzly. Even he feared Gehrig. He voiced the thoughts of many American League pitchers by saying, "I'd never think of throwing at Gehrig. You never want to get that fellow stirred up. There's something about him that tells you to lay off him or you'll get killed with a line drive."[10]

In spite of Gehrig's quirky paranoia, McCarthy looked upon him as a true team leader, not just in terms of talent but also in terms of attitude. Both gentlemen believed that players needed to be respectful of themselves, the team, and others at all times. Gehrig was known to take aside players he saw being in some way disrespectful to the reputation of the team and give them private, one-on-one lectures on what was acceptable behavior and what wasn't. He emitted team spirit from every pore.

Gehrig emitted team spirit from every pore.

His spirit and solidarity shone through during the 1931 home run race with Babe Ruth. During a game in Washington midway through the season, rookie shortstop Lyn Lary was on first with two outs as Gehrig strode to the box. He fired a shot at the right-center fence. Lary ran for second as the ball passed overhead, rounded second, glanced over his shoulder, and saw the ball falling into the glove of the center fielder. Understandably he assumed that the third out had been made, so he tapped a foot on third base and kept going straight, headed to the dugout for a drink of water before taking infield. Meanwhile Gehrig was trotting his way around the bases with his head down after watching his hit ricochet off the right-field bleachers and then back into the center fielder's glove—a home run. He had not seen Lary's mistake, and continued on around third to finish out his home run trip. As soon as he touched home plate, the Washington players screamed that he had illegally passed the runner ahead of him, an offense that carries the penalization of an out. This meant the inning was over and Gehrig's hit counted as a triple. Only then did Lary realize what he had done: He had caused the third out, cost the Yankees a run, and cost Gehrig a home run hash mark.

Lary swore that when he saw the center fielder catch the ball he had truly thought the inning was over. The press was ready to have a field day with the rookie's mistake, but Gehrig would give them no ammunition. Instead he stated to reporters with the professionalism he tried to impart to the rest of the team, "He's no more to blame than I. If I had kept my head up, I would have seen what happened and waited for him to come back and finish his run before I scored."[11] Lary's error would have been the one to push Gehrig ahead. As it was, the race between Ruth and Gehrig that year ended in a tie.

As the season drew to an end for the Yankees, they had upped their overall performance over the previous year. They lost nine fewer games than in 1930. It wasn't enough to bump them past the A's, though, who won 107 games. The Yanks finished second, thirteen-and-a-half games behind first.

While 1930 had been one of Gehrig's best performances, 1931 was one of his greatest. He led the league in hits (211), total bases (410), runs (163), and RBI. His 184 RBI is still the American League record and was twenty-nine above his total number of games played that year (155). Five times in his career his RBI total would be greater than his total games played, a wonderful achievement. In home runs he tied with Ruth at forty-six. He was second in slugging percentage (.662) and tied for second in triples (15). In walks he tied for third with 117, and he was fifth in average with .341. He set a new standard for runs produced at 301. Though he did not win the official AL Most Valuable Player Award, the *Sporting News* declared him its MVP.

Fred Lieb, the sportswriter who befriended Gehrig and his family, also considered him among the best players in the league. After the completion of the season, Lieb invited Gehrig and a number of other major league players on his first annual all-star tour of Japan to be chronicled in Lieb's employer paper, the *New York Times*, which co-sponsored the tour along with the Japanese periodical *Yomouri Shimbun*. In fact, the Japanese newspaper specifically requested Gehrig. The tour was seventeen games long, and pitted America's best against Japan's best. Among Gehrig's all-star teammates were the A's Mickey Cochrane and Frankie Frisch. Crowds packed into the stadiums much like the crowds in the Midwest had done when Gehrig and Ruth barnstormed. In the sixth game of the tour, Gehrig was struck on the hand by a Japanese college pitcher, causing a fracture that forced him to sit out for the remainder of the tour.

He wasn't upset, though. First of all, the fracture would heal before spring training and, second, he had more time to learn bits of Japanese to say to his Far East fans. "Hello," "goodbye," "thank you," and "home run" were included in the vernacular he amassed. Being that it was his first visit to a foreign country, he went a bit overboard in his role as tourist. He would leave the island with $7,200 worth of ivory, silk and jewelry for his mother. To put that into better perspective, the tour paid him only $5,000.

Even with all these gifts for his mother, Gehrig was beginning to wonder if he would ever find a woman of his own. On the boat ride to Japan, Gehrig would disappear for hours. Only Lieb knew where he was: Gehrig had stowed away with Lieb's wife Mary in a lifeboat on the upper deck to privately discuss Mom's constant control over his love life. Once he had brought home a very lovely young lady to meet his parents. She was intelligent, funny, pretty. He was so hung up on this girl that he was considering proposing to her. When Mom got wind of his intention, she actually went to the girl's hometown and nosed around until she found something incriminating enough to ruin the relationship. With his other girlfriends, Mom was no less successful in breaking them apart. No potential bride, it seemed to him, would ever pass Mom's approval test. All of this and more he talked about with Mary Lieb.

Mary was a sharp woman, and advised, "If you wait around for a girl that will suit Mom, you'll still be unmarried at fifty!"

"Yeah," Lou sighed reluctantly. "You're right."[12]

Chapter Nine
Beginnings, 1932-1933

McCarthy cracked the whip with a distinctly more audible snap in 1932. Second place was unacceptable to a team with the offensive prowess of Lou Gehrig, Tony Lazzeri, and base-stealing champ Ben Chapman. There were no complaints among McCarthy's loyalists because they realized the Yankees were again in transition after the loss of vets, the aging of others, and the arrival of pitchers like Vernon "Lefty" Gomez and Johnny Allen. Rookie Yanks felt the same fear of failure and intimidation that Gehrig had nearly ten years prior. Among those fearful kids was Charlie Devens, a righty pitcher who trembled when he thought of being put into a World Series game. Gehrig didn't comfort him, something Devens would hold against Gehrig ever after. "To me," Devens said, "he was without a light touch, a remote and inward-looking fellow. He never had much to do with young players like myself."[1] Perhaps Devens was jealous of the way Gehrig treated a certain other rookie, and that jealousy blinded him to Gehrig's true nature.

Frankie "Crow" Crosetti was a recruit from San Francisco who had his eye on shortstop. His quiet nature and humbleness appealed immensely to Gehrig. "Lou made me feel like I belonged," Frank said of the tenderness Gehrig bestowed on him.[2] They shared rides to and from the stadium. They shared a large respect for McCarthy and his spit-shine perfectionism. During one exhibition game, Gehrig noticed the gravel in Crosetti's voice and the shivers of a fever in his body from a wretched cold. Since McCarthy demanded that players hold exhibition games in the same esteem as regular season games, Crosetti dared not ask for the day off. Gehrig knew this. He spoke to McCarthy, then returned to Crosetti with the news that McCarthy would let them leave. Gehrig took Crosetti to the best nurse in town.

Mom Gehrig had a remedy for everything. Crosetti coughed once and she knew immediately what medicine to use: a large meal followed by a large glass of hot wine. After he swallowed the last drop, she tucked him into one of the guest beds and he slept soundly until the next morning. He woke up to find with stunned joy that he was strong and was as playful as a baby tiger.

"He was great," Frankie would say of Lou. "His folks were great."[3]

The two men also collaborated on the old sandlot trick of the hidden ball. Crosetti was quite adept at the trick and adjusted his version to include Gehrig over at first base. Gehrig's assignment in the charade was to avoid looking at Crosetti and sometimes, for flair, he would yell encouragement to the pitcher, who pretended to have the ball in his glove and stared intently at the catcher's mitt. Crosetti, meanwhile, had the ball hidden in his glove and would distract the runner on second. When the runner took his leadoff, Crosetti tagged him out. Gehrig roared with delight. Kid tricks were more pleasurable to him than dirty baseball. No one got a spike in his leg.

Another new Yank Gehrig became close with was Lefty Gomez. He made everyone on the team laugh with his quirky remarks and goofy grin. One Yankee concluded, "Best thing to happen to Gehrig was running around with Gomez. Gomez could loosen anybody up. Lou felt at ease with him."[4]

Still, the best friend Gehrig had was Bill Dickey, the ever-reliable catcher. Dickey is often given credit for being the brains behind the operation on the field. His knowledge and sensibility in any given situation were impeccable. If a pitcher shook him off or threw a pitch he didn't call for, Dickey had ways of letting the pitcher know he would not tolerate mutiny. Dickey simply didn't stand for pitchers who thought of only their stats and not of the benefit of the team. Gehrig loved that about him. In 1932 Dickey married a gorgeous blonde named Violet Arnold. Though he and Gehrig still found time for fishing and cards, Dickey was for the most part absorbed in his role as husband. If Gehrig felt abandoned by his friend, he did not let on about it. "You know, guys," he told reporters time and time again, "I don't really need much else. I get everything I want at home."[5]

After a while, however, even Gehrig didn't believe this, but he didn't know what to do about it.

Gehrig swam in a small dating pool. Socializing was not emphasized or practiced in his household. When he was growing up, long work days resulted in little time to entertain. Friendships were few and far between for the Gehrigs. The few friends Gehrig had besides the Yankee mates were from his college or high school days, and he occasionally did the usual activities with them, fishing or playing a round of cards. The people he saw the most were his parents. Fred and Mary Lieb were some of the few visitors in the Gehrig household, and Lieb was able to observe things about Gehrig's home life that most reporters could not. For instance, he observed that Gehrig was not as close with his father; that was perhaps the most obvious thing. When Gehrig returned home from road trips, Mom would be there to pick him up at the station and he would rush up to her, kiss and hug her, and excitedly rattle off his many adventures to her in German like a little boy returning from camp.

Friendships were few and far between for the Gehrigs.

Little socializing left plenty of time for baseball. Achieving accomplishments that boosted the team's performance were at the forefront of Gehrig's mind; setting a record or improving his stats were fringe benefits. One accomplishment that did both occurred on June 3, 1932, in Philadelphia's Shibe Park. He would become the first American League player to hit four home runs in a single game, which is no easy afternoon, especially against Connie Mack's A's. George Earnshaw had pitched his way to sixty-eight wins in the regular season and four successful World Series campaigns throughout his career. He was no slouch, but Gehrig made him seem that way. In the first inning, Gehrig took him deep to right, 331 feet away from home plate. He did it again in the fourth, putting the Yanks ahead 4-

2. In the bottom half of the fourth the A's rallied to catch up, and then Gehrig dropped an easy pop foul that would have been the third out. That gave the A's the chance to pull ahead, and they did, leading 8-4. Steaming from his bonehead mistake, Gehrig stepped up to the plate in the fifth and cracked a pitch over the right field fence for his third home run.

Earnshaw cursed, and his manager Connie Mack flashed the signal for veteran Leroy Mahaffey to come out of the bullpen. Earnshaw dragged himself into the dugout. The next time Gehrig was up, Mack said to him, "Watch Mahaffey for a minute, son. I want you to see how he handles Gehrig. You've been pitching to him all wrong." Earnshaw turned to watch Mahaffey offer up to Gehrig. Crack. The ball sailed over the infield, over the left-fielder's head, and dropped on the other side of the fence 334 feet from home plate.

Regardless of which team the crowd was rooting for, everyone realized the historical and breathtaking feat of five home runs in one game.

Earnshaw said flatly, "I see now, Mr. Mack. Mahaffey made him change directions. May I shower now?"[6]

Of course, Gehrig still had one at-bat left to try for the all-baseball record of five home runs. Mack tried again to stop Gehrig by replacing the pitcher, this time putting in Eddie Rommel. Crack! The ball sailed over the infield in a beeline for the deepest part of center that reached its zenith at 450 feet from home. Al Simmons, who was filling in for the ailing regular center fielder, raced toward the fence, jumped as the ball began to descend behind the fence, and desperately stuck his glove out to just the right spot. The ball slapped into his glove. Groans resounded throughout the stadium. Regardless of which team the crowd was rooting for, everyone realized the historical and breathtaking feat of five home runs in one game. Had it not been for Simmons' vertical reach, Gehrig would have made history. Three other Yankees had hit home runs that day, driving the final score to Yankees 20, A's 13. That's the part Gehrig truly cared about—his team had won.

Prior to Gehrig's big day, only two men in the history of baseball had hit an equal amount of home runs in a single game: Ed Delahanty of the Phillies in 1896 and Bobby Lowe of Boston in 1894. Gehrig had, however, set a different record that day. It was the fourth time he had hit three or more home runs in a single game. Gehrig's name, though, would not be the one at the top of the headlines the next day, because that same afternoon John McGraw, the grumpy little manager for the Giants, announced that he was retiring. Some of the baseball followers familiar with the McGraw-Gehrig relationship theorized that McGraw may have purposely released his announcement just after the Philadelphia-New York game ended as a form of revenge. In truth, McGraw had made the decision the day before. He had offered his first baseman Bill Terry the managerial duties, and Terry accepted. That the announcement came the same day as Gehrig's feat was published was coincidence. At the age of fifty-nine with a powerfully successful thirty-year career as a manager, McGraw's retirement was a bigger story than Gehrig's homers. McGraw used his place in center stage to voice the reasons he chose to retire, among them was this comment: "Nowadays, the game has become a case of burlesque slugging with most of the players trying to hit home runs."[7] Gehrig politely kept quiet in response to the jab, and he resigned himself to seeing McGraw's face instead of his own on the front page of every paper. After all, he was no stranger to being overlooked. For years he was hidden by the barrel of a man with spindly legs they called Babe and never complained.

"He'd probably figured there's no use trying to outmaneuver Ruth as far as publicity goes," Tiger Charlie Gehringer said. "Whatever town the Yankees were in, all of their writers would flock to Ruth. Gehrig was probably a better all-around player by far, but he'd get no special attention even though he'd hit just about as many home runs."[8]

As the years passed and the difference in their slugging abilities grew vaster—Ruth's ability declining, Gehrig's improving—Gehrig found the courage and self-respect to no longer go along with the king of the show. Ruth didn't respond well to anyone upping him, especially in the hitting niche, and he tried his hardest to keep the trident in his hand. The tension ate away at their friendship.

During one train-ride bridge game, Ruth got himself progressively drunker and, to irritate Gehrig, he would make bad bids. Ruth topped his bad bids with a not-so-gentlemanly gesture in Gehrig's direction. Finally, Gehrig put down his cards. "Figure up what we owe you," he said to everyone at the table. "Bridge game's over." Once again Gehrig openly stood up to Ruth.

One of the contributing factors to the deterioration of Ruth and Gehrig's relationship was McCarthy's favored-son treatment of Gehrig. It was no secret that Ruth and McCarthy did not get along, and Gehrig's transference of the respect he once had for Ruth to McCarthy penetrated Ruth's pride. McCarthy was not one to rave about his players, but he would rave about Gehrig long after his career had ended. "What a wonderful fellow that Gehrig was," he said. "Always hustled. Never gave a moment's trouble. Just went out every day and played his game and hit the ball."[9] In Ruth's opinion, McCarthy had no right to be head of a major league baseball team having never played in the majors. Ruth argued that he himself was the obvious choice for Yankee manager. Ben Chapman overheard him making such comments one day and responded wryly, "If you become manager, send me to St. Louis."

"Ha, ha, you laugh now," Ruth responded. "Just wait until I talk to Ruppert."

But all Ruppert said to Ruth's request was, "How can you manage the Yankees when you can't even manage yourself?"[10] Years of beer guzzling and hot dog binges and an apparent vow against exercising left Ruth overweight and lacking youthful agility.

One of the first things McCarthy had noticed when he took over the Yankees was that Gehrig was the key to success. In 1932 Gehrig solidified his opinion. With the help of the brightest Yankee star, the team won the pennant by a margin of thirteen games with a season win total of 107 games. It was the sixth time in seven years that the Yankees led the league in runs. Their boost to first place was owed much to the improved pitching staff, which included Gehrig's new friend Gomez. Their rival for the Series, as fate would have it, was the Chicago Cubs—McCarthy's former employer.

◆ ◆ ◆

From the start, there was overt vengeance on both teams. For one thing, McCarthy was still bitter about being canned by the Cubs. For another, Mark Koenig, a former Yankee teammate in 1927 and favorite of Ruth, had been traded to the Cubs midseason in 1932, and despite a solid performance was paid only half a pennant-win share. The news angered Ruth, and he made some critical comments to a sportswriter that found their way into that writer's column. The Cubs players sent along their scornful rejoinder in the press. The Yankees had some responses to that. And so on... At the start of the Series, the players exchanged insults during pregame practice. Ruth started it by yelling out to Koenig, "Hey, Mark! You'd better get four-for-four today or they'll cut you to a quarter share!"[11] Usually one to stay out of the muck, Gehrig himself threw out a few steamy handfuls. As the Series went on, the muck throwing remained heavy.

Before the third game, played in Chicago, a reporter asked Gehrig for his predictions on the game regarding Babe Ruth. "He's on fire today," Gehrig said. "He ought to hit one today, maybe a couple."[12]

In the first inning of play, amid the roaring tumult of insults between players and from the thousands of fans, Ruth knocked out a three-run homer off of Charlie Root. Gehrig echoed it with a solo shot. The Cubs were not letting the Yankees off easy in front of the home crowd, and the Cubs rallied to tie the score at four all. The home run Ruth had hit gave him new material to throw back at Root during his next at-bat. In the fifth inning, no runners, no outs, Ruth came to the plate yelling insults in Root's direction. He took two strikes. Root snarled something, to which Ruth responded by pointing and yelling a phrase or two of his own. The noise in the stadium overpowered Ruth's yell, so only those nearest to the plate heard the words he uttered. The next pitch was a changeup that Ruth sent so far over center field fence that many claim no one has hit a ball further out of Wrigley Field. In a shower of debris from the crowd, Ruth made his rounds and slapped a foot on the plate with a wink and a handshake for Gehrig. He encouraged Gehrig to do the same thing, who laughed and nodded.

As Gehrig expected, the first pitch from Root was dangerously close to his head. Gehrig didn't take the grin off his face as he set up for the next pitch. He had learned by now how to take brush-backs. Tommy Henrich, Gehrig's teammate from 1937 to 1939, best described Gehrig's approach to pitchers who tried to hit him, "Lou treated it like, 'Sooner or later you'll have to throw the ball over the plate, and when you do I'll cream you.'"[13] Sure enough, Gehrig slammed Root's next offering over the wall. The buzz over Ruth's home run was still so high that no one really noticed Gehrig going around the bases. Root had given up four home runs—to the same two players—in an hour's worth of play. Though the Cubs manager Charlie Grimm replaced war-weary Root, the Yankees still came out victorious with the final score of 11-6.

The talk of the paper men that day, as usual, focused on what Ruth did. Speculation was rampant over just what Ruth was pointing at before his second home run. Some ventured that he had pointed out to Root where he was about to hit the ball—he had called his shot. Ruth did not deny or confirm this, and Gehrig didn't care much one way or the other. In fact, Gehrig joked, "What do you think of the nerve of that big monkey? Imagine the guy calling his shot and getting away with it."[14] If police investigators had descended on the scene and taken statements from witnesses, the fantasies would have dissolved rapidly. All those who were close by as Ruth was at bat claim that Ruth was not calling his shot, rather he was gesturing at Root while yelling some trash talk. Cubs catcher Gabbie Hartnett said Ruth held up one finger to indicate that it only took one pitch to hit. Frank Crosetti, who was standing near enough to hear Ruth and Root, said Ruth was saying that he still had one strike left. Gehrig, standing in the on-deck circle saw Ruth point at Root and warn him, "I'm going to knock the next pitch right down your throat."[15]

Called shot or none, the Yankees flattened the Cubs' Series dreams in four straight games. Gehrig was the "undisputed hero" of the Series, whether or not the papers awarded space to his Series stats instead of to what turned out to be Ruth's last grab at immortality. In the Series, Gehrig racked up an astounding batting average of .529, nine hits, nine runs, three homers, eight RBI. Gehrig's 1932 Series stats win nearly every debate on the best individual performance in Series history. "I just didn't think a player could be that good," Cubs manager Charlie Grimm told reporters after the Series ended.[16]

Even with the praise from Grimm, Gehrig still received little notice from the October 1932 papers. Such was Gehrig's fate. "I'm not a headline guy, and we might as well face it," he said. "I'm just a guy who's in there every day. The fellow who follows the Babe in the batting order. When Babe's turn at bat is over, whether he strikes out or belts a home run, the fans are still talking about him when I go to bat." Overall Gehrig's 1932 season was superb. He finished in the top four in the league in many of the major offense categories: .349 batting average, thirty-four homers, 151 runs, .621 slugging, 370 total bases.

As spectacular as Gehrig's 1932 World Series performance was, something else amazing happened during the Series: Lou Gehrig fell in love.

Eleanor Grace Twitchell was two years younger than Lou Gehrig and the daughter of Frank Twitchell, who had made his fortune as a food supplier to Chicago restaurants and park vendors. She was raised in an Irish-Catholic household of substantial means in Chicago, and was well-educated, well-connected, and quite the bubbly social butterfly who enjoyed smoking and drinking just as much as clothes, literature and opera. When the market crashed, Frank's business went bust, as did his marriage (he moved away from Chicago shortly afterwards). Eleanor was forced to support herself with a secretarial job for the Chicago World's Fair Century of Progress. Lesser means did not prevent her from continuing to enjoy some of the activities she had come to love in her upbringing. She rode horses, played golf, danced, and partook in the latest fads. By the time she met Lou Gehrig a second time at a party the night before the third game of the 1932 Series, she was tamer and more mature than she had been when they were first introduced in 1928. A mild heart condition combined with having to earn all her money had slowed her social pace.

Through the years between their initial meeting and their second, she had loyally gone to watch her White Sox play. When the Yankees were in town, she unknowingly watched her future husband at work. "I hated him," she would confess in her autobiography. "I hated all the Yankees. I sat there in the ballpark and hoped Gehrig would fall down and break a leg. Once I yelled at him, 'Strike out, you big goof!'"[17] Of course, Eleanor never really "hated" Gehrig, and she had found herself drawn to his career and followed it closely after the first time they met.

The day before the third game of the 1932 Series, Eleanor ran into her well-connected friend Kitty McHie who was lugging armloads of beer to her apartment. She invited Eleanor over later. After all, Lou Gehrig, a friend of a friend, was going to be there. Eleanor needed no more incentive.

She made him feel comfortable and he made her swoon. They were falling for each other.

The woman who had not made much of an impression on Gehrig's memory in 1928 captured his full attention that night in 1932. Eleanor describes, "The 'shy one' suddenly became the bold one, singled me out, and spent the whole time giving me the shy man's version of the rush."[18] For the duration of the party, Gehrig stuck to her side faithfully, asking for the chance to bring her food or a drink. He watched her intently whenever she happened to chat with another man. She was the perfect woman for him. She loved baseball and she didn't make him feel like the oversized, bumbling ape that he often thought he was. She made him feel comfortable and he made her swoon. They were falling for each other. Everyone could see it. Kitty ordered the other guests not to interfere with the magic going on in her living room. The end of the night came too early for Eleanor. Gehrig had a self-imposed midnight curfew on game nights—something Eleanor would have to get used to. Before he left, he asked to walk Eleanor home, a request she gladly granted, her heartbeat thundering in her ears as they stepped out of Kitty's apartment and were alone together for the first time. Her palms sweated a little at the thought of kissing the handsome man she had been watching from afar for years. But he left her that night at her door with an unceremonious "Goodnight" and an excellent view of his back as he returned to his hotel. Disappointment pulled heavily on her heart.

She thought for sure she had ruined it, repulsed him somehow. A week passed and there was no word from the World Series hero. She sighed heavily and resolved to stick to ordinary boys from there on out. Then she got a package. It was a diamond-cut crystal necklace Gehrig had bought on his trip to Japan. Quickly she called up Kitty for advice. "Send him the sweetest thank-you note you can immediately," Kitty said. "That thing represents the Taj Mahal to him."[19] A few days later, Gehrig found in his mail a note from Miss Twitchell and rushed to a private spot to read it. He quickly wrote her back. Their letters criss-crossed the country at a rapid pace that fall. "The notes were fairly noncommittal for a couple of people who were already taken with each other," Eleanor said of their correspondence. "We hadn't begun to confide in each other, at least not just yet."[20] That would come later, Gehrig entrusting her with his secrets and she with hers. Along with the letters, Gehrig also conversed with his new girlfriend via long-distance phone calls, quite a pricey activity in 1932. In their many conversations, he managed to convince her to travel to New Rochelle to meet his family, and in return he went to Chicago to meet hers. Not surprisingly, Gehrig got along better with her family than she did with his mother.

Because it was the offseason, not many of Gehrig's teammates knew of his new romance, though it was possible that Gehrig might not have offered up that information if it had been the regular season. To his teammates, he was the mama's boy forever dedicated to bachelorhood. Some teased him about his various dates with women that never prospered. The little intimacy he had known with a few women he held sacred. Bill Werber, a fellow Yankee, said of Gehrig, "Lou was monogamous even as a single fellow. He didn't mess around."[21]

The one thing Eleanor didn't worry about in dating a big-name baseball player was Gehrig's faithfulness. They were apart for most of their courtship, and the enormous amount of trust such circumstances demand is enough to crack less-dedicated couples. This couple, however, was destined to be together. He lovingly called her "pal," and she enjoyed the pet name because it was "sort of man to man."[22] Pals confide in each other, and Lou began to do that around the time contract negotiations started for the 1933 season. In February 1933 Gehrig was in a stalemate with Colonel Ruppert over a salary hike. Gehrig wrote to Eleanor frankly about his feelings and hopes, saying that he would work things out, and if it ended up that the only solution was to quit baseball, then he could always be a truck driver or a chauffer. To this she replied she was in full support of him whatever the outcome. Meanwhile Ruth, once so arrogant when it came to demanding a salary raise, was told he would have to take a drastic pay cut because of the poor economy and because he was not the same player he used to be. While Ruth voiced his opinion about the forced pay cut to reporters, Ruppert pointed out that Ruth was still the highest paid player in baseball. Gehrig ended up not getting his salary increase, but he didn't complain. At least he had negotiated well enough with Ruppert to maintain his salary from the year before.

In 1933 with the help of a ghostwriter Gehrig penned an article for *Liberty* magazine titled "Am I Jealous of Babe Ruth?" Among the points he touched on was the issue of the "called shot." Gehrig wrote that he was actually happy that everyone remembered Ruth's home run instead of his own because he didn't want people thinking he was trying to imitate Ruth by knocking out a homer directly after he did. All he was trying to do, he said, was put the ball in play. If it happened to go over the fence, so be it. "The Babe and I are not competitors," he wrote, "never have been. We haven't fought each other; we've fought together for the good of the ball club, so that when one hits a home run the other is able to say to himself with satisfaction, 'That's one for us.'" He explained his relationship with the Babe in more detail. "The sports writers continually remind me that Babe Ruth is my inspiration. But he isn't. He's my pal, and he has been my advisor. But my mother is my inspiration." To sum up his persuasive essay, Gehrig told readers, "I have no trace of the inferiority complex towards Ruth that writers love to talk about...there's only one Ruth, so why argue with the facts?"[23]

Gehrig might not have been jealous of Ruth, but Ruth may have been envious of him. At the time, Gehrig was entering the climax of his career. The next couple of years belonged to him. Ruth, on the other hand, was just shy of calling it off. A "cooling" between the two had started the year before, and a number of incidents over the course of 1933 and 1934 would cause the cooling to turn to a freeze. One such incident occurred in 1933 when Ruth's daughter Dorothy came to visit the Gehrigs as she did many times. Mom had grown quite attached to Dorothy, but she wasn't so fond of Dorothy's new stepmother Claire. It was Mom's contention that Claire intentionally neglected Dorothy, preferring to coddle her own daughter, Julia, instead. The truth of the matter was that Dorothy favored a few dresses and sweaters and always chose them to wear instead of the other clothes with which she was blessed. When Dorothy came to visit the Gehrigs one day in 1933, she was dressed in clothes that Mom had seen time over time, and Mom determined that she was being dressed in a manner that was unfit for the Sultan of Swat's daughter and commented, "Why doesn't Claire dress Dorothy as properly as she dresses Julia?" When Claire heard about the comment, she told Babe, who in turn confronted Lou. "Tell that mother of yours to mind her own business!" Ruth snapped at him. Gehrig did not take well to anyone criticizing his mother, regardless of the circumstances. This was to be only the first major conflict in their relationship.

As the 1933 season progressed, the Yankees were the obvious pennant winners. Dan Daniel of New York's *World Telegram* was looking for an interesting story. He found it in the stats of Lou Gehrig. In early July Daniel finished breakfast in a Washington hotel where he was staying with the Yankees and walked out into the lobby with his story idea swirling in his head. Coincidently, Gehrig was sitting in the lobby, and Daniel approached him to ask if Gehrig knew how many games in a row he had played.

Gehrig honestly had no idea, but Daniel figured it at about 1,250 consecutive games. He just wasn't sure whether Gehrig's first game was the day he replaced Wally Pipp on June 2, 1925, or the day before. Gehrig couldn't recall either, so Daniel promised to have his office verify Gehrig's first game. After all, Everett Scott currently held the record at only 1,307 games. If Gehrig played every game in 1933 he would beat that in no time.

The *World Telegram* office reported back the streak had begun the day before Gehrig replaced Pipp, when he went in as a pinch hitter on June 1, 1925, which meant Lou's streak was up to 1,252 games. That total did not take into account unofficial games, such as exhibition games, that Gehrig had played. If those games had counted, the total would have inflated to about 1,471.

Daniel made Gehrig promise not to do anything rash that would result in injury or otherwise bring the streak to a halt and therefore ruin his story. On August 16, Gehrig tied Scott's record. The next day, he broke it, and the game was stopped after the first inning for a special ceremony at home plate in which the American League president presented him with a silver statuette. That night he received a congratulatory telegram from Colonel Ruppert: "Accept my heartiest congratulations upon the splendid record of continuous service and accomplishment which you have just completed. My best wishes are with you for many additional years of success."[24]

The most famous exhibition games that would not count toward his streak were the All-Star Games, a tradition that began in 1933. *Chicago Tribune* writer Arch Ward came up with the idea for the game as a way to promote the Chicago World's Fair. The concept behind the game has remained intact throughout the years: Fans vote for their favorite players by position in each league, and those chosen players faced off in the All-Star Game. Gehrig won the American League first baseman spot by a landslide, and he would win the spot every year until 1939. Off he went to Comiskey Park for the July 6, 1933, All-Star Game. Ruth, naturally, also went.

Before the game began, young Edwin Diamond, the son of a sportswriter, was introduced to some of the All-Stars, among them Gehrig, Ruth and Al Simmons. After he obtained their autographs, he posed with them for a picture. This picture, Diamond claims, is evidence of the gnawing tension between Ruth and Gehrig. In the picture, Gehrig, arm draped around the boy's neck, is smiling broadly, while Simmons is standing on the other side of Edwin with a grin. About a foot to Gehrig's right is Ruth, staring off into space, arms akimbo, no hint of a smile. Clearly Ruth did not want to be there. Edwin claims it was because he was at odds with Gehrig. Ruth did, however, want to be playing in the All-Star Game, proving so by smacking out the very first All-Star home run, much to the delight of the promoters and the fans.

Every opportunity he had, which included the All-Star trip, Gehrig visited Eleanor in Chicago. They were persuing each other with zest. During the Yankees' first swing to the Windy City in 1933, they breakfasted one morning at the Drake Hotel, then spent the rest of the day dreaming and planning the rest of their lives together. Finally at Eleanor's home, Gehrig attempted to propose to her but was so nervous he could barely get the words out. She finally had to intervene and asked if he was requesting her hand in marriage. When he said that was exactly what he was doing, she instantly replied with a yes.

The dreaming and planning they did was essential to climb the mountainous obstacle they knew lay immediately in front of them—Mom Gehrig. They agreed to keep the engagement under wraps, revealing it only to Eleanor's immediate family until Lou could get back to New York to tell his mother himself. She didn't deserve to have to read about it in the papers. Despite their secretiveness, the news somehow leaked back to Mom before the Yankees returned home. Needless to say, she was furious. It wasn't so much because he didn't tell her personally; it was more that he was the only big egg in her basket, and she was not going to let him go without a fight, a bitter-sweet sentiment in her son's opinion. "Mom is the most wonderful woman in the world," Lou told Fred Lieb. "She broke up some of my earlier romances, and she's not going to break up this one."[25]

Gehrig suggested that Eleanor invite Mom out to Chicago for a few days as a way for the two women to get to know each other. He hoped that Eleanor would impress Mom if she saw his fiancée in her natural environment, just the way she had impressed him. Her impression of Eleanor turned out to be very different than her son's, however. Whereas he viewed Eleanor's social adeptness and sophisticated tastes as a refreshing and attractive change from what he knew, Mom viewed it as the apple of temptation. Eleanor knew how to order her steak in restaurants, but she didn't know anything of finding the perfect cut to broil at home. And she didn't know how to starch a shirt or dust an end table, or so Mom claimed. Mom refused any advances Eleanor tried, unimpressed by her jokes or her familiarity with Chicago's upscale eateries and entertainment. They parted ways, Mom defiant toward her son's choice of fiancée, Eleanor exasperated. When Mom was on a train back to New York, Eleanor sat down to write a desperate letter to Lou, telling him how awful the meeting with Mom went and saying she didn't know if she could go through with the marriage.

> *Eleanor knew how to order her steak in restaurants, but she didn't know anything of finding the perfect cut to broil at home.*

Unwilling to let the love of his life go, he composed a letter to her that assured her all would work out fine, he would make sure of it, and he would love her until his dying day if she stuck with him. His letter proved that he was committed forever to Eleanor, and she decided to stay in the fight with him.

When it came time for the conversation between mother and son, Gehrig sat his mother down and bluntly told her he was going to marry Eleanor and there was nothing she could do to stop it. For her part, Mom went on and on about how Eleanor didn't know how to take care of him like she did, that she and his father were too old to go back to work (to which Gehrig reiterated his pledge that he would always take care of them), and that Eleanor was really only after his money.

In the end, Gehrig put all of his mother's fears to rest, but was also very stern with her. He and Eleanor would marry, they would move in to their own place, and Eleanor would be the number one woman in his life.

The news of Gehrig laying down the law to Mom was comforting to Eleanor, but she still feared the influence Mom had over him and wrestled with the fear that Mom would eventually break him. Her fears reached their peak one Sunday night when Gehrig failed to call her at the usual time. For hours she paced around her house, caught between frantic and livid. When he finally called, he whispered that he had taken Mom to see "The Silver Cord," a play about a domineering mother who ruins her son's wedding. He hoped that Mom had taken the hint. Eleanor giggled with delight and forgot the hours of pacing and worrying she had done. He was serious about making it work between them.

Dedication despite opposition was nothing out of the ordinary for Lou. On August 16, 1933, he tied Everett Scott's consecutive games record. The same fanaticism he displayed in preserving his engagement he displayed on the field. While he continued to prove his worth on the diamond, the Great Depression continued to ravage the nation, demonstrating that no job was completely safe. Consequently Gehrig played in more consecutive games than anyone else ever had and was dubbed the new Iron Man of Baseball, or more famously, the Iron Horse. Elon Hogsett, a Tigers pitcher, was witness to how the opposition attempted to sabotage Gehrig's durability, "We used to try to step on his feet at first base and everything. But he'd play with a broken thumb, broken fingers."[26]

No one among the opposition was fool enough to believe that eliminating Gehrig from the lineup was a small or even medium feat. "To hurt Gehrig," John McGraw once said, "you'd have to run over him with a locomotive."[27] In his personal life, his tenacity was stronger. For Eleanor to lose Lou, she would have had to poison his dinner.

◆ ◆ ◆

Their wedding day was set for September 30, 1933, the next to last game day of the season. The Long Island home of Eleanor's aunt and uncle, Blanche and Gene Austin, was to be the site for the wedding. The plan was for Eleanor to move in with the Gehrigs until she could locate a home for her and Gehrig to live in together after the wedding. In early September, she hugged her mother goodbye and headed for New York. She had formulated a game plan on how to handle living with Mom: Avoid direct confrontation at all costs. Mom was bound and determined to show her son "that girl from Chicago" was no good for him, and she regarded Eleanor with icy glares and used every opportunity to highlight Eleanor's severe lack of domestic training and knowledge of German culture.

From the day that the couple announced their wedding day, Mom proclaimed that she would not attend.

Mom got an odd kick out of conversing with her family in German, forcing Eleanor out of the conversation entirely. Mom once complained about Eleanor's reaction to the family conversations in German to Fred Lieb. "Eleanor always thinks we are talking about her," Mom told him, "but, goodness, there are things to talk about that a son has in common with his parents, but Eleanor just won't understand."[28]

The drastic differences in the home lives each woman was accustomed to became evident immediately. Among the first things Eleanor noticed about Mom was her inability to just be, to sit and do nothing productive and just socialize. If she wasn't cooking, she was cleaning, then she tended to the pets, and to finish off the evening she sat in the living room and knitted at a furious pace while chatting. Mom played well the role of ultimate house wife. Eleanor didn't sew or scrub pans or fix Gehrig's favorite German dishes. In Mom's eyes Eleanor was of no practical use at all.

From the day that the couple announced their wedding day, Mom proclaimed that she would not attend. Gehrig enlisted the help of Fred Lieb in getting his mother there. Before a game a few days prior to the wedding, Lieb approached Mom sitting in her usual seat in Yankee Stadium. After listening to a cruel personal attack on Eleanor, Lieb sternly told Mom that he would pick her up at her house and that when he honked she had better be ready.

Then, two nights before the wedding as the Gehrigs sat in the living room, Eleanor endured another round of denigration from Mom. Finally she got up from the couch and discreetly motioned Lou to join her in the kitchen for a private conversation. He saw her bottom lip quiver as she told him she could not stay one more day in the same house as his mother. He pleaded with her to stay but she insisted that as soon as his parents had gone to sleep that he take her to Aunt Blanche's.

When Mom and Pop were asleep, Eleanor and Lou snuck out to the driveway and pushed the car to the street. A safe distance from the house, Lou started up the car and they began to drive. A few blocks into their journey, Eleanor told him in a rage of sobs that the engagement was off. Mom had won. Gehrig stopped the car, tears gushing from his eyes as well. He begged her to change her mind and stick with him. Only a few more days, he pleaded. No, was her answer. They cried all the way to the Long Island ferry.

Together they sat on the ferry boat, listening to the live band entertain the sparse number of passengers. As they wiped their eyes the first few notes of a familiar song drifted easily over the still night air, a gift from destiny. It was their special song. Listening to the music Eleanor realized the heartache of not having Lou would be greater than having him with his controlling mother. Before the band had finished the song, the engagement was reinstated, upon the condition that Eleanor stay with her aunt and uncle until the wedding.

The next morning, on September 29, Eleanor and her mother, who had come in for the wedding the previous night, were at the new apartment coordinating the plumbers, carpet layers, carpenters, and furniture delivery crew. Eleanor was in a common house dress and apron, hair falling out of a loose bun, sweat glistening all over her face. Suddenly Gehrig burst into the apartment. Mom was making threats and he was fed up. He presented Eleanor with a surprising idea: Why shouldn't they get married right then, immediately. After all, the fancy Long Island wedding wasn't really his style anyway, and this would completely remove the problems with Mom. Eleanor quickly agreed to the new plan.

Gehrig immediately dialed the mayor of New Rochelle, Walter G. C. Otto, to officiate the wedding, and a couple of friends to come over to witness. The ceremony was not what would be called a sparkling specimen of sophistication, what with Gehrig in his shirt sleeves and Eleanor in her sweaty dress with workmen hammering, buzzing, and making a racket in general. One workman caught on to what was happening and yelled out to the others to stop their construction. There was a wedding going on in the living room. They stopped their noise, removed their hats, and stood still as the mayor finished the joining of Yankee great Lou Gehrig and his Chicago bride Eleanor Twitchell. Within ten minutes, they were announced husband and wife and kissed to the cheering of a handful of friends and strangers. Then Eleanor ran to change into a clean dress for the trip to the ballpark, for nothing except death would keep Gehrig from playing. They paused for a picture on their apartment building's stoop, then they were whisked to the ballpark accompanied by a police escort Mayor Otto had arranged.

Before scampering to the locker room to change into his uniform, Gehrig found Fred Lieb in the stands and motioned for him to come down to the dugout. He informed Lieb of what he had just done, but asked for his help once again. His mother now refused to attend the reception the next day and he needed Fred and his wife Mary to drag her along. Fred agreed to get her there.

The Saturday paper mentioned the Gehrigs' nuptials without much fanfare, which was quite fitting for the groom. That night the couple held their reception, upscale compared to the wedding, accompanied by friends, family, and baseball associates. In a picture taken of the celebration, Lou and Eleanor are flanked by Mom and Pop as well as many of their guests; all were smiling or laughing as if they had never had more fun in their lives. Mom may have been a little upset that Lou and Eleanor married in secret to avoid any possible ornery behavior on her part, but not a trace of anything but happiness can be found in her facial expression. Fred Lieb did not have to pry her from her home to get her to Long Island, and when he pulled into her driveway afterwards he agreed with her that she had behaved very well at the reception.

Gehrig also did very well for himself in 1933. Along with a wife, he garnered another season of spectacular stats. He would have preferred the wedding gift of a league pennant, but he had to settle for the Yanks finishing second even though they scored more runs than any other team. The sum of Gehrig's season was a respectable .334 batting average that included thirty-two homers and 139 RBI. He was a close second to win the coveted Triple Crown hitting award. By the end of the season, his streak reached 1,350 games.

> *Gehrig also did very well for himself in 1933. Along with a wife, he garnered another season of spectacular stats.*

Pennant earnings and a World Series bonus would have helped Mr. and Mrs. Lou Gehrig out a lot, especially since Gehrig transferred every last dime in his savings account into a trust benefiting his parents. He wanted to prove to his parents that marriage would not make him abandon them. For the rest of their lives, they would receive a handsome monthly allowance. Additionally, Gehrig handed over the deed to the house they lived in and a set of keys to the new car he had bought for them. The gesture broke his wallet, but it was a potion that eased the pain between Mom and Eleanor. What he had left, he surrendered to Eleanor's control. He gave her the checkbook, telling her, "Our old age is in your hands."

With the wedding battle and the baseball season both over, Gehrig and Eleanor had the time to discover each other. They came from such distinctly different backgrounds that it took a while for each to adjust to the other's perspective on the world. They started out by partaking in each other's hobbies. Gehrig's favorite, of course, was fishing—deep sea fishing. One chilly morning, they set out on a boat with some friends to the waters off New York's shore. Not long after dropping anchor, Eleanor got a bite. Half an hour into the pull-and-give reeling, Eleanor's arms were sore and she wanted to give her pole up to one of the strong men surrounding her, but she figured if she was going to be a part of Lou's world she would have to reel in what felt like a humpback whale alone. After another half hour of fighting the fish they finally lifted it onto the deck. It was a beautiful and rare blue fin...and they threw it back in.

As payback, Eleanor later requested that her new husband attend the opera with her. "I was no 'society girl,'" she wrote in her autobiography, "whatever the newspapers said in their flights of fancy; but I had grown up with more involvement in 'society' than Lou."[29] Fine art and high-grade performing arts were a part of that society she knew well. She chose Wagner's *Tristan and Isolde* as her husband's first opera, though she had reservations about it since it was rather heavy and four hours long. Gehrig agreed to go so long as it was kept a secret. If the boys on the team heard about him attending the hoity-toity opera, he would never have heard the last of it. Once at the opera, the first measure of *Tristan and Isolde* had him at full attention. With the emotion in the voices and the soaring music, he was hooked. Wagnerian operas became his favorites since he understood the German. His pleasure in opera was so great that he bought the librettos to all the operas during the winter and followed along during Saturday afternoon radio broadcasts from the Metropolitan Theater.

Literature was next on Eleanor's agenda. Gehrig had received a good education, but Eleanor had a better one. She exposed him to philosophy, one of her many passions, and to classic books such as Tolstoy's *Anna Karenina*.

"So he discovered my world of opera and literature," Eleanor wrote later, "and I discovered him. I discovered that this was no automation, no unfeeling giant. The experiences were new to him, but the feelings had been deep inside him waiting for the masterwork that might bring them out."[30]

This is not to say that Gehrig entirely replaced his likes with hers. He still clung to B-grade Westerns, for instance. There was a night when he proclaimed just after they had finished supper that he was going to the movie house to take in a show. He did not invite Eleanor, which she thought was odd but she gave no complaint. She could tell by the way he shuffled to the door unsure of himself that it was a test, a way to announce that he was his own man with his own prerogatives. A short time later, Gehrig returned to the apartment without a word. He had gotten about a block away and decided he had been too harsh, but he wasn't sure how to correct his behavior. Eleanor chuckled to herself and offered him an out. "Why didn't you bring in the evening paper?" she asked. He bounded out the door to retrieve the paper, returning with a much happier demeanor.[31]

It took a woman like Eleanor, extremely patient and compassionate, to bring out in Gehrig all that he could be. She improved him outwardly by taking him to Abercrombie & Fitch for a wardrobe makeover. Knowing her husband would refuse to buy clothes at the normal Abercrombie & Fitch markup, she asked the floor manager to quote prices at half-rate, but she paid the full price when Gehrig wasn't looking. Then she began the arduous task of improving his self-esteem. She began to build him up in his own eyes, telling him how much he meant to her, to his family, and to baseball. She urged him to make time to sign autographs and answer questions from reporters after a game. He was a celebrity, an important figure in baseball, and people wanted to know him better. Dinner could wait. With her help, his fame and appeal to fans grew, and it didn't turn him into the conceited and arrogant athlete he had thought it might. He rather enjoyed his fame once he understood it. His teammates, especially Bill Dickey, noticed the positive influence Eleanor had over him. Dickey often credited Eleanor for bringing her husband out of his shell and into the warm light of self-confidence.

> *It took a woman like Eleanor, extremely patient and compassionate, to bring out in Gehrig all that he could be.*

Chapter Ten
Taking the Reins,
1934-1935

As the couple prepared for their first season of baseball as husband and wife, Eleanor worked hard to build up Gehrig's self-esteem. "What he needed badly," Eleanor said, "was confidence, building up; he was absolutely anemic for kindness and warmth."[1] While the Gehrigs enjoyed their marriage immensely, they were not without their own fights and arguments. The problem was that Gehrig, no matter who was ultimately at fault, would often go for days without speaking to Eleanor after a fight. While she would go crazy wondering what she had done to make him so despondent, he was generally chastising himself for losing his temper and would wonder if she was going to walk out on him. When he revealed this, it broke her heart, for she had to start all over again building up his self-confidence and his trust in her assurance that she would never leave him.

In February 1934, the true baseball life Gehrig knew and Eleanor had to get used to began with the six-week long spring training. They left earlier than most of the other teammates so Gehrig could squeeze in some fishing time off the Florida Keys. Afterward they stopped off in Miami to lunch with the wife of Jimmy Walker, the former New York mayor. Then Eleanor placed a call from their hotel to her Aunt Blanche and Uncle Gene who were snowbirding in New Orleans, where Frank Twitchell, Eleanor's father, then lived. Blanche frantically told Eleanor that her father had suffered a stroke and that she needed to get to New Orleans as soon as possible.

Eleanor gathered a few essentials and caught the next train to New Orleans to be with her father. Within hours of her arrival, he slipped away. For the first week of training, Gehrig slept alone, wishing he could be at his wife's side to comfort her. As much as he wanted to be with her, he couldn't release his grip on the game long enough to be with Eleanor in her time of grief. She assured him that she was fine, however. After all, she was with family and he needed to tend to his business while she took care of the family affairs in the wake of her father's death. She returned to Florida before long and was there to kiss her husband goodbye before he traveled north with the team. Wives did not travel with the team on the tour back to New York. Instead they dispersed to their various hometowns across the country to wait for the season to start. Eleanor drove from St. Petersburg to New York alone.

At the age of thirty, Gehrig was already being referred to in the papers as "the veteran" first baseman.

The home opener led on to the rest of the season, which was split into groups of weeks when the boys were on the road and when they were home. Roughly every two weeks Gehrig and Eleanor either said hello or goodbye to each other. It was tough on a young marriage, but they made the most of their time together. When Gehrig traveled by train back home, he got off at the Harmon station, which was closer to the house he and Eleanor had purchased in Larchmont. It became their ritual that she would wait for him at Harmon to drive him home. She normally drove him everywhere, to and from the train station, to and from the ballpark. She insisted on it. She also insisted that he no longer park blocks away from the stadium. She drove him right up to the players' door, making him get out of the car and face a mob of reporters and fans asking for a minute of his time. With Eleanor's prodding, he learned how to ease into the role of celebrity and became much more comfortable around reporters and their notepads.

At the age of thirty, Gehrig was already being referred to in the papers as "the veteran" first baseman. In the baseball world back then, thirty was considered one foot in the convalescence home. Eleanor was not going to tolerate the fate most declining players faced—being traded from one team to the next while their price tag was still relatively high, bouncing their families all over the nation. The couple made a pact that Gehrig would retire the year he turned thirty-five—1939—regardless of whether he could still hit above .330 and stretch to catch a high throw to first. Retirement was still a ways off, though, and Eleanor settled into the rookie season of her career as a baseball wife.

Since the press had pegged her as a "society girl," a woman who loved the life that was of a superior caste than baseball, some of the other players' wives had the wrong impression of her. Whereas she was a nervous rookie who wasn't sure where to go and latched onto those few people she knew already, these women viewed her as too uppity to associate with other baseball wives. "She thought she was better than we were," one wife lamented.[2] Who knows if Eleanor actually did portray such characteristics. Perhaps the other wives were influenced by Mom Gehrig, who avoided her new daughter-in-law with measured precision at the ballpark. In private life, Gehrig did not spend a whole lot of time with his parents. He had warned his mother that would be the case. Mom, of course, took to heart the lack of time with her son.

Taking things to heart was a Gehrig family trait Eleanor had to deal with. Quickly after the start of the 1934 season, she learned that her husband's mood after a game depended on how the Yankees did. If the Yankees lost, the hours after the game would be achingly silent while Gehrig played an endless reel of all the foolish mistakes the team had committed, particularly his own mistakes, over and over again in his mind. There was no use, she found, in trying to cheer him up. He would have to do that alone in his own time. If the Yankees were victorious, he was his normal self, which is to say he greeted her with words.

"On the ball field," Eleanor explained, "he wasn't just dedicated; he was fanatical."[3]

A ballplayer has to be fanatical in order to pull off a feat of endurance. A consecutive games streak is no easy task. It demanded playing hurt, playing sick, playing stressed, playing regardless. "He lived in a rough, tough world, but it never got to him," Stan Lomax, New York broadcaster, said. "That's the way he was."4 Eleanor referred to the streak as "the tyrant" over his life. Since becoming a starter Gehrig had survived a number of threats to his streak. In 1927 he pulled a groin muscle and then later sprained an ankle. He played. In 1929 he had chipped his elbow, making it excruciatingly painful for him to throw. Still he played. At the end of the 1929 season he underwent surgery to remove the chip. In 1934 came the closest call to ending the streak. June 29 was an exhibition game in Norfolk, Virginia. Youngster Ray White was on the mound for Norfolk. White's aim was off—intentionally say some. The ball struck Gehrig right on the temple, and he went down with an audible thump.

McCarthy gasped, "There goes the pennant." Gehrig was unconscious for a full five minutes before the team trainer Doc Painter could revive him. As Gehrig was carted off to the local hospital for x-rays, his self-appointed defender Ben Chapman yelled vicious names at White. The next time Chapman was up to bat, he slammed the ball into White's stomach. Meanwhile Gehrig lay on a gurney listening to the attending doctor tell him that while there was no fracture, he had suffered a concussion and should stay at the hospital as precaution. Gehrig, however, did not listen.

The next day, an official game against the Senators, Gehrig borrowed a cap from Ruth, cut a slit in the side to accommodate the goose egg on his head, and went to bat when his turn came. Reminiscent of his alleged bender days in the minors, his throbbing head did not stop him from hitting like crazy. He knocked out three triples, and was poised to do more damage when the game was called because of rain. "That beaning in Norfolk improved my hitting," Gehrig joked.5 Later in life he had a more serious view of his decision to play. He admitted that refusing doctor's orders was not the wisest choice. "Some of my friends advised me to rest for a week or so. I felt I had to go right back in, so there wouldn't be a chance of my becoming plate shy."6

It is important to note here that Gehrig himself was the first to admit that his streak wasn't "pure." That is, he didn't play the entirety of every single game. A few weeks after the Norfolk incident, Gehrig was playing in Detroit's Navin Field on July 13. As he was running out a single, he suddenly doubled over. He finished out his run as best he could hunched over. By only a second or two he beat the throw to first base. Earle Combs came to his aid. Gehrig said he must have caught a cold in his back. When McCarthy and Doc Painter arrived, they walked him off the field. Gehrig had played enough for the game to count.

Back in the clubhouse, Doc gave Gehrig a treatment of heat and massage on the rubbing table. No matter what Doc did, though, nothing eased Gehrig's pain. That night Doc stayed with Gehrig in his hotel room, continuing heat treatments. The pain was so defiant that Gehrig sweated through his clothes instead of sleeping. Sometime around dawn he was so exhausted he managed to get a couple hours' shuteye. At 10:00 am he forced himself to go to the ballpark despite Doc's insistence that he not play. Gehrig approached McCarthy with a favor to ask. He wanted McCarthy to let him lead off in the top of the first, then let him return to Doc Painter's table. He only needed the plate appearance for the game to count in his streak.

Knowing that the Iron Horse would never ask for such a favor if the pain was not unbearable, McCarthy listed Gehrig in the lineup as shortstop in place of the leadoff hitter/shortstop Frank Crosetti for the first inning of play. Somehow he managed to lob a single and make it to first safely. Then he was back under Doc Painter's care. The cold worked itself out and the next day he was back to playing normally.

These "colds" in his back, also known as lumbago, a form of rheumatism, would strike him three or four times over the next five years. Some have wondered whether or not these were harbingers of worse things to come, but modern science says that the lumbago was a condition unrelated to his future illness.

In addition to a little help from his friends on the team, Gehrig's consecutive games streak was due to his extraordinary stubbornness and extraordinary luck. He would insist on playing with a minor broken bone or pulled muscle, but he also let fate help him out on occasion. For instance, in the 1934 season he collided with a Boston runner, slightly tearing a muscle in his right shoulder. Unable to move his catching arm more than an inch in any direction, he was useless as a first baseman. But luckily the injury occurred in late innings, so the day's game already counted toward the streak, and the next day was a rain-out, followed by a travel day. By the time the team was ready to play again, Gehrig's shoulder had healed well enough to allow him to play.

> *Luck and stubbornness drove his streak, but not his success.*

Luck and stubbornness drove his streak, but not his success. "My success came from one word—hustle," he told anyone who would listen. "There is no excuse for a player not hustling. Every player owes it to himself, his club, and the public to hustle every minute he is on the ball field. And that goes for the star as much as for the kid who is fighting to get a regular job. If I have achieved any success on the diamond it has been because I have been willing to give everything the old college try."[7] Every major leaguer respected his approach to playing. How could they not when he dominated on defense and offense? His hitting was as solid as his pride. On June 25, 1934, he became the fourth Yankee ever to hit for the cycle. Ten days later, he roped out his fourth grand slam of the season, setting a new club record. By the end of the season, he would amass forty-nine homers, thirty of which were hit in Yankee Stadium.

Those forty-nine home runs topped the league. His faltering relationship with Ruth crumbled a little more as Ruth, the Sultan of Swat, etched out only twenty-two. It was generally understood that Ruth was not going to return to the Yankees the next season, and the press, who loved to compare Ruth and Gehrig, asked Gehrig for his thoughts on the strong possibility of Ruth's departure. Gehrig answered politically, "He meant a lot to me, to the Yanks, and to baseball. I'd be sorry to see him go."[8] Of Ruth's thirty-nine years of life, he had spent twenty in the major leagues, but not once did he earn the most prestigious of all batting awards, the Triple Crown. To win, a player has to lead the league in home runs, RBI, and batting average. It's a rare, and therefore very prestigious, honor. At the age of thirty-one, with eleven years' experience, Lou Gehrig earned the grail, the first Yankee ever to do so. He also received kudos from the *Sporting News* as its choice for MVP once again.

The last day of the season was a very special day for Gehrig indeed. A Triple Crown, a peoples' MVP, and the anniversary of his marriage. Eleanor had a special dinner waiting for him when he got home that night. She said it was to celebrate his awards and her getting through her rookie season as a baseball wife. Later that night he gave her the Triple Crown award, saying he never could have earned it without her.

That fall Gehrig was invited on another all-star tour of Japan, and he and Eleanor decided to extend the trip into a sort of delayed honeymoon. First they headed to Chicago to visit relatives and friends, then they continued by train through the Rockies, up to Vancouver to meet with the other players to set sail on a plush cruise ship to Japan. Staring at mountains from a train car was fun to Eleanor, but staring at vast blue ocean got boring quickly. One day she was walking around the deck trying to find something to do when she spotted Claire Ruth. At the time, the Ruths and Gehrigs were not associating with each other, and Eleanor knew this full well, but she decided that it was the least she could do to be congenial. It wasn't the wives who were at odds, after all. To her delight, Claire was congenial in return, and they talked for a while about the trip, about hair and nails, and about the despicable A's—the typical, everyday banter about which Yankee wives would converse. Then Claire boldly offered an invitation to Eleanor to go back to her cabin. Eleanor accepted, saying that she couldn't stay long, however.

Two hours later, Eleanor emerged from the Ruth cabin, tipsy on champagne, full on caviar, and laughing at the conversation with Claire and her big-belly partner Babe. She didn't immediately notice the search party approaching her. They took her to her husband, who was standing at the stern with a head shipman and a crowd of searchers preparing to drag the waters for a body. He brightened immediately when he saw her alive and he dismissed the crew. When she told him where she had been, however, she saw a distinct shadow spread over his face. She knew she had made a horrible mistake when all she had meant to do was mend a broken tie. She had not taken into account just how much Gehrig detested the thought of her in the private cabin of Babe Ruth. If he could ever forgive Ruth for disrespecting Mom, he would never forgive him for keeping Eleanor out of sight for hours. Gehrig knew Ruth's womanizing habit all too well not to believe that the Babe didn't at least think of Eleanor inappropriately, even if he may not have tried anything.

Gehrig did not speak for the rest of the day, or night. While they were dressing for dinner, Ruth stopped by their cabin with his trademark "Hiya, keed," hoping that the visit from Eleanor was a sign that the Gehrigs had extended a welcoming hand of friendship. He was wrong. Gehrig turned his back on his teammate, literally and figuratively. Eleanor watched helplessly, and soon Ruth left. "They never did become reconciled," Eleanor wrote in her autobiography. "And I just dropped the subject forever."[9]

Ruth didn't let Gehrig's cold-shoulder treatment go without retaliation. A few days into the tour in Japan, Gehrig showed up late to an early morning ceremony, and Ruth laid into him in front of everyone. The cold war commenced with fervor. "They were never friends again," Bill Dickey said in response to the press' probing on what happened in the Ruth cabin. "Lou just never forgave him."[10] Of course, Eleanor he did forgive. As proof, one day the players were separated from their wives every daylight hour, so he sent her a simply perfect telegram: "I miss you today. I love you."[11]

With his duties toward the all-star tour fulfilled and the bonus money filling his pockets, Gehrig took his wife on the third leg of their journey. As Eleanor put it, they returned home "by way of the rest of the world."[12] First they swung through Singapore, Bombay and Cairo, where they had a personal encounter with camel lice while visiting the pyramids. Then they journeyed on to Naples, Rome and Munich, where they encountered the tumultuous whirlwind of the Hitler machine. (Based on his experience in Munich and from his devoted newspaper reading, Gehrig would prophetically tell his Yankee teammates in 1935 and 1936 that America should prepare for a war in Europe. Most of his teammates laughed off his comments.) Finally, they visited Paris and London, then returned home thoroughly exhausted.

Gehrig loved their journey, since it was the first real traveling he had ever done, but he loved home and having Eleanor to himself even more. They frequented the opera once again, and his newest favorite—the ballet. The Iron Horse found ballet tantalizing, specifically because of the well-honed athleticism and slender, sharply defined muscles of the dancers. On his first visit, Gehrig whispered to Eleanor, "It takes me fifteen minutes before a game to warm up, but it takes these ballet dancers hours."[13] He sat enthralled watching the dancers leap with grace and glide poetically across the stage.

The return home was not as congenial for the Ruth family, however. Yankee GM Ed Barrow had notified Ruth that he would be offered a provisional contract for the 1935 season. The Sultan of Swat would have to prove himself during the season before getting paid by the Yankees. Ruth had failed to produce hits the last couple of seasons, and Barrow and Colonel Ruppert had had enough.

While the provisional contract really wasn't a surprise to anyone, most everyone had mixed feelings about it. Gehrig, for example, was saddened by the end of a long, historic era. On the other hand, he knew that with Babe Ruth out of New York, the limelight would be focused on him. Since marrying Eleanor, he had learned to appreciate his celebrity status.

Emil Fuchs, the president of the Boston Braves, Ruth's old team, appealed to Ruth immediately after hearing the news of the Yankees' mediocre offer. He promised Ruth a spot on the team that would allow him to play and coach. Ruth accepted, and the Sultan of Swat left New York City.

As the end of an era played itself out in the press, life went on for the New York Yankees. McCarthy named Gehrig team captain, the first captain named since Everett Scott in 1925. Regardless of Gehrig's newfound roles on the team, as captain and as brightest star, he faced the same fear and trepidation he dealt with every year while waiting for his contract to arrive in the mail. When his 1935 contract arrived, he didn't sign it blindly and return it immediately as he usually did. This time the salary total caught his attention. The amount offered was $39,000. Gehrig decided, for the second time in his career, to ask for more. He and Ruppert met to discuss his salary. They negotiated each other into a stalemate. While Gehrig pushed for $40,000, Ruppert was deadset on the original offer. For weeks they were stalled, Gehrig missing the whole of spring training in 1935. As usual, though, Gehrig gave in to authority and signed for $39,000. It was to be the highest amount he would ever make playing for the Yankees.

Missing spring training did not diminish his role or credibility as captain in McCarthy's opinion. Being captain was more than just a title. He actually had responsibilities, which ranged from taking the lineup card to the umpire just before the start of the game to being the role model for the entire team. This was perhaps the easiest part of being captain for Gehrig, since he only had to continue what he had been doing for years.

People also urged him to fill the publicity gap Ruth had left in his wake. They wanted him to do something colorful like the Babe used to do. Ruth forgot people's names and that was colorful. But when Gehrig forgot something important, it turned into a punch line. He did a radio spot for Quaker Oats' now discontinued Huskies cereal during the popular national show Robert L. Ripley's *Believe It or Not* which was aired live. In the spot he was interviewed for a few minutes by the host, and then asked, "Tell me, Lou, to what do you owe your tremendous strength and fine condition?"

Lou promptly replied, "Wheaties!"[14]

The last syllable no sooner rolled off his tongue than he realized he had just endorsed the famous cereal of Quaker Oats'

rival General Mills. After the embarrassment, he saw no solution but to send back to Quaker Oats their compensation check with a profuse apology. A representative contacted Gehrig telling him not to worry about his on-air flub. They had received more free press from his mistake that they ever would have if he had said the name correctly. Gehrig still felt too bad to accept the check, so they compromised. Gehrig would do the spot again and accept the check for that.

Shortly after, Gehrig was back on Ripley's show to right his wrong. And when the host carefully and slowly asked him for his top choice of empowering breakfast cereals, Gehrig was right on cue.

"My favorite is Huskies," he stated clearly. "And I've tried them all."[15]

It quickly became apparent that Lou Gehrig would never have the flawless flair of Babe Ruth. "Gehrig did not have the Babe's color," Paul Krichell wrote. "He did not have his flare for finding the headlines. Lou could hit a home run and get less attention than the Babe striking out."[16] Eventually, people warmed up to the harsh fact that the Babe was through, and so was his show. They learned to love the unique qualities of the quiet man who confused cereals and played every single God-given game. "He has a quality of sincerity that is rare," Shirley Spencer, a handwriting analyst, reported in 1935 after examining a sample from Gehrig.[17] Rare and great in his own right, that's what he continued to be. And eventually he also got endorsements right the first time. For instance, Gillette Safety Razor Company employed his promoting services by having him "write" an ad for their razor blades. "Like a rookie ballplayer," his ad read, "Gillette Blade steel has to be hardened and tempered. When it comes to cleaning up on stubborn bristles— with the greatest of ease and comfort—Gillette hits a home run with the bases loaded!"[18]

Eleanor did what she could to further the popularity of her husband. She enlisted the help of their friend Fred Fisher, a nationally known professional songwriter who had befriended Gehrig based on a common German heritage, a love for eating fresh crab meat off a newspaper on the living room floor, and for—surprise—fishing, to write a song for Gehrig. Together they wrote and released the single "I Can't Get to First Base with You." The ditty tickled her husband to no end, though the song was at best a mediocre hit with the public. Eleanor felt the need for such antics to keep the joy in their marriage—they had learned that they were unable to have children. The exact reason is unknown because Gehrig was so ferociously private, though some have speculated that the mild heart condition Eleanor was afflicted with may have been the culprit. At one point the couple had seriously considered adoption. "Mom wouldn't have any of that," Gehrig told Fred Lieb. "She said she didn't want a grandson if it wasn't a Gehrig."[19]

Chapter Eleven
A New Buster, 1936-1937

Just as Gehrig was percolating in the spotlight, in glided a kid from San Francisco named Joe DiMaggio. DiMaggio hit more successfully in his first few games than some rookies did in a month. In the outfield he seemed to float effortlessly across the grass to easily nab a drive. His natural talent was captivating, and the aura of confidence he exuded was undeniably commanding. People couldn't help but stare at him in wonder. DiMaggio's elegant grace on the field, rare for an athlete as young as he was, was mesmerizing, completely unlike Gehrig's rocky beginnings. Whereas Gehrig famously flashed a dimpled grin, DiMaggio's scowl rarely left his face, giving him that cool, tough-guy edge, and he was just as reserved as Gehrig. Despite the scowl, Joe DiMaggio had youthful good looks. Combine that with his talent, and he was the new media buzz.

"The man I felt sorry for was Lou," Lefty Gomez commented. "Joe became the team's biggest star almost from the moment he hit the Yanks. It just seemed a terrible shame for Lou. He didn't seem to care, but maybe he did. They got along, but how could you ever know how Lou really felt?"[1]

While Gehrig was a little envious of DiMaggio, it was not an all-consuming jealousy. He even admitted to reporters not long after the rookie's arrival, "I envy this kid. He has the world before him. He has everything including the mental stability."[2] It's interesting that Gehrig added this last note, the "mental stability." It could be read as if he was saying that DiMaggio had the knowledge to get him through any situation on the field or escape the intimidation from big, mean pitchers. But thinking back to Gehrig's rookie season, his biggest problem wasn't intimidation. While he did have trouble knowing what to do in some situations, that wasn't his biggest problem either. It was his self-confidence. Perhaps that's what Gehrig truly meant by his comment. He envied DiMaggio for not suffering from the constant self-doubt that still plagued him, even as a seasoned veteran.

DiMaggio and Gehrig had a few important similarities. Foremost, they were both quiet, ill-at-ease with small talk, and fiercely private. Though DiMaggio loved his privacy, he basked in the limelight when he frequented hot night spots such as Toots Shor's and the Stork Club. His chain smoking was another thing he shared with Gehrig, but DiMaggio's addiction garnered more attention for two main reasons. First, Gehrig tried to hide his habit whenever possible. During away games, Gehrig was often seen ducking into the tunnel leading to the clubhouse between innings to drag on cigarettes. DiMaggio saw no such need to hide his habit. Second, despite chain smoking and another addiction—coffee—DiMaggio's unmistakable grace on the field seemed unphased no matter what chemical he put into his body.

The differences between the two stars, however, were dramatic. Principally, DiMaggio wasn't afraid to doggedly pursue what was his. Within a couple of years in a Yankee uniform, DiMaggio demanded a $45,000 contract. Ruppert laughed and said, "Lou Gehrig doesn't make that much." Without flinching, the young star retorted, "It's too bad that Gehrig is so underpaid."[3] In the end, however, even Joe DiMaggio settled for less—$25,000.

DiMaggio and Gehrig got along about as well as two quiet, reserved men can. They always respected each other. DiMaggio hit third in the lineup, directly in front of Gehrig. During one game in 1936, the home plate umpire called a strike on DiMaggio that looked like a ball. When DiMaggio looked back at the umpire to protest with his eyes, the umpire snapped, "Turn around!" From the on-deck circle came the slightly high-pitched voice of Gehrig, "Ah, leave the kid alone. If you'd call 'em right he wouldn't have to turn around."

"When you are a rookie, you never forget that," DiMaggio

said of the incident later in life.[4]

To DiMaggio, Gehrig was the mightiest hitter he'd ever seen. To Gehrig, DiMaggio was an incredible player with an amazing future waiting for him.

While there are those who believe that Gehrig resented the rookie stealing the press coverage he had rightfully earned—they cite a number of publicity stunts Gehrig attempted in 1936—most of the impetus for a PR grab by Gehrig came from others. For example, Gehrig's agent Christy Walsh, who had come up with the barnstorming tours for Gehrig and Ruth, convinced him to get in a loincloth and pose for still photographs. As he was posing and flexing, Walsh was busy spreading the rumor that Gehrig was replacing Johnny Weissmuller in the popular Tarzan movies. The rumor and the pictures spread to every major newspaper in the country, and Weissmuller stepped up to make a statement. "I guess they'll be making me a ballplayer next," he said in unbridled amusement. "I'll need some first baseman lessons."[5]

For an already self-conscious man, the laughter of an entire nation was overwhelming. He immediately cancelled any future Tarzan gigs, telling Walsh that if this was what it took to get noticed, he was fine in obscurity. After all, why couldn't he just be himself?

Gehrig's self was marked by humble dedication, and that was shown in his continuing consecutive games streak. "It was strange," his wife would say in her reflection on his streak, "because there was no particular reason to keep playing without a break, no particular compulsion—except the fascination to add one more day, one more week, whatever you lost."[6] When a player pushes himself so compulsively, the list of losses can lengthen quickly, which is why some cautioned him to slow down and take it easy. Babe Ruth was among those who told him to take a vacation.

"He thought I should take a few days off and go fishing when I felt the strain was wearing me down," Gehrig told the press. "Well, the strain hasn't got me yet. And can you imagine me fishing when the Yankees are playing ball?"[7]

He was correct. Would America honestly accept the image of Iron Horse Lou Gehrig "gone fishing" when there was work to be done on the field? He would emphasize his determination to keep playing despite detractors. "I have the will to play. Baseball is hard work, and the strain is tremendous. Sure it's pleasurable but it's tough."[8] He was not giving up, and his streak approached 2,000.

"How does the streak make you feel?" a reporter asked him.

"I'm very proud of it, like a postman might feel after making his rounds for 1,800 days or so."[9]

"How long do you think you can keep it up?"

"Ballplayers can last just as long as their legs last," Gehrig said, "and my legs are strong as they ever were."[10] His whole body was as strong as it ever was. Around this time a few doctors became so fascinated with his endurance and strength that they asked him if they could run tests on him. Gehrig agreed, and he found himself surrounded by a host of medical professionals and their various gadgets. They found that his resting heart rate was seventy-two beats per minute, and after strenuous exercise his rate returned to normal within ninety seconds. They X-rayed his hands and found seventeen assorted fractures that had never been checked out by a doctor. Every finger had been broken at least once. One of his little fingers was permanently crooked because he had bandaged it himself.

He never said a word to anyone about the breaks because he was too worried about losing his spot in the Yankee dynasty. In 1936, the Yankees had a new royal court to boast. Gehrig, DiMaggio, Lazzeri, Dickey, and Selkirk made up the offense nicknamed the Bronx Bombers. The offense was nicely complemented by the pitching staff led by Red Ruffing. The two ends worked flawlessly together, and the team clinched the pennant by September 9, the earliest of any team in history. In his first year, DiMaggio knocked out twenty-nine home runs, justifying the media circus dedicated to him in the papers. Meanwhile Gehrig's forty-nine homers topped the league and included fourteen off of a single team—Cleveland. He earned a .354 average with 152 RBI, while having the highest number of walks. To top it all off, he was chosen by the Baseball Writers Association as the official American League MVP for the second time in his career.

Despite his accomplishments, Gehrig was crowded out of the spotlight by the hot-hitting rookie. Story after story focused on the hitting ability and fielding prowess of the young outfielder. DiMaggio could have the papers, however, because Gehrig was about to appear on the cover of *Time* magazine. He shared the cover with Carl Hubbell, the pitcher he would face when the Yankees played the Giants in the 1936 World Series. Back in the 1934 All-Star Game, Hubbell dominated the American League team with his signature screwball, which slid right past the leftys he faced. Gehrig, Ruth, and Jimmie Foxx all had been whiffed by that pitch. Hubbell and his screwball won the National League MVP in 1936, after having won twenty-six games. Gehrig anxiously awaited the first game.

Despite his accomplishments, Gehrig was crowded out of the spotlight by the hot-hitting rookie.

That first game was unproductive for Gehrig. He couldn't lift the ball past the infield. In his fourth plate appearance, a Hubbell toss smacked into him, although it had very little force. After the game reporters asked Hubbell why he threw at Gehrig. "I slipped and the ball got away from me with nothing on it. Maybe it's lucky it hit Lou instead of going over the plate."[11] Gehrig's power could have unraveled the seams of the baseball had the gingerly thrown pitch been in the strike zone.

After the second game, Yankees 18-4, and the third game, Yankees 2-1, a record crowd of 66,669 packed into Yankee Stadium on October 4 to watch the fourth game. The Yankees were leading the Series. Hubbell was on the mound again. In the last seventeen games in which Hubbell had started, he had won every single one, including the first Series game. Odds were measured, bets were placed, but no one could accurately gauge what was to happen.

In the third inning, with one runner on and a full count on

Gehrig, Hubbell delivered a high-and-tight pitch that would have been called a ball if Gehrig had let it be. Instead he leaned back a little and swung hard. Hubbell watched helplessly as the ball sheared its way through the October afternoon into the right field bleachers. It was the first time all season anyone had hit a home run off Hubbell with a runner on base. With Gehrig's two-run shot, the Yankees were able to beat out the Giants 5-2, and they went on to win the World Series. Years later, Gehrig was asked to recall this momentous slug. "He was all pitcher, that Hubbell. If he had stopped us that day, with that incredible pitch of his, he would have been very tough in a seventh game. I've had thrills galore, but I don't think any of them top that one."[12] In the 1936 Series, Gehrig had a respectable performance, though it wasn't anywhere near the level of his 1928 or 1932 Series performances, with a .292 batting average, two homers, and seven RBI. Age may have tweaked his average, but strength kept up the number of runs he could bat in. "He seemed as strong as a slab of New Hampshire granite," Fred Lieb wrote of Gehrig.[13]

Bucky Harris, who played against Gehrig, seconded that notion by saying, "When that guy came to bat, all you could do was hold your breath."[14]

About this time, Gehrig's agent Christy Walsh really began to focus on ways for the Iron Horse to stay in the limelight and earn a living after retirement, which wasn't far off for the thirty-three-year-old Gehrig. Babe Ruth made a good paycheck by appearing in short films and radio spots. Walsh began to translate such a choice into terms Gehrig would accept. Gehrig had already nixed the idea of Broadway, so he looked further west. Playing upon Gehrig's love for Westerns, Walsh arranged for Gehrig to appear in a low-budget cowboy flick produced by Sol Lesser of Principal Productions. In March 1937 Gehrig traveled to Hollywood to meet Lesser and to partake in tests to see what kind of character he would best portray. The best character was, appropriately, himself. He signed a one-picture deal for the yet-to-be-written movie which would be filmed after the 1937 season ended. No one could convince Lou Gehrig to shave any time off his season, even if it was to star in his own movie.

The streak must continue. That was Gehrig's motto. "He stayed in many games, grinning crazily like a macabre dancer in a grueling marathon," journalist Jack Sher wrote.[15] Sher claimed it was Gehrig's obsessive nature which stemmed from pride in his work, not his talent, that drove his streak. But to many, Gehrig's obsessive nature *was* his talent, a talent he shared unselfishly with his team. Because of it, the pride he took in his work brushed off on his teammates. Stanley Frank, a reporter who traveled extensively with the Yankees, once wrote, "Lou was the most valuable player the Yankees ever had because he was the prime source of their greatest asset—an implicit confidence in themselves and every man on the club."[16]

By 1937 he had established himself as not only one of the most upstanding players in Major League Baseball, but also one of the most upstanding young men on the eastern seaboard. The Young Men's Board of Trade of New York certainly thought so. They awarded him for setting a fine example for boys. Previous honorees included the district attorney and later New York governor and presidential hopeful Thomas E. Dewey. "To my mind there is no greater inspiration to any American boy than Lou Gehrig and his career," sportswriter Paul Gallico wrote. "For if the awkward, inept, and downright clumsy Gehrig that I knew and saw in the beginning could turn himself into the finest first-base-covering machine in all of baseball, through sheer drive and determination, then nothing is impossible to any man or boy in this country."[17]

In truth, Gehrig was an upstanding citizen of America, not just the East Coast. In his time, the Negro Leagues were flourishing, and he paid attention. During the postseason he played alongside folks from all races and saw first-hand that talent did not depend on skin color. "I have seen many negro players who belong in the big leagues," he told reporters. "I don't believe there's any room in baseball for discrimination. It's our true national pastime and a game for all."[18] Gehrig also had a grip on baseball's place in American culture. "I do feel we contribute to the spirit of the country and its mental attitude toward life. It would be a dull place if everyone was a salesman, a contractor, or politician."[19] For all these beliefs and more, Gehrig was the captain of the greatest team in baseball at the time and the role model for countless children.

1937 proved to be a somewhat anticlimactic season. The Yankees were on top and everybody knew it. One of the peak moments, however, came during the All-Star Game. Dizzy Dean from St. Louis proclaimed himself the best pitcher in the National League. Indeed Dean was at the peak of his career. His homemade "fogball," a version of a curve that broke left, was hard for lefty batters to whack. He planned to use his favorite pitch to embarrass the American League sluggers in the 1937 All-Star Game. The day of the game, Gehrig told his teammates, "Don't be surprised if I knock one out of the lot off Diz. I told Eleanor when I got up this morning that I felt like a million dollars." Dean may have heard about the comment, but if he did he didn't put any stock in the claim.

Later that day, Diz was confronted with the truth. Third inning, full count, one runner on, and Gehrig stepped up to the plate. The fogball failed to impress. Gehrig hit it into the right field stands. Gehrig ranked this accomplishment nearly as high as the World Series homer off of Carl Hubbell.

Once again the Yankees won the league pennant and Gehrig was a big help. He finished the season with a .351 batting average that included thirty-seven home runs, and he amassed 159 RBI. The 1937 World Series was to be a rematch of the crosstown rivalry with the Giants. The Yankees had destroyed their competition throughout the season so thoroughly, however, that fans viewed the match-up as rather boring. Yankees fans were complacent with winning. Giants fans were weary from trying to win against the Yankees...but constantly losing. As a result, the 1937 Series was one of the poorest attended ever.

The fourth game was the only one the Giants managed to win. In that game Gehrig hit another homer off Hubbell, a solo shot, but it didn't help the Yankees as they lost 7-3. "A fellow has to get lucky sometime," Gehrig said after the game. "But it didn't do us much good, did it?"[20] Still that home run was a special mark for all time. It was Gehrig's tenth Series homer, and the one run it produced bumped Gehrig's lifetime Series RBI total to thirty-four, one higher than Ruth's.

Perhaps the Babe took the loss of the high mark for Series RBI personally. As Gehrig happily pranced off to Hollywood to film his movie, Ruth emerged from relative obscurity to give an interview that consisted of some overly harsh words about his former teammate. "This Iron Man stuff is just baloney," he growled. "I think he's making one of the worst mistakes a ballplayer can make. The guy ought to learn to sit on the bench and rest. They're not going to pay off on how many games he's played in a row. When his legs go, they'll go in a hurry."

Gehrig had a simple, calm retort. "I don't see why anyone should belittle my record or attack it. I never belittled anyone else's. I'm not stupid enough to play if my value to the club is endangered. I honestly have to say that I've never been tired on the field." In his classy way, he never singled out his attacker.[21]

With the 1937 World Series under his belt, Gehrig submerged himself in the Hollywood environment as Eleanor waited in New York and the rest of the country waited for the premiere of his movie. When he wasn't filming, Gehrig was doing the many things required of movie stars, such as attending luncheons, re- ceptions and conferences and doing promotional work. He par- ticipated as energetically as he would for baseball's sake. The one thing he absolutely refused to do when asked was pose with swimsuit-clad models for a promotion. He calmly informed his agent that he was married and didn't do that sort of thing. Walsh promised to back off, then secretly stole one of Gehrig's night shirts. He had it signed by the mavens of the film, including Jean Harlow, Joan Crawford and Mae West, and mailed it to Eleanor. Gehrig was furious when he found out. Eleanor thought the prank hilarious.

Come spring, Gehrig brushed the Hollywood cowboy dirt off his face and changed into his warm-up garments in time for training. The movie, titled *Rawhide*, was due to premiere in St.

Petersburg during spring training so Gehrig and all of his team-mates could watch the movie together. As a special bonus, the St. Petersburg mayor arranged for a parade the day of the pre-miere complete with a roped-off Main Street, a marching band, a clown, and press galore all the way to the movie house.

Rawhide (no affiliation with the classic television series) starred Gehrig and Smith Ballew. The movie had a simple premise: urban cowboy saves the day in troubled rural life. In the movie, Gehrig is frustrated with his Yankee contract nego-tiation and decides to forgo baseball and live on his sister's peaceful ranch outside the western town of Rawhide. He ar-rives in the midst of a war between the ranchers and the cor-rupt local co-op and its hired thugs. The town's attorney-at-law Larry Kimball (Smith Ballew) has been trying unsuccessfully to find a rancher willing to join forces with him and take down the co-op. Cue Lou.

At the climax of the movie, Kimball and Gehrig corner the thugs at the town tavern. Chaos ensues, with Gehrig stationing himself by the pool tables to bombard the bad guys with pool balls. He even body-slams a bad guy on the bar.

In the end, Gehrig and Kimball round up the rest of the Rawhide ranchers and drive the corrupt co-op out of town. Con-veniently, just after the battle is won, Gehrig wins his salary ne-gotiations and is able to return to the Yankees.

Critics of the day derided the film as worthless. The *Daily Mir-ror* proclaimed Gehrig as "no actor at all." For good reason crit-ics ignored the film and many people snickered just seeing the movie poster. As far as entertainment goes, *Rawhide* is less than satisfying, but for the purposes of researching Gehrig the man and what he was like off-field, *Rawhide* is as good a source as many biographies. Granted, *Rawhide* is terrible if compared to, say, a Clint Eastwood western, but the great thing about *Rawhide* is that generations born far beyond Gehrig's time are able to see him move, speak, and have fun. This latter is most important for die-hard fans. To those whose connection to Gehrig sprouts from impersonal photographs and video bi-ographies showing snippets of him slicing, running or posing, *Rawhide* is more an *important* movie than it is a good movie.

Fans get to see Gehrig do a lot of those small, everyday things that aren't the slightest bit intriguing until heroes do it: drive a car, fold his hands, clap to a beat, put up hay, wax macho, interact with kids, laugh. His New York accent also comes through, which is something that modern-day fans have only caught in the very few reproductions of his voice that have survived the many decades after his death. To non-New York ears, his whimsical "glad'd'no'ya" does not go unnoticed.

The most apparent thing about Lou Gehrig in *Rawhide* was that he may have had impeccable timing at the plate, but his ability to deliver lines was more like a dime-store wall clock sputtering on its last drops of battery juice. After seeing *Rawhide*, it goes without saying that Lou Gehrig picked the right day job.

After seeing Rawhide, it goes without saying that Lou Gehrig picked the right day job.

Rawhide does not skimp on the cowboy-flick clichés: galloping-horse chases, bloodless gunfights, a celebratory barbeque with red-checkered tablecloths, songs randomly intermixed with action. Smith Ballew was a singer and orchestra leader before crossing over to movies. Not surprisingly, the songs were led by his character. In one song Gehrig does get the privilege of singing an entire verse solo. Actually, he lip-synched to a voice that was laughably nothing like his own. The song was "A Cowboy's Life (Is an Easy Life)."

> *I played the major league for years*
>   *with versatility;*
> *I rarely missed a fly I chased*
> *And now the flies chase me.*

Classic.

At the end of the movie, Gehrig is sitting in a wicker chair on the ranch house's front porch when he's handed a telegram from the Yankees: "Your terms acceptable. Report at once for spring training." Gehrig hops up from his chair and declares, "That's what I've been waiting for!" He then jauntily turns around and hurdles over his chair to rush into the house, pre-sumably to pack. This small moment when he jumps over the chair with beautiful ease stands out because this was early 1938. In about a year and a half he would be retiring tearfully from baseball for reasons even he did not fully comprehend. In less than three years he would be crippled by a disease he could never beat, but never knew he couldn't.

Some fans have been seeking pictures, stories, videos, any-thing in which they can spot some monumental moment in which his humanity and all the reasons why he is fascinating come to the forefront. It may sound a bit too imaginative, but this moment in *Rawhide* is what fans have been waiting for. That is why Lou Gehrig's life has been romanticized by so many—his beautiful, calculated, yet seemingly natural display of strength, and the tremendous irony of it. If for no other reason than to see this moment or to watch him hurl a dude like a sack of potatoes, Gehrig fans should enjoy *Rawhide* at least once.

Chapter Twelve
With Honor Intact, 1938-1939

"You can't make dough saving yourself," Gehrig declared in spring training 1938. "I'll be out there hustling as hard as ever and taking my chances."[1] He may have been fearless, but the chances he was taking were starting to wear on Eleanor. She kept mum about her worries and hoped that he would soon take a seat before he got seriously injured. At the start of the 1938 spring training, Gehrig was a little overweight, but nothing that a few weeks of extra hard training and practice couldn't fix. By the time the season started Gehrig had chiseled himself back into his normal Iron Horse self.

On May 31, 1938, he was due to play in his 2,000th consecutive game. He woke up as usual, grabbed an apple for breakfast, and prepared to leave for the stadium and the history marker game that awaited. Eleanor nervously fluttered about their house, debating with herself on whether she should confess her fear of catastrophic injury. As Gehrig was about to leave, she blurted out, "Stop now. Stop at 1,999."

He blinked. "What? Why in the world would I do that?"

"People won't remember 2,000. It's too blah. The books are full of neat, even numbers like that. But people would remember 1,999."

"You're talking crazy. I can't stop. Not now. I've come so far, El."

She sighed, and came to the decision to speak the words she had tried so long not to. "Luke, I'm afraid. Every day I watch you get ready for a game, and I fight the voice in the back of my head that says, 'Today is the day he gets hurt. Today is the day he'll be eliminated.' Please, stop before that paranoid voice turns out to be a prophet of truth."

Lou gathered her in a hug. "I understand your fear, pal. But you know that one day this stunt of mine will end. I would prefer that I end it of my own volition, and not because of injury. I'm strong and I've got a good thing going. I'm not going to quit. I'm playing today."[2]

She was not at the stadium to see the ceremony at home plate in which they draped a horseshoe of flowers around his neck as a way of saying "Congratulations, Lou." She was at home preparing a celebratory meal and chilling champagne for the hero of the house. There was little she could do to persuade him to take it easy, she realized, so she decided to help celebrate.

By August, his average had fallen to .277, a staggering low for the Iron Horse.

Her fears did not subside, and they had good reason not to. Not long after the 2,000 mark, during a game against Cleveland, Gehrig was suddenly struck once again with lumbago. Later in the season, he reached for a low throw to first from teammate Spud Chandler and inadvertently jammed his thumb hard into the ground.

Injuries heal quickly. Batting slumps, however, are a more serious problem. Sometimes slumps are brief and don't take much of a toll, and sometimes they are much more damaging. Gehrig fell into one of the latter midway through the season. Occasionally he had a multi-hit game, but those days were few and far between, not enough to boost his batting average. His teammates gave him the standard encouraging remarks such as "It's bound to turn around" and "Just ride it out" as McCarthy searched for flaws in Gehrig's stance and swing. One of his remedies was having Gehrig try a lighter bat, but it was no help. His teammates suggested a number of other adjustments he could try. Nothing worked.

"Hell, I'm not hitting with all those changes of stance and

other things," he was quoted as saying. "I've tried just about everything. So I might as well go back to my old way."[3] Even that didn't work. By August, his average had fallen to .277, a staggering low for the Iron Horse. Throughout it all, Gehrig never hinted at any physical ailment that could possibly have been causing his slump, and he never openly voiced his frustration with the slump.

Despite overt examples that he was far below standard, Gehrig continued carrying a shield of pride. "I'm all right. I can play," he professed in August. "And I'll promise you this: when the day comes that I don't think I can help the ball club, I won't be in there, record or no record."[4] Later that month he finally got the big payoff. He started hitting at a .400 pace, and his spirit was revived like the first bloom of spring. "Now my confidence is as strong as ever," he said joyfully. "I can't wait for game time. I may be down, but Gehrig has not quit on Gehrig."[5] When the season ended, his streak stood at 2,122 games, but his batting average had fallen to .295. Even with the slump, however, he still racked up impressive stats: .991 fielding percentage with 1,283 putouts and fourteen errors; only seventy-five strikeouts in over 758 appearances at the plate; 170 hits; 114 RBI; .523 slugging percentage. Babe Ruth didn't do much better in his twilight years, but Gehrig had just cause to be worried. He was still young, first of all, and he was used to slamming out somewhere between thirty-five and forty-five home runs every season; in 1938 he ripped only twenty-nine. It was normal for him to bat in over 150 runs, have a minimum .600 slugging percentage, keep his batting average hovering around .340. Any player of that caliber would tense up if he got the numbers Gehrig did in 1938.

The Yankees won the World Series in 1938 against Chicago. Normally Gehrig would have been exhilarated; he had gone to the Series seven times in his career and won every time. Instead, he fretted over his slump which had caused him to get a mere four hits in nineteen plate appearances during the Series, even though he brought in four runs with those four hits. His overall slugging percentage, though, fell dramatically to a .286 (his next-lowest Series slugging percentage was .435, from

1926). His batting average also slipped to a .286. It was his lowest Series batting average mark ever. The Yankees swept the Cubs in four straight, with a notable lack of a Gehrig homer. Gehrig was so bothered by his performance that he got completely drunk at the Yankee victory party, a rare occurrence for the normally temperate man.

During the offseason, Gehrig noticed his strength and coordination dwindling. He felt the coldness of ruin on the approach, a feeling that somewhat intensified when he received the news that his adoring owner, Colonel Ruppert, had died at the age of seventy-one. Inspired by the death of his boss and friend, Gehrig finally agreed to see a doctor. The specialist guessed that Gehrig had a gallbladder condition and recommended a bland diet. While Eleanor seriously questioned the diagnosis, Gehrig, always one to submit to an authority figure, followed the doctor's advice.

During the offseason, Gehrig noticed his strength and coordination dwindling. He felt the coldness of ruin on the approach.

Gallbladder condition or no, Gehrig was determined to overcome it before spring training and remain reliable for his employer. He exercised outside to let the crisp New York air tingle his lungs, went fishing, and skated at the Playland Ice Casino. When the Yanks re-signed him for 1939 with a salary $3,000 less than in 1938, Gehrig accepted the contract without question.

By spring training 1939, he wasn't much better. A black hole was sucking out his strength. Yet, in his Gehrig way, he forced himself to endure more physical training, thinking that if he could just push himself through one more lap, one more practice swing, he could rekindle his power. It was all in vain. The muscle power and the coordination were both disintegrating.

He clung to his shield of pride in defiance. Reporters asked him to comment on whether he had any doubts about himself for the upcoming season. "None at all," he responded. "Why should I? What are you talking about? I'm still a young fellow, even if I have been around in baseball for a long time. I just had a bad year last year. Anybody can have a bad year. This year I'll make them forget about what happened in 1938."[6]

"Are you worried about your hitting?" a reporter asked.

Gehrig chuckled. "I've been worried about my hitting since 1925. But you know that I have never hit in spring training. I just have to work harder than ever."[7]

McCarthy had his own set of remarks on this issue. "The guy bats in 114 runs and scores 115 [in 1938] and everybody asks what's the matter with him," he said. "I wish I had more players on this club that would be so far off their play."[8] Privately, however, McCarthy believed that something was terribly wrong with his star player.

The sportswriters, voiced through one New York-based newspaper, revealed their standpoint:

> Most of the baseball writers obviously feel that if this is not the end for Lou, it is at least the beginning of the end. They do not find it pleasant to chronicle it because Lou has been a great and popular figure for fourteen years and it is not an easy thing for them to write anything that may seem to be knocking the props from under him as he tries to hold his job. Whether or not Lou finally is reaching the end of his amazing career, there is no means of knowing at this range. There have been times in the past when it seemed he couldn't go on much longer, but somehow he always managed to rally at a critical point and go slugging on his way.[9]

There were other signs that Gehrig was fading. Tony Lazzeri, also heading into his twilight at the time, observed Gehrig's small bout with a wild pitch during training. Gehrig managed to dodge the pitch by leaning back, but when he did, he began staggering uncontrollably backward. He didn't stop until he crashed into another player. One day veteran Wes Ferrell watched Gehrig moving along a golf course. Whereas the other players wore golf spikes for walking across the greens, Gehrig wore sneakers with smooth soles so he could easily slide his feet across the grass. He wasn't picking up his feet and putting them back down; he was shuffling, leaving a path of bent grass in his wake. "God it was sad to see," Ferrell recalled remorsefully.[10]

Gehrig did have a "rally" in the 1939 preseason. He hit two singles and two home runs in one game in Norfolk, Virginia. On paper it looked good, but McCarthy settled the flames of excitement. He told reporters, "The singles were all right. The home runs were fly balls over a short right field fence."[11] By March Gehrig was hitting .100, barely. Fans jeered him when he came to bat. "Easy out!" they chanted. Opposing pitchers who had been very cautious around the slugger began taking advantage of his weakness. On the first day of the 1939 season, April 20, Boston's Lefty Grove intentionally walked DiMaggio in order to obtain an out off the weak Gehrig—the ultimate insult to a hitter. Gehrig did manage to hit the ball...directly to the middle infield, right into an easy double play. The second game of the season wasn't much better for Gehrig. He missed a slow-moving grounder that in 1934 he could have stopped with his eyes closed. Throughout the month of April, the Yankees played eight games; only three days did Gehrig get a hit.

McCarthy knew that the only person who could stop Gehrig from playing was Gehrig.

"You could see his timing was way off," DiMaggio recalled later. "Then he had trouble catching balls at first base. Sometimes he didn't move his hands fast enough to protect himself." McCarthy echoed DiMaggio's observation and the fear Eleanor felt when he said, "You could see his reflexes were shot. I feared Lou might get hurt if I didn't get him out of there." But McCarthy knew that the only person who could stop Gehrig from playing was Gehrig.[12]

In the stands, Eleanor could see and hear the public's reaction to Iron Horse Gehrig striking out on fat pitches down the middle. She heard the gasps when he barely got his glove up in time to prevent the ball from smacking into his face at first. She saw the fans shake their heads as they penciled in "K" next to his name on their scorecards. "They had marveled for thirteen years at his sublime strength; now they were marveling at his stunning weakness," she said.[13]

The view from the dugout was all the more intense. Friend and teammate Lefty Gomez recounted, "To see that big guy coming back in the dugout after striking out with the bases loaded would make your heart bleed."[14]

The 1939 season was unfolding as statistically the worst ever in Gehrig's career: eight games, thirty-four plate appearances, four hits, one RBI, two runs, zero home runs, zero doubles/triples, .143 batting average, .143 slugging percentage. In fielding he committed two errors compared to sixty-four putouts, and earned a .971 fielding percentage. The most heartbreaking stat was his GDP, grounded into double play. In sixteen years, Gehrig had never been caught in a double play. Less than two months into the 1939 season, he had been caught twice.

Many insisted that the strain of playing such a long string of games was too much and his body was retaliating. But those who had been watching him closely knew it had to be more than strain, more than a slump. James Kahn, a reporter who often wrote on Gehrig, pointed out in one article:

> I think there's something wrong with him. Physically wrong, I mean. I don't know what it is. But I am satisfied that it goes far beyond his ball-playing. I have seen ballplayers "go" overnight, as Gehrig seems to have done. But they were simply washed up as ballplayers. It's something deeper than that in this case, though.
>
> I have watched him very closely and this is what I have seen: I have seen him time a ball perfectly, swing on it as hard as he can, meet it squarely—and drive a soft, looping fly over the infield. In other words, for some reason that I do not know, his old power isn't there. He is meeting the ball, time after time, and it isn't going anywhere.[15]

As Gehrig's best friend and roomie, Bill Dickey knew before most people, including Kahn, that Gehrig was suffering from some type of physical ailment. One day Gehrig could not get the cap off of a ketchup bottle. A man who could bench press like a linebacker could not get a simple cap off of a bottle. Dickey had to do it for him. Another day Dickey was reading a newspaper in their hotel room and heard Gehrig stumble. Dickey put down the paper to see what Gehrig had tripped on, but there was nothing there except flat floor. Gehrig had a bewildered look on his face. In a similar incident, Gehrig fell over while trying to dress in the locker room. Clubhouse attendant Pete Sheehy offered his hand to him, but Gehrig shook his head. More than anything, he didn't want pity.

Then, late one game, Gehrig made a very routine putout at first base for the third out. It took him much longer to make the play than it should have, though. His teammates congratulated him on a job well done. His heart sank. They were congratulating him for making an easy play—something he was supposed to do error-free anyway.

Events had finally come to a head for Lou Gehrig. The night of April 29, 1939, was the most important night in his career. That day he had gotten a hit off Senators' Ken Chase, hit number 2,721, consecutive game number 2,130. As night fell, the big conversation finally happened in the Gehrig household. Gehrig looked at his wife with pained eyes and asked if he should quit.

She asked if he was still getting satisfaction from playing. Gehrig, however, knew that his satisfaction didn't matter. He was hurting the club.

They spoke no more. They both knew. The time had come.

The next game day was May 2, 1939, in Detroit. That morning Gehrig waited for McCarthy in the team's hotel lobby. All McCarthy had to do was look at Gehrig's posture and he too knew the time had come. The conversation was brief, and McCarthy ended the excruciating talk with the only honor he could give his fallen star, "Whenever you want to play, you just say the word. That spot at first is yours when you're ready to take it back."[16] Gehrig nodded in reply, then went back to his room.

Later he walked alone and silent into the locker room. Dickey was among the first to catch on that something was up. Gehrig, he said, was ambling around the locker room "dragging his feet and with his head low."[17] Soon all the players and the reporters who traveled faithfully with the team knew the day had come. No one had to tell them. Gehrig agreed reluctantly to pose for photographs with his replacement, the agile young Babe Dahlgren. Dahlgren, focused only on his chance to prove himself, was thrilled for the opportunity to break into the lineup and smiled away in the staged pictures. Beside him, Gehrig wore an obviously forced grin.

As game time approached, Gehrig walked the lineup card to the home plate umpire and returned to the dugout to sit by himself. The game started, and come Gehrig's usual turn at bat, the stadium announcer said, "Dahlgren, first base." The concession vendors stopped their peddling, the fans looked at each other in shock and stunned silence. Dahlgren turned to Gehrig, for the first time comprehending what was happening. "Come on, Lou, stop your fooling. Grab a bat."

Lou gave him a partial grin and encouraged, "Go on out there and knock in some runs."[18]

Dahlgren choked back his remorse for being "the culprit," as he later called himself, who took a legend's spot and headed for the plate. At that moment, the crowd knew that history had been made, a record seemingly unbreakable had been set. Every last witness, Yankee fan or foe, rose to his feet and applauded earnestly for the Iron Horse. The applause lasted so long that Gehrig had to step out of the dugout to give the obliging tip of his hat. Gehrig sat out for the first time since June 1, 1925—2,130 consecutive games—a record that surpassed Everett Scott's by 823 games, approximately six seasons of playing time.

The applause died, and Dahlgren finished his at-bat. Meanwhile, Gehrig sat on the dugout steps with his cap bill low to hide his moist eyes. Lefty Gomez had a knack for cheering up anyone. He slapped Gehrig on the shoulder and said, "Buck up, Lou. It took them fifteen years to get you out. Sometimes I'm out of there in fifteen minutes."[19] Apart from Gomez's comment, the team let Gehrig be.

As painful as it was, he had made the right decision, and he tried to find solace in that. After the game, reporters pounced on the story. For the first time, Gehrig did not have to share the spotlight with any other player or manager. The day's big story was him, all headlines were his. Reporters asked if he thought the rest would do him any good.

"Maybe it will, maybe it won't," he responded softly. "Who knows?"[20] Though he may have had some ounce of hope that whatever was draining his strength was temporary and reversible, deep inside him he must have sensed otherwise.

He tried to bury the pain, covering it up with Yankee pinstripes every game day. But it wrenched his gut and bent his psyche. More than once he was spotted crying in the corner of the dugout. His teammates continued to let him be, the only condolence they could offer him. "It's just as well he made up his mind to get out," McCarthy told reporters. "I never wanted to hear people shout at him, 'Ya big bum, ya!' if Lou made an out or messed up a ball. Lou's been too grand a fellow, too big a figure in baseball for that sort of thing."[21]

"No man," reporter Cy Peterman wrote, "not Cobb, not Ruth, not even Mighty Matty was more of a team player than Gehrig." Peterman wrote this in the same article in which he relayed these Gehrig words: "Some of you newspaper guys may not believe it, but this consecutive games record has been meaningless to me. I do want to say that I appreciate the fans' encouragement and the fact they have not gotten 'on me,' however."[22] This is not to say that Gehrig wasn't proud of his achievement. Quite the contrary. He meant that he did not play because the fans wanted to see how long he could go or because he was trying to establish for himself a record that could stand long after he was gone. He played because it was his duty and his honor on behalf of the Yankees. Not being able to perform his duty tore him apart.

While Eleanor waited for the opportune time to convince her husband to see a second doctor, Gehrig continued to tour with the Yankees, fulfilling his obligation as team captain to hand the lineup card to the home plate umpire before the game. Then he plopped onto the bench to watch the boys play the game he couldn't. Every game day he forced his limbs into his uniform to take that walk to home plate and back, until June 12 when he decided to do more than walk. The Yankees were playing an exhibition game with one of their farm teams, the Blues, at Ruppert Field, later and better known as Municipal Stadium, in Kansas City. The majority of the fans there had never seen a major league game, and few had seen Lou Gehrig play. The game was important enough to draw 23,000 attendants, and the Blues, in the midst of a bang-up season, had a lineup that boasted soon-to-be star Phil Rizzuto. Joe DiMaggio's brother, Vince, played second base. Johnny Sturm was the catcher, and a big fan of Gehrig. Before the game, Sturm greeted Gehrig with a congenial "Guten tag." The two men had a lovely conversation in German. "How are you feeling?" Sturm asked him. Gehrig's reply was monosyllabic—"schlect," terrible.[23]

Gehrig insisted, despite protest from both teams, on playing because he felt like the fans wanted to see him. He batted eighth and played third base. In the second inning he grounded to second. The next inning he caught a line drive that nearly knocked him out of his cleats. At that point he decided to leave the game. It was the very last time anyone would ever watch him play baseball.

◆ ◆ ◆

Eleanor Gehrig once said there were two things, which she called "tyrants," that ruled over life with her husband: the consecutive games streak, and then this strange physical ailment that had yet to be identified. When one ended, the other settled in. In June 1939, all anyone knew was that Gehrig was having his worst season ever. He continued to collapse on the field, in the locker room, for apparently no reason. Eleanor was beside herself with worry of a brain tumor and desperately wanted him to realize the absurdity of his doctor's diagnosis of a gallbladder condition. Soon it was clear there was danger he would fall walking out to the home plate umpire, so McCarthy ensured that he was accompanied by a player or coach. His hair grayed rapidly at his temples. He lost so much weight in a matter of weeks that his clothes hung from his frame. The wrinkles on his face deepened. Still Eleanor was scared to broach the subject of a second opinion with him.

On the advice of a friend, she placed a call to the Mayo Clinic in Rochester, Minnesota. Even today Mayo is recognized for its breakthrough research and medical expertise. "I tell you, it's not exactly like calling your family doctor to make an appointment for a routine checkup," she wrote in her memoir. "I was making a long-distance call to people I didn't know, except by reputation as the most distinguished medical detectives in the country, maybe the world, and it had nothing to do with a routine checkup." Eleanor's call was transferred immediately to Dr. Charles Mayo, who had been following Gehrig's career, particularly the mysterious depletion in his strength. He urgently told Eleanor, "We'll welcome him with open arms. Get him here."[24]

Eleanor agreed to send her husband, on the one condition that she be the first and only one to know his full prognosis. Dr. Mayo was hesitant, saying (in the typical sexism of the day) that it was Mayo's policy to give full disclosure to the head of the household. He assumed Lou Gehrig was the head. Eleanor corrected him by pointing out her husband had given her full control over household finances, therefore she was the only viable head of household. Dr. Mayo had no choice but to grant her request, as it was the only way to get Gehrig to his clinic.

After speaking to Dr. Mayo, Eleanor arranged Gehrig's trip from Chicago, where the Yankees were to play, to Minnesota, all in secret. The only thing left to do was convince her prideful husband to go to Minnesota. She feared he was still set on the gallbladder diagnosis, but to her relief he met her request with, "Yes, pal."[25]

On June 13, 1939, Gehrig arrived at the Mayo Clinic, first meeting Dr. Harold C. Habein. Without even touching a stethoscope to Gehrig's chest, Dr. Habein knew what was wrong. He could tell by the walk, the way Gehrig hunched his shoulders inward. Habein's own mother had died from a full-blown battle with a rare and crippling disease called amyotrophic lateral sclerosis (ALS).

At the time, little was known of ALS. Many referred to it as creeping or infantile paralysis because it is characterized by a deterioration in muscle control. The victims become incapable of movement, first in certain appendages, creating limps and difficulty standing. The disease eventually affects speaking. Sadly, many creeping paralysis victims were considered idiots because of their disabilities and seen as a source of shame to their families. It was common to lock the victims in attics or wood sheds, anywhere far away from public view. It would take a beloved celebrity to suffer from the horrid disease for the public to learn about it and respect it. What was known at the time about ALS was mostly kept in medical circles, the most important details of which were that ALS had no known cause and no known cure.

Eleanor was told that the cause for ALS was unknown, but it was painless, non-contagious, and cruel in manner of attack.

Dr. Habein consulted with Dr. Mayo and discussed his early diagnosis. Dr. Mayo instructed his colleague to make absolutely certain that it was ALS.

On June 19, Gehrig's thirty-sixth birthday, Dr. Habein's fear was confirmed and the diagnosis was official: It was ALS. The Mayo Clinic called Eleanor in secret before they spoke to Gehrig. The full prognosis was harsh: expect rapid paralysis, incapacitation of speech/swallowing, no loss in mental capabilities, and certain death within three years. Eleanor was told that the cause for ALS was unknown, but it was painless, non-contagious, and cruel in manner of attack. The nervous system, and thus muscle function, is affected; the mind is left intact. In other words, the victims are fully aware of what is going on as they gradually lose control over their own bodies.

Before he left for the Mayo Clinic, Gehrig had promised Eleanor that he would call her as soon as he knew the "verdict" from the doctors. By the time he called, Eleanor had already been informed by the doctors. While she waited she had the Liebs come stay with her for moral support. When her husband's call came in, she took it in the privacy of the bedroom. The Liebs waited patiently in the living room. After a while,

Eleanor emerged, pale and a little shaky. "I guess I need a drink," Eleanor told them, "a real stiff drink. You know what that Dutchman just told me? 'Don't worry, Ellie, I have a fifty-fifty chance to live'—just as though he were asking about the weather in Westchester County."[26]

Eleanor delved into all the research she could find to better understand the obstacle she and her "Luke," as she fondly called him, were up against. She quickly became a clinical expert. Later in life she passed along all she knew in her autobiography.

As Eleanor requested, Gehrig was not given the full prognosis. "Lou was besieged by fears and doubts about his own life," Eleanor said. "And he also had a premonition of his own—that [his success] couldn't last, that it was all a tantalizing trick of some kind, never really meant to be. When they gave him the news at Mayo, he must have thought, 'Christ, here it comes.'"[27] He was told that he had ALS, but he was also told that there would be no severely bleak impact on his life. Gehrig must have been relieved, as odd as it sounds, to know his ruined career was not his fault, that he was not just getting old and washed up, but that he had a disease. For the three days after his diagnosis, the Mayo doctors took him fishing in the lakes surrounding Rochester to help him come to terms with his diagnosis before sending him back to his life. Gehrig surely felt the need to figure out how to break the news to Eleanor, unaware that Eleanor knew more than him. When the group returned to the clinic, Gehrig sat down and wrote a letter to his wife:

> Mornin Sweet:
>   Really, I don't know how to start and I'm not much at breaking news gently. But I am going to write it as there is no use in keeping you in suspense. I'll tell it all, just as it is.
>   As for breaking this news to the papers, I thought and the Dr.s approved, that they write a medical report and then a laymen's interpretation underneath, and I would tell the papermen here that I felt it was my duty to my employers that they have first-hand information and that I felt sure they would give it to the

newspapermen. That seemed the most logical way to all of us here and I felt it was such vital news that it wouldn't be fair to have Joe [McCarthy] and Ed [Barrow] read about it in the papers.

However, don't be too alarmed or sympathetic, for the most important thing for me is no fatigue and no strain or major worries. The bad news is lateral sclerosis, in our language chronic infantile paralysis. There isn't any cure, the best they can hope is to check it at the point it is now and there is a fifty-fifty chance for that. My instructions and my physicians will be furnished me by Dr. O'Leary.

There are very few of these cases. It is probably caused by some germ. However, my first question was transmission. No danger whatever. Never heard of transmitting it to mates. If there were (and I made them doubly assure me) you certainly would never have been allowed within one hundred feet of me.

There is a fifty-fifty chance of keeping me as I am. I may need a cane in ten or fifteen years. Playing is out of the question and Paul [Mayo doctor] suggests a coaching job or job in the office or writing. I made him honestly assure me that it will not affect me mentally.

They seem to think I'll get along all right if I can reconcile myself to this condition, which I have done but only after they assured me there is no danger of transmission and that I will not become mentally unbalanced and thereby become a burden on your hands for life.

I adore you, sweetheart.[28]

Dr. Habein released this statement to the newspapers after Gehrig had the chance to tell the Yankee organization:

This is to certify that Mr. Lou Gehrig has been under examination at the Mayo Clinic from June 13 to June 19, inclusive.

> After a careful and complete examination, it was found that he is suffering from amyotrophic lateral sclerosis. This type of illness involves the motor pathways and cells of the central nervous system and, in lay terms, is known as a form of chronic poliomyelitis—infantile paralysis.
>
> The nature of this trouble makes it such that Mr. Gehrig will be unable to continue his active participation as a baseball player, inasmuch as it is advisable that he conserve his muscular energy. He could, however, continue in some executive capacity.[29]

The Mayo doctors appointed Dr. Caldwell Esselstyn, a friend and neighbor of Gehrig, to be his primary physician in New York. Dr. Esselstyn's main form of treatment was the then-revolutionary vitamin E shots which the Mayo clinic sent through the mail.

Dr. Habein's statement, unfortunately, did not answer the question of how Gehrig developed ALS. The public filled in the blanks with such rumors as that he had caught something during all-star tours in Japan or his streak being too much for his body. There was a vicious rumor that ALS was contagious and had spread to the other Yankees because the team had started to go downhill. But all of this was nonsense and put to rest. The latter rumor infuriated Gehrig to the point that he sued the newspaper that printed the story for millions of dollars. "This story is beyond belief," he told reporters. "As it is now I am a pariah whom many people shun. I might just as well have been marked with leprosy. Sitting in motion picture houses, those near me get up and move away. As far as my illness is concerned, I am still in there swinging and punching."[30] The lawsuit was settled in his favor for a small amount of money and a retraction.

Bill Dickey said after Gehrig's diagnosis became public, "I knew there was something seriously wrong with him, but I didn't know it was as bad as this."[31] Everyone who was close to Gehrig felt the same way. How could this happen to such a powder keg of a man?

When Gehrig rejoined the Yankees days later, reporters clamored for a quote from him. "I have to accept the bitter with the sweet," he said. "If this is my finish, I'll take it."[32]

Whether Gehrig knew he was dying has been contested for decades. While he told reporters, "Whatever it is, I'm going to beat this thing," he told friends something else.[33] When he caught up with the Yankees in Washington after his visit at the Mayo Clinic, he was greeted happily by a group of Boy Scouts at the train station. The boys waved and wished him luck with the Series. Gehrig waved back at them, but then leaned toward his companion, Rud Rennie, and said, "They're wishing me luck—and I'm dying."[34] Eleanor insists that Gehrig never knew his full prognosis, so much so that she professed her burden of guilt in her autobiography, saying, "I just lied all the way through, and he believed it—so trustingly that he didn't read up on [ALS] himself or crowd his doctors to tell him more."[35] However, even Eleanor could not deny that Lou was astute and intuitive.

From the time his diagnosis was released, there was a public push to honor Gehrig. The idea of an appreciation day reportedly began with Bill Hirsch, who suggested it during a phone call with his sportswriter friend Bill Corum. Corum spoke of the idea in his column, and other sportswriters picked up on it, promoting it far and wide in their respective periodicals. Someone suggested the appreciation day be held during the All-Star Game, but when Ed Barrow got a hold of the idea, he quickly shot down the All-Star Game suggestion. He didn't want Gehrig to share the spotlight with any other players. Believing the idea was valid and the best thing to do, he wanted the appreciation day to be soon, and that day turned out to be July 4, when the Yankees were playing a doubleheader against the Washington Senators.

The public was ecstatic, and former Yankees, namely the 1927 team, from every nook of the country vowed to be there for Gehrig on his big day. Lou Gehrig Appreciation Day ended up being Gehrig's retirement party with approximately 62,000 guests.

In attendance were Mom and Pop Gehrig, Eleanor, and all the 1939 Yankees with manager Joe McCarthy. Other guests included Bob Meusel, Bob Shawkey, Herb Pennock, Waite Hoyt, Joe Dugan, Mark Koenig, Benny Bengough, Tony Lazzeri, Arthur Fletcher, Earle Combs, Wally Schang, Wally Pipp, Everett Scott, New York Mayor Fiorello H. LaGuardia, U.S. Postmaster General James A. Farley, and the New York baseball writers dean and MC for the ceremony Sid Mercer. George Pipgras, who played with the Yankees for eleven seasons and whose daughter was a favorite of Gehrig's, served as umpire. Babe Ruth showed up late, as was his typical fashion, and drew a loud cheer from the crowd. Gehrig was touched that there were so many people there on his behalf, but he had mixed emotions about Ruth being there. The two had not spoken in years.

During the first game, Gehrig stayed in the Yankee dugout anxiously awaiting the ceremony that would take place between games at home plate. Similarly Joe McCarthy was fretting over the words he would say to Gehrig during the ceremony. Neither man thought himself articulate, and neither looked forward to having so many eyes on him. Whereas Gehrig decided to do the best he could with the impending ceremony, McCarthy was so nervous he became irritable. But he still had presence of mind enough to notice how frail Gehrig looked, and he pulled some of the Yankees players aside and told them to watch Gehrig during the ceremony so someone would catch him in case he should start to collapse.

Finally the first game was over and workers set up a hive of microphones behind home plate. Current and past Yankee players lined up along the foul lines. Gehrig was placed near the microphones. A line of well-wishers from various occupations and fame came to the mikes to say sweet things to and about Gehrig. Some tears escaped from his eyes while he nervously, humbly hung his head and made a small circle of impressions in the dirt with his spikes.

Ruth was one of the notable speakers. Less than three years prior, Ruth had made derogatory remarks about Gehrig's consecutive games streak, suggesting that Gehrig needed to learn to sit on the bench or go fishing. In his speech on Lou Gehrig

Appreciation Day, Ruth again suggested Gehrig pursue fishing, but this time he was trying to encourage Gehrig rather than shame him.

When it came time for McCarthy to speak, he had to steady himself in front of the microphones to stop from breaking down in tears. McCarthy and Gehrig had forged a father-son type relationship and McCarthy knew that if he broke down, so too would Gehrig. The most memorable part of his speech was when he assured Gehrig that no matter what Gehrig thought of himself, he was never a hindrance to the team.

Gehrig was given a number of presents, commemorative plaques, and trophies. Some came from the bigwig guests, and some came from folks with the stadium's janitorial and grounds-keeping services. The most talked about present Gehrig received was a silver trophy with all the 1939 Yankee players' signatures on it presented by McCarthy. Inscribed on the front was a poem the Yankees had asked Times writer John Kieran to pen:

> We've been to the wars together,
> We took our foes as they came;
> And always you were the leader,
> And ever you played the game.
> Idol of cheering millions;
> Records are yours by sheaves;
> Iron of frame they hailed you,
> Decked you with laurel leaves.
> But higher than that we hold you,
> We who have known you best;
> Knowing the way you came through
> Every human test.
> Let this be a silent token
> Of lasting friendship's gleam
> And all that we've left unspoken.
> – Your Pals on the Yankee Team[36]

This trophy, though valued in 1941 to be worth $5, was one of Gehrig's most prized possessions.

When it was Gehrig's turn to speak, he became so flustered from emotion and fear that initially he had Sid Mercer speak on his behalf. "Lou has asked me," Mercer said into the mikes, "to thank all of you. He is too moved to speak." Gehrig started to walk off the field with McCarthy escorting him, and the microphones were about to be disassembled. But the crowd rose to its feet and chanted emphatically, "We want Gehrig! We want Gehrig!" Gehrig knew he had to say something, so he turned around and headed to the plate. The crowd cheered loudly as Gehrig mustered up the courage. He held up his hand to request silence from the crowd and began to speak, without notes, what would be the most famous sports retirement speech in history.

His speech, according to his wife, was as follows:

> Fans, for the past two weeks you have been reading about a bad break I got. Yet today I consider myself the luckiest man on the face of the earth. I have been in ballparks for seventeen years and have never received anything but kindness and encouragement from you fans.
>
> Look at these grand men. Which of you wouldn't consider it the highlight of his career just to associate with them for even one day?
>
> Sure, I'm lucky. Who wouldn't consider it an honor to have known Jacob Ruppert; also the builder of baseball's greatest empire, Ed Barrow; to have spent six years with that wonderful little fellow, Miller Huggins; then to have spent the next nine years with that outstanding leader, that smart student of psychology—the best manager in baseball today, Joe McCarthy?
>
> Sure, I'm lucky. When the New York Giants, a team you would give your right arm to beat, and vice versa, sends you a gift—that's something! When everybody down to the groundskeepers and those boys in white coats remember you with trophies—that's something.
>
> When you have a wonderful mother-in-law who

takes sides with you in squabbles against her own daughter—that's something. When you have a father and mother who work all their lives so that you can have an education and build your body—it's a blessing. When you have a wife who has been a tower of strength and shown more courage than you dreamed existed—that's the finest I know.

So I close in saying that I might have had a tough break; but I have an awful lot to live for.[37]

He began to back away, then remembered his manners and quickly added, "Thank you."

Applause filled Yankee Stadium for nearly two minutes. Gehrig was visibly shaken as he stepped back from the mikes. He took out his handkerchief and wiped the tears away. Babe Ruth came over to hug him, though some noticed that Lou did not return the hug or make much eye contact with Babe.

His speech has often been called the Gettysburg Address of Baseball. Eleanor revealed in her autobiography that he had spent the previous night working on his speech, writing it down, but never rehearsed it "because it was simple enough and agonizing enough and he was still shy enough, groping for some way to phrase the emotions that usually were kept securely locked up."[38] Unbelievably, for all that the speech symbolized at the time and all that it would come to symbolize, no one recorded his speech in its entirety either on audio or film. Consequently, there are differing versions of his speech published in various biographies and baseball history books. There are only clips of video of his speech that remain, which are owned by the Yankees and often played on their cable TV station, YES Network.

◆ ◆ ◆

His career was over, but that didn't stop him from setting milestones. Gehrig was the first player of any sport to have his jersey number retired. Gehrig was also the first baseball player to have the Baseball Writers' Association (BWA) waive the mandatory waiting period between retirement and induction into the Hall of Fame. Gehrig was inducted the same year he retired, in December 1939, by a unanimous vote as the sole choice for 1939. He was unable to travel to Cooperstown for an extended stay, so there was no induction ceremony, but of course he was deeply moved by the honor the BWA and the Hall gave him. Meanwhile, the New York and Chicago chapters for the BWA tried to revive the idea of an intercity high school baseball championship game, similar to the one Gehrig played in during high school. The proceeds from the game would have gone to charity and the winner would be given a trophy in Gehrig's honor. The idea never came to fruition.

The Gehrigs moved into a cozy two-story on Delafield Avenue in Riverdale, New York (a section of the Bronx). Even though he, the sole income winner, was out of a paying job, he was promised by Ed Barrow that he would still be given his money promised in his 1939 contract. Barrow said that since Gehrig retired voluntarily, Gehrig had the right to remain on the Yankee payroll until the close of the season.

But Gehrig didn't need a bribe to remain loyal to the Yanks. Though his ALS quickly made it nearly impossible for him to climb stairs, Gehrig would frequent the stadium for home games in the late summer months. A few weeks after Lou Gehrig Appreciation Day, he was named as an honorary member of the American League All-Star team. The Yankees went to the Series that fall and voted to share the bonus money with him. When the Yankees headed south for spring training, Gehrig told the press, "Sure I'd like to be going south with the Yankees. And so, I guess, would about a million other fellows. But I'm luckier than they are because I've been south with the Yankees."[39] He insisted that life on the other side wasn't all that bad. "You'd be surprised," he said, "how different a slant you get on a ballgame when you see it from the bench— I mean, after you have been playing for years. For the first time, I am looking at a complete game. For years I was so busy trying to take care of my own position that I didn't have time to take in a view of the whole game."[40]

At the end of the 1939 season, Barrow made it clear what he

He insisted that life on the other side wasn't all that bad.

thought of Gehrig's future relationship with the Yankees. He told Eleanor that her husband should get a different job. Though Gehrig was upset that his boss, for whom he had enormous respect, would say such a thing, his anger was nothing compared to Eleanor's bitterness. She was hoping that Gehrig would be asked to remain with the organization in some capacity. When he was diagnosed, the Mayo Clinic suggested that Gehrig would fit well in an office or writing position with the Yankees. Barrow's refusal to entertain this possibility angered and embittered Eleanor.

Fortunately Gehrig didn't really need the paycheck from Barrow. He would soon have a new career anyway. In the meantime, he corresponded with other ALS victims around the country. Piles of cards and letters poured in from well-wishers eager to give Gehrig encouragement. Though he tried to respond to all of them, he was overwhelmed by the volume, and eventually by the simple task of holding a pen.

He also made trips in the second half of 1939 to the Mayo Clinic for a variety of check-ups and treatments. On one such trip, he agreed to an interview with Dwight Merriam of Rochester's KROC-AM Radio, on the firm condition that the conversation stick to the subject of baseball. He spoke to Merriam on August 22, 1939, for about fifteen minutes about various issues including newly initiated night games and advice to up-and-comers. Below are some selected excerpts from this interview.

(DM = Dwight Merriam, KROC; LG = Lou Gehrig)
DM: Lou, what's your opinion of night baseball?
LG: Well, night baseball is strictly a show and is strictly advantageous to the owners' pocketbook. But as far as being a true exhibition of baseball, well, I don't think I can say it is, and it's very difficult on the ballplayers themselves. Of course, we realize that the men who work in the daytime like to get out at night and really see a spectacle, and we do all in our power to give them their money's worth. But after all, it's not really baseball. Real baseball should be played in the daytime, in the sunshine.

DM: You can't see the balls as well at night as you can in the day, is that the trouble? It's hard on the eyes?

LG: Well, you can't see what you call the spin on the ball. You see, it looks faster than it really is and your timing's slightly off.

DM: Is that why some ballplayers can hit very well at night and not so good during the day and vice versa?

LG: [laughs] No, I would say there are no ballplayers that hit better at night than they do in the daytime. Now, you look at comparative averages at the close of the season and I believe that you will see it's strictly a pitcher's game at night.

DM: More close, more low-hit games.

LG: More low-hit games and low scores. Now [Cotton] Pippen beat us a night game in Philadelphia, our first night game. He beat us 3 to 2, and we had pretty fair luck with him in two innings in a daytime game.

DM: Who would you say has been the ballplayers' ballplayer?

LG: Well, there's no question about the three greatest and most outstanding ballplayers in the history of baseball have been Ruth, Cobb, and Wagner. Now personally, Ruth was a typical fans' ballplayer. And Cobb was a typical individual ballplayer, because I believe he had more enemies on the ball field than any man in the history of baseball because he played it so hard and he thought of nobody. I mean, cutting or slashing or anything to gain his end, he went through. And yet I think Honus Wagner was the typical ballplayers' ballplayer or the managers' ballplayer, because he was always thinking of winning and doing what he could for the other fellow, for himself, and for his manager and for the fans.

DM: Do you believe the young player should receive thorough seasoning in the minor leagues?

LG: I don't think there's any question about that. There are very few major league ballplayers in the history of the game that have proven themselves capable of jumping from the sandlot or college into major league baseball, and it usually requires two to four years' seasoning and then another year's seasoning in the major leagues while they are learning. Constant reminding of different things, which plays they're making wrong, or little "pepper-uppers" is what we call them.

DM: Are you in favor of the All-Star Game?

LG: Oh, I think it's a great thing. Just great. I'm thrilled to death every time I can attend one, and you can imagine the thrill I can get when I was chosen to play in them.

DM: Do you think there will ever be such a thing as a players' union?

LG: I don't see how it possibly could work because at that rate a boy would not be rewarded for his abilities. A ballplayers' union would put everybody in the same class, and it would put the inferior ballplayer, the boy who has a tendency to loaf, in the same class, as far as salary is concerned, with the fellow who hustles and has great ability and takes advantage of his ability.

DM: Would you say ballplayers as a whole play for salary or do you think the majority play for the love of the game?

LG: I think it's a combination of both. I think every

ballplayer is so crazy about the game that he'd go out and play in his spare time if he weren't able to earn a living at it, and, of course, we must earn our bread and butter too.

DM: What advice would you give, as a baseball player, to boys hoping to become baseball players—that is, to keep their health and fitness?

LG: Well, to be able to play, you have to keep your health. And in order to be able to play, you have to be able to practice and put in a great deal of time. And you have to be a regular fellow or, in other words, you have to play the game hard, and you have to play it to win, and you have to play it clean-ly. Because if you don't fulfill these qualifications in the major leagues, why the boys just force you to become a lone wolf. They pay no attention to you. That's why you very seldom see a ballplayer who is actually conceited. He might be accused of being conceited because he might feel ill that day or he might have a member of his family, his baby or his wife or somebody, might be ill. And he might be rushing to get home and when he leaves the park there might be five hundred or a thousand young-sters out there requesting his autograph. And often he may rush right on through them in order to get to his car and get home to see his family or what-ever might be wrong. And yet a ballplayer under those conditions will be accused of being conceit-ed. I don't think I've ever come in contact with any of the boys that we could really call conceited.[41]

Chapter Thirteen
Two Quick Years, 1940-1941

Before ALS completely took over his life, Lou Gehrig tried to live as normally as possible for as long as possible. He had a few months to earn a paycheck before ALS restricted all his travel. In early 1940, New York City Mayor Fiorello LaGuardia offered Gehrig a ten-year appointment to be one of the city's three commissioners of parole, and Gehrig welcomed the job offer. LaGuardia thought Gehrig a pristine example for morals and ethics to troubled boys going through the parole commission. "I am sure Lou can help many boys," LaGuardia said, "but I also was thinking of Lou helping himself. I was thinking that in studying the boys' problems he could, for the time being, forget himself, and that would be helpful."[1] Gehrig accepted the position, but Eleanor added the stipulation that LaGuardia ask no questions when told it was time for Gehrig to leave.

As a parole commissioner, Gehrig worked with many underprivileged, poor and struggling people of almost every age, race and religion. It was ironic that many of the people he came in contact with claimed that they simply "got a bad break." But Gehrig would never sneer or preach about what "a bad break" truly was. LaGuardia had warned Gehrig not to let any offender hit his emotional weaknesses. It was the other way around in the end; Gehrig ended up inadvertently finding *their* weaknesses.

LaGuardia was extremely pleased with Gehrig's performance on the parole board—not a far cry from the pleasure he used to get out of Gehrig's on-field performance. The LaGuardias and the Gehrigs became close as a result of Gehrig's job under the mayor, but Eleanor kept to herself the wretched prognosis for Gehrig until it was time for her husband to retire completely from the working world. In the short meanwhile, Gehrig made the most out of his influence over the lives of those who were struggling. "What advice do you most often give these boys?" a reporter once asked him. His reply: "I tell them to try to get involved in some sport."

Unfortunately for all, Gehrig's tenure on the Parole Board was very short. Before long he could no longer hold a pen or light his own cigarette. He finally had so much trouble walking that Eleanor decided to call it quits. The time came for Eleanor to call LaGuardia and reveal the truth about Lou's condition. "He was horrified," Eleanor said regarding LaGuardia's reaction to the full prognosis.[2]

Gehrig would remain almost exclusively in his home most of 1940 and into 1941, confined to bed in the latter months. In all, he struggled with ALS for twenty-three months after diagnosis. The whole time he did not know the full prognosis, according to his wife. During the months of constraint, he was entertained by an array of Broadway stars, friends, and neighbors. Eleanor brought many of them to the house with the specific purpose of keeping him in social environments as long as possible to try to alleviate any depression. Some of the more memorable guests included Fred Fisher, songwriter; Pitzy Katz, vaudevillian; John Kieran, *New York Times* sportswriter; Tallulah Bankhead, Broadway actress, along with the cast of *The Little Frog*; Ed Barrow; teammates Bill Dickey, Frank Crosetti, and Babe Ruth. Virtually everyone Gehrig knew showed up at his house at some point. "Everybody who came to the house," Eleanor said, "was screened and warned: no backslapping or stuff like that because Lou was too smart for that."[3]

Gehrig became more and more paralyzed, to the point that he couldn't walk. Yet he absolutely refused to have a wheelchair, even in the worst of it when Eleanor tried to persuade him and had made plans for putting ramps in their house. "He always believed he was coming back to the Yankees," Eleanor said in 1945 when she was finally able to discuss publicly this very private part of her life. "Only one thing worried him and every once in a while he'd give utterance to it. He'd look up from his reading or whatever he was doing and ask quite seriously, almost with a note of alarm in his voice: 'Now tell me honestly, do you really think McCarthy will make a place for me?'" She would have to force herself to say, "Yes, of course, my darling."[4] His condition continued to worsen. Chewing became a tortuous chore for him, so he was put on a liquid diet, preferring milk shakes.

The last month or so of his life, Gehrig was completely bedridden. He desired only the essential people to see him: Eleanor, Dr. Esselstyn, Eleanor's mother. "Lou didn't want anyone to see him as he lost the power from that great, sturdy physique and the vitality from that great chiseled face," Eleanor explained.[5] By the end of his battle he had gone from a bulky 200+ pounds of muscle to twenty-five pounds underweight. Despite knowing full well that his body was wasting away, Gehrig never lost faith that his wife and doctors would bring him through it.

> *By the end of his battle he had gone from a bulky 200+ pounds of muscle to twenty-five pounds underweight.*

Late May 1941 was the worst of it. He couldn't converse very long or move his limbs or swallow easily. His breathing was heavy and labored. His mind may have danced with the glorious memories of swinging on parallel bars in the turnverein or watching another one sail over the right field fence, but his body remained motionless. He watched his wife hover about him, wishing he could hug her or speak endlessly of his love for her. According to Eleanor's recollection, Mom had been kept "at a distance" until Lou was on the verge of the end. In the last days of his life, Eleanor sent for Mom. "For once," Eleanor said, "she entered our house without a chip on her shoulder. She was visiting him for the last time, and I left them alone, no longer worried that she would or could exert the influence on his affairs that she had exerted for so long. And she carried it off with something that approached grace."[6]

On June 2, 1941, around ten in the morning he looked up at those by his bedside, his wife, doctor, and his mother-in-law, and smiled. "My three pals," he said in his whispered voice.[7] Those were to be his final words. The last few hours he slipped in and out of consciousness. Then, finally, at ten that night, he succumbed. "The most beautiful expression instantly spread over Lou's face," Eleanor recalled, "and I knew the precise moment he had gone."[8] His death came almost sixteen years to the day his playing streak began (June 1, 1925), and seventeen days before his thirty-eighth birthday. All flags in the city flew at half-staff, on the order of Mayor LaGuardia.

On the night of June 3, his body was laid in state for two hours as 5,000 people filed past to pay their respects. June 4 was Gehrig's funeral. The Yankee game for that day, while cancelled due to rain, had been scheduled to go on—much like how the Iron Horse had always pushed ahead through virtually any hardship. The funeral was held at 10:00 am at Christ Episcopal Church in Riverdale. Approximately 125 family members and close friends were in the church for the short service, another 200 people stood outside in the rain. Rev. Gerald V. Barry presided over the ceremony. Mayor LaGuardia, Joe McCarthy, Bill Dickey, John Kieran, Christy Walsh, two members of the Parole Board, Dr. Esselstyn, and four Mayo doctors were listed as honorary pallbearers. After the service, Gehrig's body was cremated at Fresh Crematory in Queens. Eleanor bought a plot of land in the upscale Kenisco Cemetery in Valhalla, New York, on which to erect a headstone. His ashes, and eventually hers, were placed inside the headstone.

The *New York Times*, June 3, 1941, ran the large headline: "Gehrig, 'Iron Man' Of Baseball, Dies at the Age of 37." The obituary encapsulated his career and disease and included many quotes from various then-current players and managers as well as those with whom Gehrig played in his early career. To quote one passage of the obituary, "As brilliant as was his career, Lou will be remembered for more than his endurance record. He was a superb batter in his heyday and a prodigious clouter of home runs. The record book is liberally strewn with his feats at the plate." Those feats at the plate and some other accomplishments are included here (asterisk indicates Gehrig still holds the record as of January 2006):

Columbia University
◆ Longest home run (approximately 450 feet, on South Field, 1923) *
◆ Seventeen strikeouts in one game (1923)

New York Yankees
◆ First Yankee to win Triple Crown (1934)
◆ Second Yankee to have plaque erected in Memorial Park (1941)
◆ Led team in RBI nine times *
◆ Second-highest in games played, at-bats, runs, total bases, and batting average*

American League
◆ 184 RBI in a single season (1931) *
◆ In top-ten list of MVP candidates for nine seasons—in top five for eight seasons
◆ Voted to the All-Star Game seven consecutive years (1933-1939)
◆ Won BWA's MVP Award twice in career (1927, 1936)

Major League
◆ Twenty-three career grand slams *
◆ Most career home runs by a first baseman (493) *
◆ 400+ total bases per season for five seasons *
◆ Tied record of four home runs in four consecutive at-bats (1932)
◆ Unanimously elected to Hall of Fame (1939) *
◆ 2,130 consecutive games played (out of 2,164 career games played)—second-highest total *
◆ Fifteen career steals of home
◆ Averaged one RBI per game over the length of his career*
◆ 150+ RBI per season seven times *
◆ 301 runs produced in single season (1931)
◆ Fourth-highest career RBI total (1,995)
◆ Third-highest career slugging percentage (.632)
◆ Fifth-highest on-base percentage (.447)
◆ Ninth-highest career runs (1,888)
◆ Third-highest isolated power rank (1.8080)
◆ Fifth-highest extra-base hits (1,190)
◆ 100+ RBI per season for thirteen consecutive seasons *

◆ Played in a four-game World Series four times *
◆ Received the highest number of votes for MLB's All Century Team (1999) *
◆ Retirement speech voted fifth-most memorable moment in baseball history by fans (2002) *
◆ Drove in 500 runs in three years *

Sports History
◆ First player of any sport to have jersey number retired *

Chapter Fourteen
The Remainder of His Survivors' Lives

Fred Lieb wrote, "Yet even sharing a common tragedy, Mom and Eleanor could not bury the hatchet. The hostility between the two women remained unabated long after his death."[1] Without the buffer of Lou Gehrig, the sparks flew between Mom and Eleanor.

Gehrig's parents hired a law firm to sue Eleanor for part of their son's life insurance money. In August of 1941, Gerald F. Finley, representative of Gehrig's parents, met with Eleanor's attorney Milton Eisenberg to discuss the matter. At the time, Eleanor was in Hollywood on the set of the bio-pic of her husband *Pride of the Yankees*. In a letter to Eleanor dated August 28, 1941, Eisenberg reported that Finley contended that Gehrig wasn't of sound mind when he revised his will for the last time and therefore it could be void—a preposterous claim in Eisenberg's opinion. Finley threatened to sue for the life insurance payouts to Eleanor, requesting 40% of her income. Eisenberg told Eleanor that it would be absurd for her to fork over that much money to her husband's parents, but he did recommend that she settle out of court and pay the Gehrigs approximately $2,000 "to bring this bitter feeling to an end."[2] The lawsuit, however, was drawn out for two years. On September 23, 1943, Eleanor settled and wrote a check payable to Mom and Pop in the amount of $2,525.45.

From the trail of paper left behind, it seemed everyone stayed in their respective corners for a few years. Mom and Pop moved to Mt. Vernon, New York. Though having lived and worked in America for nearly half a century, they were finally sworn in as official American citizens on May 11, 1944.

Pop's health faded rather quickly after his son's death. In early 1945, Pop suffered a heart attack. He was told to rest, but he didn't. He had a burning desire which kept him on his feet a bit longer. When Memorial Day rolled around, he convinced Mom to take him to Yankee Stadium for the game despite his doctor's objections. "That doctor sure was mad," Pop told his friends. "But I just wanted to see what it looked like again around first base."[3]

Eleanor kept herself busy by delving into another realm of the sports world. In September of 1945, she talked to a reporter about her new job as Secretary Treasurer of the newly formed All-American Football Conference. "I was a football fan before I ever saw baseball," she explained. "I like to be active and I like sports. I suppose I should be surprised to find myself in football instead of baseball. But that would be easy to answer too: the football opportunity developed first."[4] She

> *Eleanor kept only one picture on her desk, a headshot of her husband.*

kept only one picture on her desk, a headshot of her husband. Eleanor also worked hard to support further ALS research.

When Gehrig's father died on August 16, 1946, he was buried just feet away from his son's headstone. Throughout the years the Gehrig family ran into difficulties dealing with the Kensico Cemetery. Picnickers and tourists kept frequenting the gravesite, but the cemetery management wasn't keeping up the site well enough. One fan even tried to pry open the iron doors on the headstone and steal the urn. Finally, the Gehrigs looked into moving Lou Gehrig's remains to the Baseball Hall of Fame, but when the story broke in the media they backed out from the idea. Gehrig's remains are reportedly still at the Kensico Cemetery.

Gehrig's mother died in 1954. She was buried in the Gehrig family plot, as were Eleanor's mother in 1968 and her brother in 1975.

Eleanor published her memoir, *My Luke and I*, in 1976, writing about intimate details of her romance and home. Within a few years of the book's release, it was turned into a made-for-TV movie. She continued plugging away with ALS activism and attending various events in honor of Lou until the age of seventy-nine. She died on March 6, 1984, leaving an estate worth $400,000. She bequeathed $220,000 to four unidentified people, and the rest she split between the Caldwell B. Esselstyn Foundation and the Presbyterian Hospital in New York for the continuation of ALS research. She donated all of her husband's remaining baseball mementos to the Hall of Fame Museum.

Appendix A
Interesting and Rarely Discussed Tidbits

Lou Gehrig's death, though foreseen, was difficult for many. As a result, memorials and tributes sprouted up everywhere. Even today the world is paying respect to Gehrig and all for which he stood.

June 3, 1941
■ New York Mayor Fiorello LaGuardia orders flags to be flown at half-staff.

■ Gehrig's obituary appears in the *New York Times*. It includes mini-eulogies written and submitted by the likes of Joseph McCarthy, Joe DiMaggio, Earle Combs, Jimmy Foxx, and Rogers Hornsby.

■ Gehrig's locker is sealed and never used again. (The Hall of Fame now houses his locker.)

June 4, 1941
■ Gehrig's funeral. The Yankee game scheduled for this day is canceled. Officially it is a rain-out, but no Yankees player could think about baseball when the man who defined the team for so long was gone.

■ Gehrig's remains are cremated and placed inside a headstone in Kensico Cemetery in Valhalla, New York. Oddly, the headstone erroneously claimed he was born in 1905 (he was born in 1903).

June 17, 1941
■ Lou Gehrig Plaza was dedicated at the intersection of Grand Concourse and 161st Street, two blocks from Yankee Stadium. Eleanor Gehrig was on hand.

July 4, 1941
■ At 1:30 sharp before the first game of a doubleheader with the Senators, the Yankees honor Gehrig by erecting a monument in Memorial Park, behind center field of the stadium. Lou Gehrig was one of only two players so honored by that time. The plaque reads: "Henry Louis Gehrig. June 19, 1903—June 2, 1941. A man, a gentleman, and a great baseball player, whose amazing record of 2,130 consecutive games should stand for all time. This memorial is a tribute from the Yankee players to their beloved captain and teammate. July 4, 1941."

December 5, 1941
■ In New York state 222 schools vote to honor Lou Gehrig by naming a state Liberty ship after him.

January 7, 1942
■ Lou Gehrig Memorial Fund, at 420 Lexington Avenue in New York, gives money to the city to supply hospitals with much-needed ambulances at the cost of $2,000 each. The sides of the ambulances read "Lou Gehrig Memorial."

July 1942
■ *Pride of the Yankees*, the film about Gehrig, premieres in New York. It was nominated for eleven Oscars, winning three. The movie has since become one of the most widely played baseball movies, and a classic movie overall.

January 17, 1943
■ Christina Gehrig is on hand in Portland, Maine, to christen a new Liberty ship named in honor of Lou.

February 1944
■ The Fourth War Loan Sports Committee releases tallies of

which ballplayer's name has garnered the most money in war bonds. More fans purchased war bonds in honor of Lou Gehrig by an overwhelming majority—5,745 compared to second-place Mel Ott at 4,648. Bill Dickey bought $8,000 worth of those bonds in honor of his lost friend who had predicted the Second World War in the mid-1930s.

1944
■ Commerce High School presents the Army with The Spirit of Lou Gehrig, a fully equipped field ambulance that cost $2,000. Eleanor Gehrig tells the boys of Commerce at the dedication to pray for the men who would be carried in the ambulance.

War-time '40s
■ Ball fields throughout the country are renamed "Lou Gehrig Field."

March 2, 1951
■ Longtime Yankee commentator, Mel Allen, whose game broadcasts were a comfort to Gehrig when he could no longer attend games, is honored by the city of New York. He receives many gifts and $14,000. He uses part of the money to set up the Lou Gehrig Memorial Scholarship at Columbia University, which would provide five students with a full four-year scholarship each.

August 21, 1953
■ Gehrig's birthplace, a four-story apartment building that had been turned into a laundry in Yorkville, is adorned with a memorial plaque: "This plaque marks the site of the birthplace of Henry Louis Gehrig." Christina Gehrig, Bill Dickey, and Mayor Vincent R. Impellitteri are at the unveiling ceremony.

January 7, 1955
■ Phi Delta Theta Fraternity (Oxford, Ohio, chapter), begins the annual Lou Gehrig Memorial Award, given to an MLB player whose work on and off the field best represents the spirit of Lou Gehrig. See a list of winners later in this appendix.

1957
■ New York's *Journal-America* sets up the Lou Gehrig Award, a prestigious award for high school athletes. Winners are to be judged by coaches, athletic directors, and principals from public and parochial schools on their sportsmanship, courage, skill, and conduct both on and off the field.

July 5, 1964
■ Gehrig's farewell speech is played at Yankee Stadium in memorium. Eleanor Gehrig, reporter Dan Daniel, and Gehrig's only surviving teammate Frank Crosetti are on hand.

1969
■ The Baseball Writers' Association votes Gehrig the greatest first baseman of all time.

1976
■ Eleanor Gehrig publishes her autobiography, extensively discussing her private life with her late husband. The book was later turned into the made-for-TV movie *A Love Affair: The Eleanor and Lou Gehrig Story*, starring Blythe Danner and Edward Hermann.

1988
■ Starting Lineup puts out a Sports Impressions series. Gehrig is one of the players honored in this series. Eight-inch-tall ceramic statuettes in Gehrig's likeness are sold. Only 5,000 of these highly valued pieces are ever made.

1989
■ The U.S. Postal Service commemorates Gehrig with a stamp. Soon, other countries are replicating this memorial (Granada, in the Caribbean, also dedicated a stamp to Gehrig's memory). Ray Robinson's *Iron Horse: Lou Gehrig in his Time* is published; it is widely considered the authoritative Gehrig biography.

1995
■ Curt Schilling of the Arizona Diamondbacks wins the Lou

Gehrig Memorial Award for his work on the pitcher's mound and for his dedication to the ALS Association (ALSA); he names his son Gehrig Schilling. Cal Ripken, Jr., Baltimore Orioles, breaks Gehrig's consecutive games record on September 6.

1997
■ Kenneth Gatewood, artist, releases an illustration of an infant Cal Ripken dressed in a baseball uniform with a bat watched over by the spirit of Lou Gehrig. The title of the illustration: "I Can Do That."
■ Avon sells a baseball with the images of Ripken and Gehrig, accompanied by the story that ties the two men together forever.

Sept. 20, 1998
■ Ripken sets the new consecutive games streak mark in Orioles Park at Camden Yards—2,632 games. In his address to the packed stadium, he acknowledges "the great and courageous Lou Gehrig." The crowd begins to chant, "Lou! Lou!"

1999
■ Major League Baseball, with the assistance of MasterCard, collects votes from baseball fans for their All Century Team— the fans' favorite ball players throughout the history of the game. The names of the top one hundred vote-getters are announced to the public. Lou Gehrig is not only voted as the first baseman for the prestigious pseudo-team, he receives more votes than any other player who ever played in the big leagues by an overwhelming margin.

2000
■ Following the revelation of the All Century Team, Hasbro's Starting Lineup releases action figures, accompanied by a limited-edition baseball card, of ten of the top thirty players selected. Among them is Lou Gehrig. The back side of the Gehrig action figure box reads: "This set is a tribute of the magnificent sport of baseball and the greatest athletes who ever played the game."
■ A game-used 1932 Gehrig bat is cut into sections for display at various locations. The Highland Mint collects the sawdust

and packages it into small capsules. Only 500 capsules are released; within a week, all 500 are sold.

May 2000
■ ALSA begins the Lou Gehrig Challenge: Cure ALS, an in-depth research project that vigorously investigates ALS. ALSA commits to a five-year, $25 million initiative, the largest commitment by any ALS voluntary organization.

May 31, 2002
■ Project ALS Day is held at thirteen of America's big league ballparks. At each park, a celebrity guest reads Lou Gehrig's famous farewell address from home plate.

World Series 2002
■ Announced during the fourth game, MasterCard, on behalf of Major League Baseball, reveals the most memorable moments in baseball history as voted by the fans. The fifth-most popular event is Lou Gehrig's retirement speech given from home plate of Yankee Stadium on July 4, 1939. The number one Memorable Moment is the night Ripken broke Lou Gehrig's long-standing consecutive games record by playing in consecutive game number 2,131.

June 13, 2003
■ The Hall of Fame, in partnership with ALSA, commemorates the one hundredth anniversary of Gehrig's birth with a multi-day celebration at the Hall (his actual birthday, June 19, was booked with other events prior to the organization of this event).

Lou Gehrig Memorial Award Winners
1955 - Alvin Dark, SS, New York Giants
1956 - Pee Wee Reese, SS, Brooklyn Dodgers
1957 - Stan Musial, 1B, St. Louis Cardinals
1958 - Gil McDougald, 2B, New York Yankees
1959 - Gil Hodges, 1B, Los Angeles Dodgers
1960 - Dick Groat, SS, Pittsburgh Pirates

1961 - Warren Spahn, P, Milwaukee Braves
1962 - Robin Roberts, P, Baltimore Orioles
1963 - Bobby Richardson, 2B, New York Yankees
1964 - Key Boyer, 3B, St. Louis Cardinals
1965 - Vern Law, P, Pittsburgh Pirates
1966 - Brooks Robinson, 3B, Baltimore Orioles
1967 - Ernie Banks, 1B, Chicago Cubs
1968 - Al Kaline, RF, Detroit Tigers
1969 - Pete Rose, RF, Cincinnati Reds
1970 - Hank Aaron, RF, Atlanta Braves
1971 - Harmon Killebrew, 1B, Minnesota Twins
1972 - Wes Parker, 1B, Los Angeles Dodgers
1973 - Ron Santo, 3B, Chicago Cubs
1974 - Willie Stargell, LF, Pittsburgh Pirates
1975 - Johnny Bench, C, Cincinnati Reds
1976 - Don Sutton, P, Los Angeles Dodgers
1977 - Lou Brock, LF, St. Louis Cardinals
1978 - Don Kessinger, SS, Chicago White Sox
1979 - Phil Niekro, P, Atlanta Braves
1980 - Tony Perez, 1B, Boston Red Sox
1981 - Tommy John, P, New York Yankees
1982 - Ron Cey, 3B, Los Angeles Dodgers
1983 - Mike Schmidt, 3B, Philadelphia Phillies
1984 - Steve Garvey, 3B, San Diego Padres
1985 - Dale Murphy, CF, Atlanta Braves
1986 - George Brett, 3B, Kansas City Royals
1987 - Rick Sutcliffe, P, Chicago Cubs
1988 - Buddy Bell, 3B, Cincinnati Reds
1989 - Ozzie Smith, SS, St. Louis Cardnials
1990 - Glenn Davis, 1B, Houston Astros
1991 - Kent Hrbek, 1B, Minnesota Twins
1992 - Cal Ripken, Jr., SS, Baltimore Orioles
1993 - Don Mattingly, 1B, New York Yankees
1994 - Barry Larkin, SS, Cincinnati Reds
1995 - Curt Schilling, P, Philadelphia Phillies
1996 - Brett Butler, CF, Los Angeles Dodgers
1997 - Paul Molitor, DH, Minnesota Twins
1998 - Tony Gwynn, RF, San Diego Padres

1999 - Mark McGwire, 1B, St. Louis Cardinals
2000 - Todd Stottlemyre, P, Arizona Diamondbacks
2001 - John Franco, P, New York Mets
2002 - Danny Graves, P, Cincinnati Reds
2003 - Jamie Moyer, P, Seattle Mariners
2004 - Jim Thome, 1B, Philadelphia Phillies

Lou and Cal

The biggest part of Gehrig's legacy is his consecutive games streak. So superb was his mark that only one man has dared to strive for it since it was set in 1939. On September 6, 1995, Cal Ripken, Jr., surpassed Gehrig's record of 2,130 consecutive games. Before and after this fateful night, the media worked overtime on comparing these two men, but few looked passed the streak they had in common. It's about time someone did.

Of course, there are many more differences between them than there are similarities: Gehrig wore 4, Ripken wore 8; Gehrig played first, Ripken started at third then went to short then back to third; Gehrig's family was anti-sports (until Gehrig turned pro) whereas baseball was an integral part of the Ripken family; Gehrig is often classified among the top hitters of all time, Ripken rarely. In fact, if Ripken had not played in so many games straight, he very likely would never have been compared to Gehrig at all. But the men had more similarities than just stamina.

Both men had impeccable reputations and were considered pillars of their respective teams. Gehrig was born, raised, and played his entire career in the same metro area (New York City). Ripken was born, raised, and played his entire career in the same metro area (Baltimore). The year Gehrig was born, 1903, the team that would eventually be named the Yankees moved to New York—from Baltimore. Gehrig was recruited to the majors in June (1923). Ripken was drafted to the majors in June (1978). Gehrig won the American League MVP during the second season in which he played every game (1927). Ripken won the American League MVP during the second season in which he played every game (1983). Both were adamant about physical fitness, stood over 6 feet tall, and weighed 200+ pounds.

When Gehrig was due to play in his 2,000th game, his wife suggested he stop at 1,999 because she felt the number 1,999 would be more memorable than 2,000. Gehrig did not take her seriously and continued to play. When Ripken was due to play in his 2,131st game, some people suggested to him that he stop at 2,130 because a tie would give honor to Gehrig and the number would be more memorable. Ripken did not take their advice and continued to play. On the matter, he said that stopping would have implied that the record was a goal rather than a result of his deep love for the game. "Lou Gehrig would not have wanted me to sit out a game as a show of honor," he said.[1]

While he was still relatively young, Gehrig's hair began to turn gray, partly because of his disease which his wife labeled "the tyrant" of his life. Ripken's hair also turned gray prematurely, and he contributed the first gray hair to the first time he was asked a question about the streak, the tyrant of his career. Gehrig took himself out of the lineup rather than having his manager do it (May 2, 1939). Ripken also took himself out of the lineup (September 20, 1998).

Throughout their careers, both men agreed to do endorsements for various products. For Gehrig the endorsements included Huskies cereal (a long-gone Wheaties rival) and a baseball glove. For Ripken the endorsements included Wheaties and a baseball glove. Gehrig had the Knot Hole League for young baseball fans; Ripken also founded a youth baseball league with a corresponding tournament. Gehrig wrote a chapter about playing first base for a book compiled by Rogers Hornsby; Ripken wrote his autobiography centered on, of course, baseball.

While the majority of comparisons between the two men rightfully revolve around their incredible endurance, it is also interesting to know that these two Iron Horses fell into step in a variety of other ways. Though not close to being twins, they do have similarities which should be enough to make any fan say, "How 'bout that."

Appendix B
Modern-day Gehrig Fans

This chapter was inspired by those modern-day fans who have come forward with their questions, tributes, and personal stories, all regarding Lou Gehrig. They were collected through the author's Web site, http://moregehrig.tripod.com/, from February 2002 to February 2005.

Tributes from Fans
The following is a collection of personal tributes from fans to Lou Gehrig.

◆

Thank you for all the inspiration you have given me my entire life. I thank you also for being one of the best and hardest working ballplayers ever, but most of all for living your life in such a gentlemanly way that we can be proud to pass on your story to generations of Americans to come. Thanks again for being you.
-L.

◆

Great ballplayer, great human being. Look forward to seeing you in the great ballpark in the sky.
-Tom

◆

Walking through the Columbia campus, I always get chills up my spine every time I set foot on "South Lawn" (what it's now called ever since they moved the ball field uptown), knowing that I am walking, perhaps, on the same ground where Lou Gehrig circled the bases so many years ago.
-"Pen"

◆

I have been a Lou Gehrig fanatic for almost twenty-six years. My only child was born on October 10, 2002, and we named him Gehrig Daniel after Lou and my Dad. Each individual inspired my love of baseball. I felt it would be a tribute to Lou Gehrig to link his name to life and not just death.
-Matt

◆

Your contributions to baseball and to mankind are appreciated even today...you were a legend in every way.
-Ali

◆

You were one of my favorites and an idol to me. As a die-hard Yankee fan since I was a kid, I always cry when *Pride of the Yankees* comes on. A lot of fans say the Babe was their hero, that's fine. But to me, Lou showed what true pride and professionalism were and always should be. It's sad that is what's missing in today's ballplayers. Hope to name my next child after you, if that's OK with my wife.
-Jay

◆

I know there is a Heaven. How could someone who meant so much on Earth not mean even more beyond it? To me, Mr. Gehrig, you define all that is good.

Save me a place on the bench next to you.
-S.

◆

You are an awesome baseball player and will never be forgotten. We love you.
-Joelle

◆

All I have to say is that I feel that Lou Gehrig was one of the greatest baseballplayers and people that ever lived. Some may have hit more home runs or stolen more bases, but nobody then or especially now had the class and dignity that he showed.
-Greg

◆

Lou, I have always considered you one of the greatest ballplayers of all time, but only until I started researching you did I realize how selfless you were and how you defined the meaning of being a good person. Lou, I will be on your team any day.
-MJ

◆

I have played high school and Division I college baseball. I am currently a VP in a global firm. Without your guidance, I would not be in the position I am in. Your example has guided me through the years. I will pass your legacy and example to my children. You represent everything that is good about the game of baseball...and life.
-Jason

◆

Hartford Salutes Lou Lewis –
You will never be forgotten here in Hartford, Lou Lewis, the boy. Through all your trials here, in becom-

ing the self-confident legend you were yet to become, you showed us how to grow properly from the ground up and to learn to trust the values that hold our lives together. You played out the game on how to become a man, to overcome adversity and to find yourself and your powers. While you battled here with your bat and glove, with your insecurities and childhood demons kicking and screaming, somehow you found the courage to go forward and to birth Lou Gehrig, The Man.

We knew you before the world discovered you. And we will never forget the few seasons when your spikes tore up our turf in the sacred seasons of summers past. What other Lou Gehrigs may come our way, we were blessed by you and we thank you for letting us watch you win the game of life.

-Gary Goldberg-O'Maxfield

God makes sure that we never forget the greatness of those who are such wonderful examples of humanity. You touched the lives of so many that knew you then, and I'm sure that you know you have touched even more generations that have followed you. Leadership, teamwork, dedication and more importantly courage are all words that when spoken have the picture of Henry Louis Gehrig engraved into them as their defining images. Your life has meant so much to so many of us and from the bottom of my heart I thank God each and every day for your example from which I have learned so much in all of my forty-five years.

-Anonymous

Lou may have been the luckiest man on the face of the earth, but we who know his pride and excellence are the luckiest fans. Lou's final resting place in Val-

halla, New York, is a peaceful and serene place, a dignified spot reflective of the man he was. His memory will live in our hearts and minds forever.
-Kevin Kuhner

A couple of days ago, I asked a friend who her heroes were. When she returned the question, I could not answer immediately. I thought about it for a while, and the best I could come up with was my childhood hero, Lou Gehrig. Of course, I am only thirty, so I never saw him play, but his story appealed to me. I like how he was great, but played quietly in the shadows of Ruth and DiMaggio. I like how it seems that the fans respected him, but loved someone else. I like his dependability. Most of all, I like his courage, dignity, and grace in the face of adversity. The luckiest man speech moves me whenever I think about it. When I was a kid, I wanted to be Gehrig most of all. Now that I think about it, he is still my favorite hero.
-Jaime Chang

♦

Lou's performance on the field made him an American icon, but it was his tragic and untimely death that made him unforgettable. A real-life folk hero, Gehrig was a quiet man who "carried a big stick." Gehrig was a blue-collar champion. Simply stated, Lou Gehrig was a baseball player...a great baseball player. His statistics spoke volumes as well, and continue to prove his impact on our national pastime, remaining second to none by a player from his era.
-Michael Aubrecht

Personal Stories
These next stories come from actual Gehrig fans.

Lucille's story:
On a bright, late-June day, I headed a group of twenty-one family and friends on a guided tour of Yankee Stadium. Each member of our group had his or her own favorite ballplayer (in my
case, Lou Gehrig); each of us bringing our own hopes and
dreams to the outing, and I readily admit I was looking for any
and all Lou Gehrig memories or mementos. Having been Yankee fans of long standing, we knew we would see all the famous
spots in this "cathedral" of ball playing. We were anxious to see
the press box, the clubhouse, the dugout, the field itself and, of
course, famous Memorial Park. None of these places disappointed us, but there was a surprise in our tour that none of us
ever expected.

We Yankee fans know all about ballplayers who claim they
feel the presence of all the Yankee greats who have played on
that hallowed ground. I have read these quotes from both the
Yankee players and their opponents, believing it but not really
giving it too much thought. On the tour, though, I *wanted* to feel
this presence. But I knew one could not force such an issue. If
the ghosts were there and wanted to show up, they would do so
with no help from me.

All the tour stops had their highlights. A Yankee Stadium tour
is very similar to visiting a museum. The field has been roamed
on by the best baseball has to offer. The dugout has been sat,
spat, and slept in by all the Yankee legends. The clubhouse walls
are privy to all the secrets we would love to know. Although all
these places were exciting and fun to visit, they did not have that
certain something—I had not yet felt the presence.

Cathedrals in general all have their secret walkways, stair-
cases, buried bodies, and this New York baseball church, I
found out, is no exception. After visiting the clubhouse, the
next stop on the tour was the Yankee dugout. To get there one
must go through an under-the-stands tunnel. This tunnel is a
dingy, dirty, old dungeon (not unlike a NYC subway entrance),

but much to my surprise, this is *the place*. As I had made all the arrangements for the tour, I was afforded first place in line behind the tour guide. When I stepped into the tunnel, immediately chills, goose bumps and that eerie feeling that someone was watching came over me. I knew instantly Lou's spirit was there.

A picture of the poignant scene in *Pride of the Yankees*, where Lou (Gary Cooper) walks down this very tunnel right before his famous speech flashed through my mind. I realized this was it. This was real. I was feeling the presence. I drastically slowed my walk, not wanting this moment to end. The tunnel is very narrow, making it possible for me to slide my hands along the length of its walls—a gesture which fulfilled my need to feel every inch of this very special place. It was as if Lou was talking to me, introducing me to his workplace. I had an extraordinary need to be in this presence, to make this moment last. I wanted to stay in that dingy tunnel, continue to experience an undeniable closeness with my hero. I had found Lou's spirit, an indescribably emotional moment which I won't ever forget.

When the tour ended, we all congregated outside the stadium. Although I was quite curious to know if my tour mates had experienced any similar feelings in the tunnel, I am also by nature a bit of a skeptic and have a degree of self-consciousness (not unlike my hero, Mr. Gehrig). So I was not about to voice my feelings, lest they think me nuts. I need not have worried. One by one my tour mates lined up to not only thank me for arranging the tour, but also to tell me about their experience in the tunnel.

My sister-in-law, not a big baseball fan, was first in line to express her thoughts. She related how she felt all the hair on her body stand up and how she had gotten goose bumps in that tunnel. My younger sister, a huge baseball and Yankee fan, explained how she thought the whole thing was wonderful, but "the tunnel was amazing; all the greats are there." My older sister, a deeply Christian woman, noted, "They are in that tunnel."

I was starting to see a pattern, but I still wasn't convinced everyone felt the presence of Yankee greats in that tunnel. For me the clincher came when my husband, not at all a baseball fan but learning, told me he felt chills and goose bumps while walking through that clubhouse-to-dugout tunnel. Then I knew. I truly had found the presence of Lou's spirit.

Gehrig being Gehrig, so earnest and so focused on playing every day, would naturally pick this particular place in which to haunt or reside—where every player from every era for every game played at Yankee Stadium must walk, no way around it. It is quiet, out of the way, a totally nonintrusive place, so plain, simple and functional—so Lou. My mission was accomplished; I found Lou's everlasting spirit. To me it is in that Yankee Stadium clubhouse-to-dugout walkway which I simply call The Tunnel.

◆

Lonnie's story:
I am a fifty-four-year-old fellow now, but when I was only eight or nine I knew that if I ever had a son, his name would be Lou. My son, Gehrig Louis Woods, was born on the fifth of September 1977. Why Lou? I cannot really explain this. I can remember watching *Pride of the Yankees* on our little ten-inch black-and-white TV set in 1958 or 1959. I remember the tears rolling down my cheeks as Gary Cooper recited the farewell/"luckiest man" speech that Lou had given in front of 60,000 beloved and somber fans in July 1939 at Yankee Stadium. Here was a man dying a slow, agonizing death, and yet he considered himself lucky. Again, I cannot explain this.

Even though the man died nine years before I was born, I felt as if I *knew* him. He became my "hero" not only in baseball, but in everyday life also. He rarely sought the spotlight, and neither do I. He was a "quiet man," as I try to be also. I have had many, many dreams about him, have visited Yankee Stadium once, his grave twice, and the Hall of Fame three times. Because I live in Alabama, this is a long drive, but I enjoyed each visit to New York. His famous number four became my uniform number during my ball-playing days. I use it in connection with my e-mail address. I have four diamonds on my specially made wedding ring.

Years ago, during my high school days, I "lost" the book about Lou which I had checked out of the school library. I paid for it, of course, and still treasure it today. I had that book so memorized that I could let anyone read a sentence on any page and I would tell them the sentence before and after it.

Sometime around December 1968 or January 1969, I wrote Mrs. Gehrig (Eleanor) a fan letter. She responded in kind with a letter back to me. Of course, I treasure this letter to this day. I have a Goudy baseball card of Lou, bought for $4.00 in 1976 now worth over $1,000, another treasure to keep and pass on down to the kids. Now, as time goes on, I have a five-year-old grandson named Gehrig Austin. A tribute to me, his dad, and again, Lou Gehrig, the "Quiet Hero."

In closing, to this day, I cannot explain my fondness for a man who died long before I was even born and also lived many, many miles away from me. But, with a hero like Lou Gehrig, how can a person go wrong?

Appendix C
A Brief Explanation of ALS

ALS is a disease that has had a lot of research poured into it, but is one that evades even the most studious of medical professionals. What is known of it today can basically be explained in the translation of its name. "Amyotrophic" means "without muscle nourishment;" the muscles are not receiving signals from the nervous system to move, they are not receiving nourishment. "Lateral" means "to the side;" the side of the spinal cord is the initial site of damage in the body. "Sclerosis," or "hardened," refers to the hardening of the spinal cord as a result of the damage inflicted by ALS. Except for the 5%-10% of cases that involve heredity, no cause of ALS has been found. Without an absolute cause, it's hard to find a cure.

Every year in America one to two people per 100,000 develop ALS; that figures out to about 5,000 new victims per year. Once a person has been diagnosed with ALS, they usually are given a life expectancy of three to six years. The disease can strike anyone at any age, but it most often strikes the middle-aged and elderly, more commonly in men. That Gehrig was stricken relatively early in life is uncommon, but not unheard of.

Though the victims eventually cannot talk or move, they can still think, remember, compute and daydream—and they are very aware of how "trapped" they are in their own bodies. Therefore depression is a common side effect of ALS.

ALS victims also retain all five senses, including touch. Other forms of sclerosis involve numbness or tingling, but ALS does not. Instead, ALS deteriorates only the motor neurons, the little messengers sent out by the nervous system to tell the voluntary muscles to move. As with other diseases, victims' bodies react to and tolerate ALS in different ways. Some ALS victims do not make it to the three-year mark after diagnosis, while a small number of victims live for decades (Stephen Hawking, well-known physicist/author, is perhaps the most incredible example of victim survival; he has lived with ALS since the 1960s). Involuntary muscles, such as the heart and bowels, are not directly affected by ALS, although they are indirectly affected by various complications involved with ALS. The only physical pain a victim usually feels is muscle stiffness and cramping as a result of not moving.

In Lou Gehrig's case, a doctor simply had to look at him to tell he had ALS because the doctor's mother died from the disease. Many patients are not so fortunate to have an early or easy diagnosis. It is a particularly challenging disease to identify. The ALS diagnosis procedure is fundamentally a process of elimination. Because its symptoms (loss of coordination, difficulty talking, persistent weakness in an appendage) match those of many other diseases, including muscular dystrophy, the diagnosis process can be rather drawn out, the victim going through test after test.

Though there are a number of treatments for ALS, none of them has been shown to stop the progression of ALS. The best victims can hope for at this point is a regiment of drugs and devices that help in coping with the symptoms of ALS. Gehrig was given vitamin E shots, which was a revolutionary treatment in 1939. Today ALS patients have more effective treatments.

Thanks to a drug called Rilutex, muscle function can be maintained a little longer in a victim's body, and it has been shown to extend life expectancy about three months. Baclofen eases muscle stiffness. To help with the inevitable weight loss, many victims take branched-chain amino acids nutritional supplements. Phenytoin eases cramps. Tricyclic antidepressants cut down the amount of involuntary drooling involved with ALS.

New hope came recently when researchers reported on a new form of treatment referred to as the "ALS cocktail." The cocktail combines minocycline (an antibiotic used to treat several brain diseases) with creatine (a dietary supplement also used to treat brain diseases). In test mice genetically designed to develop ALS, the ones given the cocktail lived 25% longer than those who were not. This discovery was a step toward better lives for ALS victims—a small, shaky step, but still one in the right direction.

ALS was nicknamed "Lou Gehrig's Disease" because Lou Gehrig was the first famous person to be publicly diagnosed with the disease. In other parts of the world, the common name for the disease is "motor neuron disease."

Acknowledgments

Thank you to all the MoreGehrig readers for the many reasons for writing this book. I'd especially like to recognize: Lucille Lasky-Nuzzi, Lonnie Woods, Beth Skelley, Kevin Kuhner, Gary Goldberg-O'Maxfield, Crisha Mora, James Wojtkun, Alan Gooding, Carolyn DeBonnett, Tom Tierney, Rory S. Alter, Frank M. Nebbia, Gerry G., Glenn D., Peter C., Matt, Joni W., "Sharkkie," Monte G., Jake, Teo Alvarado, Kim White, Joseph Romm, Jaime Chang, Ray Isterico, Judith B., Jay G., Frank Nebbia, Ron B., Danny Shanahan, Melissa A., Russ, Amanda, Kristy H., Phil, JK, Bill H., Shawna C., Karen, Jason U., MJ, Greg C., Joelle, Ali L., Tom E., Keith B., F. K. E., Pat, Barbara S. (and her son).

Images for this book were used with permission and were provided thanks to the kind courtesy of:

National Baseball Hall of Fame Images Department
    (Gehrig photographs)
Janice Kaden (all other photographs)

The 1939 radio interview transcript was used with written permission from the quite likeable Brent Ackerman, KROC-AM Radio, Rochester, MN.

Extra Special Acknowledgments:

Only one person signed her name to the manuscript, but there were tons of people involved in some fashion during the making of this book. For starters, I thank God because I con-sider the opportunity to write about Lou Gehrig—a longtime dream of mine—to be a very generous gift on His part. You rock, I adore You. Mom, for helping me pull off a trip to "Yankee Country" and for propping me up when it got hard. Dad, for instilling a passion for the game in me. Robert, my darling, my sweet cheeks, for unfaltering love and encouragement in a very challenging journey and for letting me skimp on household chores while I wrote. Lucille and your family, who have selflessly helped me in countless ways that I could list but it would take up another 200 pages. Tara, for putting me in contact with Ray and always helping me with research whenever you could, as one writer to another. Lonnie, for hooking me up with a rare copy of *Rawhide* and for being so generous and willing to offer. Nancy, for using your amazing artistic talent to enhance this book in a way no one else could. The wonderful fellas at the National Baseball Hall of Fame Library and Image Department for helping out a raw rookie. All my family and friends who are skimming through this paragraph looking for their names (there are too many of you, I can't list you all!). My superior editor Andrew Yankech, for his patience and for making me look good. My friend, we've created a masterpiece! To Greg Pierce, for giving me the opportunity to write this book. And to all the wonderful crew at ACTA, for all the behind-the-scenes work you do.

You are all amazing, and may you be blessed many times over!

Notes

Chapter One

1. Bak, Richard. *Lou Gehrig: An American Classic*. Dallas: Taylor, 1995, p. 8.
2. *Ibid.*, p. 9.
3. *Ibid.*
4. Graham, Frank. *Lou Gehrig: A Quiet Hero*. Eau Claire, WI: E.M. Hale and Co., 1942, p. 170.
5. Robinson, Ray. *Iron Horse: Lou Gehrig in His Time*. New York: Aladdin Paperbacks, 1989, p. 37.

Chapter Two

1. Robinson, *Iron Horse*, p. 39.
2. Bak, *Lou Gehrig*, p. 18.
3. *Ibid.*
4. Graham, *Lou Gehrig*, p. 11-12.
5. *Ibid.*, p. 17.
6. Van Riper, Guernsey. *Lou Gehrig: One of Baseball's Greatest*. New York: Aladdin Paperbacks, 1949, p. 173-4.
7. Robinson, p. 42-3.

Chapter Three

1. Bak, p. 24.
2. Robinson, Iron Horse, p. 55.
3. Graham, Lou Gehrig, p. 46.
4. Robinson, Iron Horse, p. 51.
5. Bak, Lou Gehrig, p. 29.
6. Robinson, Iron Horse, p. 52.
7. Bak, Lou Gehrig, p. 28.
8. Ibid., p. 30.
9. Graham, Lou Gehrig, p. 49.
10. Bak, Lou Gehrig, p. 30.
11. Robinson, Iron Horse, p. 52.
12. Macht, Norman. Lou Gehrig (Baseball Legends Series). New York: Chelsea Publishers, 1993, p. 23.
13. Robinson, Iron Horse, p. 62.

Chapter Four

1. Krichell, Paul. "The Lou Gehrig Story." National Baseball Hall of Fame archives.
2. Graham, *Lou Gehrig*, p. 70.
3. Macht, *Lou Gehrig*, p. 24.
4. Robinson, *Iron Horse*, p. 69.
5. Rubin, Robert. *Lou Gehrig: Courageous Star.* New York: Putnam. 1979, p. 67.
6. *Ibid.*, p. 66.
7. *Ibid.*, p. 67.
8. *Ibid.*, p. 68.
9. *Ibid.*
10. Graham, *Lou Gehrig*, p. 79.
11. *Ibid.*
12. Gehrig, Eleanor and Joseph Durso. *My Luke and I.* New York: Thomas Y. Crowell Co., 1976, p. 126.
13. Rubin, p. 68.
14. Robinson, *Iron Horse*, p. 73.
15. Gehrig, Lou. "Am I Jealous of Babe Ruth?" *Liberty*, 1933. National Baseball Hall of Fame archives.
16. Robinson, *Iron Horse*, p. 69.
17. *Ibid.*, p.80.
18. *Ibid.*, p. 81.
19. *Ibid.*
20. *Ibid.*, p. 83.
21. Gallico, Paul. *Lou Gehrig: Pride of the Yankees.* New York: Grosset & Dunlapp, Inc., 1942, p. 88.
22. Robinson, *Iron Horse*, p. 86.

Chapter Five

1. Bak, p. 46.
2. Rubin, *Lou Gehrig*, p. 104.
3. Bak, *Lou Gehrig*, p. 86.
4. *Ibid.*, p. 47.
5. Graham, *Lou Gehrig*, p. 106.
6. Krichell, Paul. "The Lou Gehrig Story." National Baseball Hall of Fame archives.
7. Robinson, *Iron Horse*, p. 102.

8. Luce, Willard and Celia. *Lou Gehrig: Iron Man of Baseball.* Champaign, IL: Garrard Publishing Co., 1970, p. 56.
9. Rubin, *Lou Gehrig*, p. 91.
10. Bak, *Lou Gehrig*, p. 47.
11. Robinson, *Iron Horse*, p. 105.
12. Graham, *Lou Gehrig*, p. 111.
13. *Ibid.*, p. 113.
14. Gallico, p. 76.
15. Rubin, *Lou Gehrig*, p. 86.
16. Robinson, *Iron Horse*, p. 107.
17. *Ibid.*, p. 109.
18. *Ibid.*, p. 106-7.
19. Gehrig, "Am I Jealous of Babe Ruth?"
20. *Ibid.*
21. Robinson, p. 170.

Chapter Six

1. Robinson, *Iron Horse*, p. 113.
2. Gehrig and Durso, p. 132.
3. Graham, *Lou Gehrig*, p. 118.
4. Robinson, *Iron Horse*, p. 118-9.
5. *Ibid.*, p. 113.
6. Bak, *Lou Gehrig*, p. 56.
7. Robinson, *Iron Horse*, p. 116.
8. Bak, *Lou Gehrig*, p. 56.
9. Gallico, *Lou Gehrig*, p. 96.
10. Robinson, *Iron Horse*, p. 114.
11. Bak, *Lou Gehrig*, p. 68.
12. Robinson, *Iron Horse*, p. 118.
13. *Ibid.*
14. *Ibid.*
15. *Ibid.*, p. 119.
16. Bak, *Lou Gehrig*, p. 68.
17. Robinson, *Iron Horse*, p. 126.
18. Bak, p. 71.
19. Personal audio files of DeadballEra.com, founded by Frank Russo.
20. Graham, *Lou Gehrig*, p. 19.

21. Bak, *Lou Gehrig*, p. 56.

Chapter Seven
1. Rubin, *Lou Gehrig*, p. 107-8.
2. *Ibid.*, p. 108.
3. *Ibid.*, p. 118.
4. Robinson, *Iron Horse*, p. 132.
5. Graham, Lou Gehrig, p. 122.
6. Bak, *Lou Gehrig*, p. 76.
7. *Ibid.*, p. 84.
8. Robinson, *Iron Horse*, p. 136.
9. Luce, *Lou Gehrig*, p. 61.
10. Graham, *Lou Gehrig*, p. 127.
11. Robinson, p. 140.
12. Macht, *Lou Gehrig*, p. 37.
13. Robinson, *Iron Horse*, p. 140.
14. Ibid., p. 141.
15. *Ibid.*

Chapter Eight
1. Graham, *Lou Gehrig*, p. 134.
2. Robinson, *Iron Horse*, p. 151-2.
3. Macht, *Lou Gehrig*, p. 39.
4. Robinson, *Iron Horse*, p. 151.
5. Rubin, *Lou Gehrig*, p. 118.
6. Graham, *Lou Gehrig*, p. 145.
7. Robinson, *Iron Horse*, p. 128.
8. Rubin, *Lou Gehrig*, p. 115-6.
9. Robinson, *Iron Horse*, p. 150.
10. *Ibid.*, p. 145.
11. Rubin, p. 100.
12. Lieb, Fred. *Baseball as I Have Known It.* Coward McCann &
    Geoghegan, 1977. National Baseball Hall of Fame archives,
    p. 177.

Chapter Nine
1. Robinson, *Iron Horse*, p. 158.
2. Bak, *Lou Gehrig*, p. 106.

3. *Ibid.*
4. *Ibid.*, p. 109.
5. *Ibid.*, p. 103.
6. *Ibid.*, p. 91.
7. *Ibid.*, p. 93.
8. *Ibid.*, p. 115.
9. *Ibid.*, p. 114.
10. *Ibid.*, p. 122.
11. *Ibid.*, p. 94.
12. *Ibid.*, p. 24.
13. "Lou Gehrig," *Yankeeography*. YES Network. New York. 2003.
14. Robinson, *Iron Horse*, p. 27.
15. Bak, *Lou Gehrig*, p. 97.
16. Macht, *Lou Gehrig*, p. 41.
17. Gallico, *Lou Gehrig*, p. 103.
18. Gehrig and Durso, *My Luke and I*, p. 135.
19. *Ibid.*
20. Rubin, *Lou Gehrig*, p. 120-1.
21. Bak, *Lou Gehrig*, p. 107.
22. Gehrig and Durso, *My Luke and I*, p. 6.
23. Gehrig, "Am I Jealous of Babe Ruth?"
24. Robinson, *Iron Horse*, p. 170.
25. Bak, *Lou Gehrig*, p. 119.
26. *Ibid.*, p. 110.
27. Rubin, *Lou Gehrig*, p. 125.
28. Lieb, *Baseball as I Have Known It*, p. 179.
29. Gehrig and Durso, *My Luke and I*, p. 160.
30. *Ibid.*, p. 165-6.
31. *Ibid.*, p. 161.

Chapter Ten
1. Gehrig and Durso, *My Luke and I*, p. 166.
2. Robinson, p. 191.
3. *Ibid.*, p. 166.
4. Robinson, *Iron Horse*, p. 231.
5. *Ibid.*, p. 234.
6. Macht, *Lou Gehrig*, p. 46.
7. *Ibid.*, p. 47.

8. Robinson, *Iron Horse*, p. 193.
9. Gehrig and Durso, *My Luke and I*, p. 190.
10. Bak, *Lou Gehrig*, p. 123.
11. Gehrig and Durso, *My Luke and I*, p. 195.
12. *Ibid.*, p. 196-8.
13. Robinson, *Iron Horse*, p. 191.
14. Rubin, *Lou Gehrig*, p. 102-3.
15. Robinson, *Iron Horse*, p. 127.
16. Krichell, "Lou Gehrig Story."
17. Robinson, *Iron Horse*, p. 213.
18. Gehrig, Lou. "For Cleanup King I Nominate..." print advertisement, Gillette Safety Razor Co., Boston, MA.
19. Lieb, *Baseball as I Have Known It*.

Chapter Eleven
1. Robinson, *Iron Horse*, p. 216.
2. *Ibid.*
3. *Ibid.*, p. 215.
4. Bak, *Lou Gehrig*, p. 126.
5. Robinson, *Iron Horse*, p. 217.
6. Gehrig and Durso, *My Luke and I*, p. 206.
7. Graham, *Lou Gehrig*, p. 195.
8. Bak, *Lou Gehrig*, p. 135.
9. Robinson, *Iron Horse*, p. 218.
10. *Ibid.*, p. 174.
11. *Ibid.*, p. 221.
12. *Ibid.*, p. 222.
13. *Ibid.*, p. 226.
14. Sher, Jack. "Lou Gehrig, the Man and the Legend," *Sport*, 1948. National Baseball Hall of Fame archives.
15. Robinson, *Iron Horse*, p. 173.
16. Bak, p. 140.
17. Gallico, p. 127.
18. *Ibid.*, p.151.
19. Macht, *Lou Gehrig*, p. 45.
20. Robinson, *Iron Horse*, p. 230.
21. *Ibid.*, p. 224.

Chapter Twelve

1. Robinson, *Iron Horse*, p. 234.
2. *Ibid.*, p. 234-5.
3. *Ibid.*, p. 237.
4. Graham, *Lou Gehrig*, p. 204.
5. Robinson, p. 234.
6. *Ibid.*, p. 195.
7. Robinson, *Iron Horse*, p. 245.
8. Macht, *Lou Gehrig*, p. 49.
9. Graham, *Lou Gehrig*, p. 197.
10. Robinson, *Iron Horse*, p. 247.
11. Gehrig and Durso, *My Luke and I*, p. 212.
12. Robinson, *Iron Horse*, p. 246.
13. Gehrig and Durso, *My Luke and I*, p. 16.
14. Robinson, *Iron Horse*, p. 237.
15. Gehrig and Durso, *My Luke and I*, p. 209-10.
16. *Ibid.*, p. 214.
17. Gallico, *Lou Gehrig*, p. 16.
18. Robinson, p. 253-4.
19. Rubin, *Lou Gehrig*, p. 144.
20. Robinson, *Iron Horse*, p. 255.
21. *Ibid.*
22. Peterman, Cy. May 2, 1939. National Baseball Hall of Fame archives.
23. Robinson, *Iron Horse*, p. 257.
24. Gehrig and Durso, *My Luke and I*, p. 6-7.
25. *Ibid.*, p. 8.
26. Lieb, *Baseball as I Have Known It*, p. 181.
27. Gehrig and Durso, *My Luke and I*, p. 27.
28. *Ibid.*, p. 13-4.
29. *Ibid.*, p. 12.
30. Rice, Grantland. National Baseball Hall of Fame archives.
31. Graham, *Lou Gehrig*, p. 209-10.
32. *St. Louis Daily Globe Democrat*. June 22, 1939. National Baseball Hall of Fame archives.
33. Macht, *Lou Gehrig*, p. 54.
34. Graham, *Lou Gehrig*, p. 211.
35. Gehrig and Durso, *My Luke and I*, p. 19.

36. *Ibid.*, p. 220.
37. *Ibid.*, p. 221.
38. *Ibid.*
39. Graham, *Lou Gehrig*, p. 238.
40. *Ibid.*, p. 225.
41. KROC Radio, Chronicles, vol. 1, Rochester, MN, 2000. Transcribed by Sara Kaden Brunsvold.

Chapter Thirteen
1. Lieb, *Baseball as I Have Known It*, p. 182.
2. Gehrig and Durso, *My Luke and I*, p. 20.
3. *Ibid.*, p. 19.
4. Gehrig, Eleanor. "Talks of Lou's Fading Days." Newspaper interview from Sept. 26, 1945. National Baseball Hall of Fame archives.
5. Gehrig and Durso, *My Luke and I*, p. 223.
6. *Ibid.*, p. 224.
7. Gehrig, E., "Talks of Lou's Fading Days."
8. Gehrig and Durso, *My Luke and I*, p. 228.

Chapter Fourteen
1. Lieb, p. 184.
2. Eisenberg, Milton M. *Personal correspondence to Eleanor Gehrig*, Aug. 28, 1941. National Baseball Hall of Fame archives.
3. *New York World Telegram*. June 4, 1945. National Baseball Hall of Fame archives.
4. Gehrig, E., "Talks of Lou's Fading Days."

Appendix A
1. Wallace, Joseph, Neil Hamilton, and Marty Appel. *Baseball: 100 Classic Moments in the History of the Game*. Dorling Kindersley: New York, 2000, p. 297.

Index

Also Available from ACTA Sports

STRAT-O-MATIC FANATICS
The Unlikely Success Story of a Game That Became an American Passion
Glenn Guzzo
This is the true story behind the creation—and re-creation—of America's most popular sports board game ever: Strat-O-Matic. This book looks at the hobby from every angle: the numerous crises that nearly engulfed the small company as well as fascinating anecdotes from real players of the game.
320 pages, paperback, $14.95

BEHIND-THE-SCENES BASEBALL
Real-Life Applications of Statistical Analysis Actually Used by Major League Teams...and Other Stories from the Inside
Doug Decatur
For the baseball fan wondering why, when and how analytical managers and GMs make key decisions in a game and over a season, this insider's book explains the practical uses of statistics in baseball.
320 pages, paperback, $14.95

THE BALLGAME OF LIFE
Lessons for Parents and Coaches of Young Baseball Players
David Allen Smith and Joseph Aversa, Jr.
Good coaches and good parents both try to teach kids the same things: persistence, hard work, how to handle pressure, and how to be a good winner. Baseball can help young players learn these lessons, but only if the coaches and parents stay focused on them.
112 pages, paperback, $9.95

The Hardball Times Baseball Annual
The writers of www.hardballtimes.com
A complete analysis of the entire baseball season from the first pitch to the last out, including a breakdown of the playoffs and World Series. Available each year in November.
320 pages, paperback, $17.95

The Bill James Handbook
Bill James and Baseball Info Solutions
Simply put, The Bill James Handbook is the best and most complete annual baseball reference guide available today. It contains a myriad of stats on every hit, pitch and catch in Major League Baseball. Available each year on November 1.
426 pages, paperback, $19.95

Available at bookstores or from ACTA Sports
(800) 397-2282   www.actasports.com